GRAY IS THE NEW BLACK

D0047946

ALSO BY DOROTHY RICE

The Reluctant Artist (2015)

DOROTHY RICE

Gray Is the New Black

⊖ ⊖ ⊖

A Memoir of Self-Acceptance

OTIS BOOKS

THE MFA WRITING PROGRAM

Otis College of Art and Design

LOS ANGELES ▚ 2019

Gray Is the New Black *is a work of creative non-fiction. The people, places and events are drawn from the author's memory. As such, the narrative in its entirety reflects the author's emotional truth. Some names and identifying details have been changed to protect the privacy of others.*

Book design and typesetting: Hannah Martin

ISBN-13: 978-9980-2-4302-7

OTIS BOOKS
THE MFA WRITING PROGRAM
Otis College of Art and Design
9045 Lincoln Boulevard
Los Angeles, CA 90045

https://www.otis.edu/mfa-writing/otis-books
otisbooks@otis.edu

For my husband, Bob
and my sisters, Roxanne and Juliet

and for Mocha and Marmalade Jam
furry companions

Part One

1

Sometimes I hate my sisters for how they make me feel. Then I hate myself for being a peevish bitch. I love my sisters. They're my best friends. But I wasn't looking forward to dinner out with the two of them and their boyfriends. I was forty pounds overweight last summer and not in the mood for self-reflection.

I don't remember the occasion. Maybe just to meet my older sister's latest boyfriend. She'd had a few since her last divorce. Toads for the most part. I didn't, yet, know enough about this one to have passed final judgment.

We'd chosen the Tower Cafe, a Sacramento institution on the busy corner of Broadway and Land Park Boulevard, beside the still operating Tower Theatre, with its Art Deco rooftop spire, a familiar beacon visible from the elevated freeway. My husband, Bob, and I pushed through the front doors. The restaurant was packed, the babble of competing voices and the eclectic decor – a frenetic mash-up of ethnic, mystical and urban jungle – added to the sensory overload.

"*Hola, hermosa*," my younger sister, Juliet, called out to me, waving both bare arms overhead. She and her boyfriend, Bill, were seated at a table for six, one with a bird's eye view of the massive dessert case, long as two coffins laid end to end. As we approached, Juliet stood, prancing with excitement. I squinted, checking out her outfit, tiny white shorts and an equally tiny turquoise top – the perfect color against her unblemished, caramel complexion.

"I *know*," she said, with a mischievous twinkle in her eyes, "Clinton Kelly says no shorts on women over 40, but I *love* my short-shorts."

Juliet, four years younger than me, was on the cusp of 60, but I'm betting Clinton would have made an exception to the rule for her. On a good day, she can pass for 35. No lie.

"*Besos*," she said, air kissing both my cheeks.

Speaking Spanish is a thing we do, a remnant of having lived in Mexico for a year when we were kids, and, like most Californians, we'd both taken years of Spanish in school. Her boyfriend Bill stood to hug me and shake my husband's hand. Bob and I took the two chairs opposite them.

"It's so good to see my beautiful twin," Juliet said.

There is a strong likeness between us, or there used to be. In the past, we were often mistaken for one another. A total stranger would start talking to me in the grocery store or on the street, until I'd say, "You must think I'm Juliet." That hasn't happened in years.

"I wish," I grumbled, giving her the stink eye.

"You make such great faces," she said, laughing. "I love it. Reminds me of Dad."

Even in the 100-plus degrees of a Sacramento summer, I wore a long-sleeve denim shirt to cover my jiggly upper arms and leggings under a long black jersey dress to keep my thighs from sticking together. I was a nun next to my near-naked sister.

I had no right to resent her – she eats like an anorexic bird and works out like an Olympian. Which made me feel guilty and mean-spirited. Which made me resent her even more. Which made me feel like crawling back into bed and calling it a day.

Sisters.

"I went to the best cardio class this morning," Juliet said, her light eyes bright with enthusiasm.

I knew where this was going and narrowed my eyes, hoping she'd take the hint and drop it.

"I'm going again tomorrow. You should come."

"So you can watch me have a heart attack?"

"Oh, don't be silly." She flapped a dismissive hand.

Bill and Bob studied the menus.

Bill is a good guy, a retired fireman, solidly built and solidly handsome. He looks like he played football back in the day. He's also a political and social progressive. I didn't expect that. Which goes to show my biases about big guys who look like ex-footballers. He's been with my sister several years. They still hold hands under the table and make sappy eyes at one another. Good for them.

My husband, Bob, is tall and lean. Great legs. He makes up for the lack of hair on his head with body fuzz. The first time my mother met him, she plucked at the tufts sticking out from under his collar.

"Does that go all the way down?" she asked, classic Mom.

"Yep, and back up the other side," he said.

That lifted Mom's eyebrows. My older sister, Roxanne, took to calling him "hirsute" after that. She's the family comedian.

It's probably a good thing Bob has lost most of the hair on his head, all but a Friar Tuck fringe. Otherwise, he'd be entirely too appealing, and I'd be forced to take better care of myself to ward off the competition. We've been married nineteen years, his second marriage, my third. We each brought two children to the party. Now we track our anniversaries by the age of our one child together, a surprise to us both on the cusp of 45. At the time of the Tower Cafe soiree, our daughter was spending a last summer at home, before leaving for college.

Rocky – Roxanne – and her current boyfriend arrived. Alan

was a bespectacled, aging hipster with skinny ankles. I have a thing about men with weak ankles, or maybe it's just men who have the nerve to be smaller than me. We all stood for another round of greetings. Roxanne hugged me too tight and for too long, tickling my ribs in the process. I pulled away and swatted her hands as if they were a swarm of pesky gnats.

"Aw, there's my prickly little sister. She just loves to be touched, doesn't she, Bob?" Rocky said, winking at him.

Bob wasn't so hesitant about hugging her back. He's an only child. My sisters are the closest thing he's got to siblings. Sometimes I wonder if he wouldn't prefer one of them to me. I would if I were a man.

Roxanne is shorter than Juliet and me. She wears her hair shorter too, a swingy bob that brushes her shoulders. The three of us are four years apart, a time span carefully planned by our mother based on the advice of child-rearing guru Dr. Benjamin Spock, who recommended four years as the ideal spread to discourage sibling rivalry. It didn't always work when we were kids, but it feels about right now. At 63, I'm in the middle.

Bob studied the menu. "Should we share something?" he asked.

The portions at the Tower are huge. But the suggestion felt personal. There was no way I could order my own entrée after that.

"We're splitting the Chinese Chicken Salad," Juliet said.

"Well then." I turned to Bob with a tight smile. "Why don't we do the same?"

"You sure? Will that be enough for you?"

"I'm not about to starve any time soon."

"That's not what I meant," he said, with that scrunched-up look he gets, as if his forehead were constipated with thought. His younger son, when he was a little boy, once ran a finger over the deep ridges and asked his father, "Does it hurt?" It looks like it might.

Our orders and two extra plates arrived. I dug into my salad. Juliet poked at her crispy noodles, pushing them into their own tidy little haystack and making another discreet pile of almond slivers, segregating the high calorie ingredients from the more benign veggies. Roxanne's technique was different. She disassembled her sandwich and squeezed piles of condiments on top of everything until her plate resembled a work of modern art more than anything recognizable as food. My sisters have mastered the art of pretend eating. It's not a skill I've ever been moved to perfect.

I eyed the dessert case and sighed, imagining that if I suggested we all split a few items, I'd be met with nervous glances and the unspoken subtext, "Aren't you trying to lose weight?"

"I like her hair color," Juliet said.

"Whose?" I asked.

"The girl behind the dessert case. I thought that's what you were looking at."

"Oh, right, cute."

"Gray hair on younger women is really a thing right now. Isn't Grace's like that now?" Roxanne asked.

Grace, my older daughter, 27 at the time, had recently gone from blond to gray.

"It's very *au courant*. Is that how you say that?" Roxanne said, mangling the French. Roxanne likes to try on new words, usually ones she's picked up reading and isn't sure of the pronunciation.

"I think Rocky should stop coloring her hair, go natural," Alan said. "I love gray hair on women." He had even less on his head than my husband.

"Like Meryl Streep or Helen Mirren," Roxanne chimed in. "Don't you think they're gorgeous?"

"You know I do, babe," Alan said. "It's just this youth-obsessed culture that's brainwashed women into thinking they have to look like teenagers for the rest of their lives. Such a waste of time. And all those harsh chemicals are bad for your health."

Rocky leaned over the table and held out her hands, extending one to me, the other to Juliet.

"I think Alan's right," she said. "How about we all do it together."

"Go gray?" I asked, wondering if they'd cooked this up in advance. I squinted at Alan and got a smug, tight-lipped smile in response. I didn't take my sister's hand, though I did tap her fingertips.

"Yeah, why not?" she said, "I want to do it, but I could really use some moral support from my sisters, my best friends in the whole world." Roxanne batted her lashes, laying it on thick. "We can find out what makeup and colors go best with gray hair. It'll be fun, another adventure." She beamed encouragement.

Alan's hooded gaze flicked round the table. Bob chewed with concentration. Juliet smiled her polite, let's-change-the-subject, smile.

"You dye your hair, honey?" Bill asked, studying Juliet's cascade of dark chocolate curls.

"She *is* nearly 60," I said.

"Thanks for the reminder," Juliet said.

"*Awkward*," Roxanne said, making a show of coughing into her napkin.

"My younger sister is gray. I think it makes her look old," Bill said, matter-of-fact. His own hair is a snowy white. "For what it's worth, I love your hair the way it is, dear. You look fantastic." He and Juliet kissed.

I smeared butter on a roll and tore off a big bite, angry on behalf of Bill's sister. Why is it that men become more distinguished with age, while for a woman, going gray isn't a natural consequence, but rather a political statement, or an admission that they've given up on their appearance?

"What do you think, Bob?" Roxanne asked, raising an inquisitive brow at my husband.

He peered right, left, then right again, as if checking for the nearest exit. "Don't pull me into this," he said.

"Wise man," Bill said.

"But seriously," I said. "Would you care if I went gray again?"

"It's your hair." Bob paused for a moment, chewing with studied determination. "I do like it long. But I can see how you must get tired of dealing with it."

"So, if I kept the length, you wouldn't mind?"

"Like I said, it's your hair."

I knew he'd prefer I keep coloring it. I also knew he'd never tell me what he really thought, about this or anything else.

"I'm in," I said, eyes on Bob's face. He remained expressionless as he sipped his iced tea.

"I'm so excited." Roxanne grabbed hold of my hand. "You?"

"Super excited," I said, deadpan.

Rocky turned her high beams on Juliet.

"Yeah, no, count me out." Our younger sister shook her head. Her long, dark hair swished

I pictured Juliet at ninety, still rocking the hula girl hair, with a body to match. I envied her that likelihood. Yet in my future fantasy scenario, a thick gray braid trails over one shoulder. It tickles the keyboard as I tinker with my latest murder mystery, a series of cozies featuring a modern-day Miss Marple and her guinea pig sidekick. Since girlhood I'd dreamed of being a prolific author. Given my age, a dozen cozies now seemed more doable than, say, your *War and Peace* type of book.

The waitress brought our check and a to-go box for Juliet's uneaten salad.

"Lunch for tomorrow," Juliet said.

"Did you get enough?" my husband asked, eyeing my spit-cleaned plate.

My cheeks burned. It was only a measly half a salad.

I hadn't forgotten that dessert case. It would have been nice to take a little something home to savor in front of the TV. But I wouldn't give my sisters, or Bob, the satisfaction.

As we wound our way through the tables towards the door, Rocky hooked her arm through mine.

"I already talked to my hairdresser about putting in highlights and lowlights for starters."

I was all for that. The last time I went gray, I'd gone cold turkey. The first year was rough, and just when it was nicely grown out, I gave up and went running back to the salon. Why did I do that? Oh, that's right, it was after another demoralizing sister get-together.

"Earth to Bozo," Roxanne said, breaking into my sour reverie.

She raised her hand for a high five. I smacked her palm, determined to show Bill, my husband, my bony-ass little sister, even the hipster chick behind the counter, that I would rock the hell out of gray hair. I'd look just like one of those "mature" fashion models in the Chico's catalogs, just like that, only of a certain age *and* plus-sized. I'd be spotted on the street and offered a modeling contract. Just picturing the possibilities was as satisfying as the slice of turtle pie I'd had my eye on.

Almost.

⊖ ⊖ ⊖

On the drive home from the restaurant, I was lost to daydreams, picturing myself a year or two down the road, gray again, naturally. My hair would look amazing. If gray could be hip on hipsters, why not seniors? In my mental movie, I was fit and trim as Juliet, with an age-appropriate designer wardrobe. No white Daisy Dukes for me, a look I couldn't even pull off at sixteen.

"You sure you're okay with this?" I asked Bob.

"What's this now?" he said, drumming the steering wheel.

"My hair, going gray."

"Oh, that. You know Rocky won't follow through."

"She might."

"Roxanne? When has she ever stuck with anything? The woman goes through men like toilet paper."

Having left two husbands myself, the going-through-men-like-toilet-paper allusion struck a little too close to home.

"What's that got to do with this?" I asked.

"You know what I mean. I give it two weeks before she's distracted by the next brain fart."

Bob was probably right. Roxanne always has some new plan for transforming her life. Building a "capsule" wardrobe and downsizing into a tiny home being some of the most recent. Efforts to simplify in a world that tends to pointless clutter. She's a font of enthusiasms. It's one of her most endearing traits.

For the moment, my sister was enthusiastic about going gray, which I suspected had more to do with the new boyfriend than any deeper impulse. Her motivations didn't bother me. I had my own reasons. It wasn't only what Bill had said about his sister looking old, or what Bob hadn't said. I was still licking my wounds from the last time, five years ago. When my dad died, I'd begun to contemplate my own mortality. I was struck with an, "it's now or never" fervor to own my age, my dreams, my life, before it was too late. I decided to go gray. When my roots were a few inches long, I cropped my hair short. It was not a flattering look. But my hair grows fast. Within two years it was long enough to pull back into a streaky French braid, twisting strands of gray, white, gun-metal and brown.

I'd been happy with the hair.

Whooshing down the I-5 towards home, the synchronicity struck me. My last hair epiphany had also resulted from a conversation at the Tower Cafe. That time it was just me and my two sisters. A different perky young waitress had taken our orders.

"What a beautiful family. Your daughters look so much like you," she'd said, beaming right at me.

At least that time Roxanne hadn't blurted out, "*awkward.*"

After the waitress left us, Juliet said, "Don't listen to her. She's an idiot. There's no way you look like our mother."

Easy for her to say.

That one misguided compliment had sent me back to the hairdresser. What had taken me years to attain was undone in under two hours. We'd been three dark-haired sisters ever since. In the intervening years, no one else had mistaken me for their mother, or if they wondered, they kept the thought to themselves, like when it's on the tip of your tongue to congratulate a woman on her pregnancy when you realize she might just have a big belly.

Gray hair or dark, Juliet still looked twenty years younger than me. Chances are she always will. Sister envy be damned. If I wanted to go gray, that's what I should do. I'd planned to wait until I was at my ideal weight, figuring a decent body would mitigate for the awkward hair stage. But I'd been waiting five years for that to happen and hadn't managed to budge more than five pounds, and not always in the right direction.

Bob pulled into the driveway.

"It's too hot for a bike ride," he said. "I think I'll go swimming. Work off some of that meal. I am *stuffed.*"

Half a damn chicken salad, and he was stuffed.

I unstuck myself from the car seat and plucked at the staticky folds of my dress. By the time I reached the kitchen, Bob was already out in the backyard, barefoot and shirtless, uncovering the pool. I sidled into the pantry and palmed six of his favorite low-fat chocolate chip cookies. Not nearly so tasty as a slice of Tower Cafe cake, but it was all we had.

I got cozy on the couch, the stack of cookies hidden in the folds of my dress. I bit into one. It would have to do. I undid my bun, finger-combed my long, falsely dark hair and pointed the remote at the television.

⊖ ⊖ ⊖

Bob was right. I hate it when that happens.

Within months, Rocky had abandoned the let's-go-gray-together plan. Alan was history, too. I didn't begrudge her for either decision. She'd tried. Her hairdresser's approach was to take my sister's hair lighter by degrees, so that her roots wouldn't be so stark. The result was a sort of twiggy blonde. I thought it suited her, but Roxanne felt faded out.

"I think it makes me look tired," she said.

Maybe it did. Maybe she was tired. I don't know. Her hair. Her decision.

My hairdresser, a gorgeous woman from the Philippines, wouldn't even go as far as Roxanne's colorist.

"Oh, no, you not ready for that. At least ten, twenty years more," she said.

"But I'm already in my sixties."

"My mother is 87. I still color her hair every three weeks. It makes her feel pretty. That's what you want, right? To feel pretty."

I let Isabel color it one more time, for old time's sake. But I did not aspire to the Diane Feinstein look. I'd also been wondering whether hair keeps growing after you die, the way fingernails and toenails do. I pictured myself ten feet under, with long, unkempt nails and a half-inch halo of white roots. What would the archeologists of the future think of me? I don't know why that seemed compelling. Lacking cheerleaders among the living, I was clutching for moral support from the scientists of the future.

On a friend's recommendation – she was going through the hair change, too – I made an appointment with her stylist.

Paul was 22, with expressive brown eyes and a sweet smirk that made me think he knew he was adorable, but it hadn't gone to his head.

"Let's have a look at what you've got going on here," he said, sifting through my mass of hair, parting it this way and that, feeling the strands, moving in closer then backing up, giving its nuances so much consideration, I felt as if I'd gotten my money's worth before he even started. I'd been touched *and* seen. Not a common sensation post-forty.

"You have amazing hair," he said. "A-mazing. And I'm excited to be part of your transformation. Let me show you something."

He pulled a phone from the pocket of his overalls, cavalierly unbuckled on one side so the strap hung down and swayed as he moved around the chair.

"This is what I'm picturing for you." He showed me several photographs of an attractive older woman, wavy hair nearly to her waist, silver and gray streaked with darker strands up near her face, trending to dark streaked with light, as it cascaded down.

"I love it," I said.

"Isn't she gorgeous?" Paul said, blushing. "That's my mom."

"Did you do her hair?"

"I did. And I can do the same for you." He paused, hands on my head again, fingertips providing a gentle massage. I melted into the chair. "You've got a *ton* of hair, and a ton of variation. It's still super dark in the back, while your crown is almost white, then there's everything in between. I would feel much better if you let it grow another six weeks, at least, so I can really see how your gray is coming in before we get into this. Can you do that for me?"

Of course, I could. It was all so professional. My hair was a long-term project, a worthy campaign. He was an artist and I his canvas.

"Let's get you shampooed," Paul said.

It was the best shampoo I'd ever had, followed by a deep conditioning treatment. His tobacco-scented fingers kneaded my scalp, temples and neck, followed by the best haircut and blow-out ever. I hadn't known it could be so good. Even with half an inch of white framing my face, I looked damned elegant. When he was done, he put a mirror in my hand and swiveled me around, so I could admire his artistry from all angles.

"Doesn't she look gorgeous?" he said, presenting me to the salon at large.

The other stylists, and a handful of clients who peered out from under their foils, nodded approvingly.

"You're good to go, Goddess," he said.

I assumed that was what he called all his female clients. Still, I was charmed, seduced into believing that I really could be someone's goddess. I tossed my hair all the way to the car.

When I got home, Bob glanced up from the computer screen and smiled. I shook my mane.

"Well?" I said, spinning on my heel.

"It's subtler than I expected," he said.

"I haven't done anything yet."

"Well, I like it," he said. "It's still long."

2

The last week of August, Bob and I flew to New York with our daughter, to help her move into the dorm at Columbia College, nearly 3,000 miles from home. My family had always gone to public schools, three generations of University of California graduates, and proud of it. The Ivy League had been Carolanne's dream. I'd never seen a teenager work so hard, to the detriment of a social life, or any activity that wouldn't add to her impressive resume. She'd set a goal and achieved it. I didn't understand, but I was proud for her all the same.

Bob and I returned to our empty five-bedroom house in the suburbs. We'd needed the space when we conjoined households. An unexpected pregnancy at 44, followed by what amounted to a modern-day shotgun wedding, brought us together three weeks before Carolanne was born, a newborn and four anxious step-siblings under one roof for the first time. For years, we were in survival mode. Our relationship became the least of our worries.

It was down to the two of us now, both retired – rattling around in a house we'd bought to accommodate our hastily blended family of seven. I wondered what would keep us together now.

There was an added weight to what we said, and didn't say, to one another. As if we were actors in a reality TV show about empty nesters, trying to act natural while a team of videographers followed us from room to room. The camera caught the tightened lips, the sniff and quick shake of my head when Bob said something that infuriated me. The notion that we could do anything we wanted—run around naked, have sex in the kitchen, shout obscenities at one another, sleep in separate bedrooms, eat beef—hung in the air, juxtaposed against the routines we'd established and now stuck to as if we had no other choice, as if someone might see.

The first night home, I pulled on my *I Love Lucy* pajamas and settled into the right side of our barge of a bed, my side. I arranged three pillows against the head board, picked a book from the teetering pile on my bedside table and switched my distance glasses for readers.

"I see you've already taken to the bed," Bob said, glancing at the clock as he passed through the bedroom on his way to the bathroom. "I guess it's not too early."

It was on the tip of my tongue to thank him for granting me permission to read in bed. If we hadn't been alone in the house, I might have. Sensing those hidden cameras, I restrained myself. I would *not* play the part of the shrewish wife.

Bob undressed in the walk-in closet, stripping down to his boxers. As he crossed the bed to his side, I snuck a peek over the tops of my glasses, taking in the muscles in his thighs and calves, his lean arms and tanned biceps. He climbed into bed, plumped his three pillows, picked up his phone and began scrolling, chuckling from time to time, chin bouncing on his chest. I didn't ask what was so damn funny. Nor did he tell me. After a few minutes, he set his phone down on the bedside table and turned out his light.

"I miss my baby," he said. He rubbed his fists in his eye sockets in mock despair and kicked at the covers like a petulant child.

I laughed as the sheets puffed with air. I missed her, too. But for Bob it was different. I wasn't the only one who thought so.

"How is Bob going to survive without Carolanne?" a neighbor had asked. "I can't believe he's letting her go. What's he going to do with himself?"

His only daughter. His baby. His sweetie. His reason for living.

Sometimes, watching them together, I would get this pang in my chest. The way he put an arm around her to pull her to his side. The way he kissed her forehead and said, "Goodnight, sweetheart," a wellspring of devotion in his every word and gesture that felt palpably different than the routine niceties we exchanged.

Bob pulled the covers up to his chin and scooted closer, his body a curved crescent beneath our blue and white quilt.

"I'm fussy," he said, burrowing deeper and pulling his knees up so they grazed my side.

I could have snapped off my light, set my book down and snuggled beside him. We might have cuddled, whispered in the dark, perhaps even made love. I couldn't remember when the last time was.

"Poor baby," I said, turning the page in my book.

My lone bedside light cast a yellowy circle. The house beyond our bedroom was still and dark. No creak of footsteps from our daughter's upstairs bedroom. Our entitled black cat, Luma, snored huskily at my feet. Mocha, the geriatric poodle mutt we adopted fifteen years earlier from a local animal shelter, snoozed in a basket at the foot of the bed, no longer able to jump up and join us on the parental raft. The grandfather clock in the living room chimed the half hour. The words on the page fuzzed. Bob's breath shifted in rhythm, grew deeper, less self-aware. Twenty minutes. Thirty. A snuffled snore. I set the book and my reading glasses down and clicked off the bedside light.

I had to pee. Again.

I blame the pregnancies, the weight of my babies bearing down, weakening the gaskets, the sphincter muscles designed to hold things in and let them out. I leak when I dance, jump, laugh and cough. Anything more percussive – retching, sprinting, sneezing fit – and I do more than leak. I know what my doctor would advise. Drop fifty pounds, exercise that flabby pelvic floor.

Roxanne bought me a mug that says, "Don't make me laugh, I'll wet my pants."

"God, that's perfect," Bob said, when she showed it to him. His bladder is still able to go the distance. Of course, it is.

I slid from bed and felt my way to the bathroom. The glare from the security light in the neighbor's backyard filtered through the opaque glass in the window beside the toilet. On the toilet, flannel pajama bottoms a fuzzy puddle around my feet, I hefted my gut and cradled it with both hands. My hands butted up against the puckered scars from two C-sections. The fat roll came right up to the tight, scarified tissue and stopped, hanging over the cliff. I ran a finger along the scars.

Like all mothers, I have my birth stories. My eldest arrived six weeks early, after I slipped on the popcorn-slick floor while cleaning the movie theater where I worked, and landed on my tailbone. I had my first, planned, caesarean with my older daughter, second child. Ten years later Carolanne was born. The obstetrician assured us she was small and recommended a vaginal delivery, despite the prior C-section and my age. Labor at 44 was a bitch. After the final push, I collapsed, only dimly aware as the doctor passed our damp newborn to a waiting nurse, who in turn tossed her to Bob. Before I thought to ask why they were treating my baby like a football, the ceiling began to slide. I was being pushed down the corridor, so fast the wheels rattled on the linoleum. The doctor jogged alongside the bed. She held my head up and pressed vials of yellow liquid to my lips.

"Chug it," she said. "Now another. We've got to get you into surgery."

My uterus had burst during delivery. Along with the baby, blood gushed onto the doctor's front and soaked her booties.

Now that child was eighteen and clear across the country.

Whenever we're reminded of her birth, Bob pales as if he's experiencing it all over again. Blood. Panic. Fear.

My fingers grazed the scant tendrils that flecked my pudgy pubic mound, a pale triangle diminished by the press of thighs and belly. Nearly hairless, the once coarse thicket of dark hair rubbed off by years of chafing against restrictive clothing. There was a buffed sweetness to my beleaguered crotch, or so it seemed in the forgiving light of the toilet at night. As if my body were reverting to girlhood, the maturation process moving in reverse now that the procreative imperative had been realized.

I stifled a laugh.

The notion of innocence regained, of coming full circle, was appealing, a rationale for my relative chastity. There were others. My body embarrassed me. It didn't look, or feel, the way it once did, the way I wished it still did.

I'd been dieting for over forty years, since gaining that first freshman twenty, a consequence of the unaccustomed availability of unlimited quantities of pizza and fries, a soft serve ice cream machine, no mother to insist I eat my veggies. I've counted calories, points and grams of carbs, fiber and protein. I've popped pills, fasted, cleansed and eaten nothing but cabbage soup. Sometimes I succeeded in losing enough weight that people noticed and said nice things. Enough that I had a valid reason to shop for new clothes. Yet no matter the number on the scale, or how thin I appeared in the mirror or photographs, it was never enough.

Nor did it last.

Dissatisfaction with the size and shape of my body had been a constant, a tedious subplot to whatever else was going on in my life. I'd spent my entire adult life either binging or dieting, fluctuating ten, twenty, forty pounds, several times a year. Months of dogged effort to reach that magic number. Only to put it back on, and then some. I could have compiled a slide show, me through the years, expanding then contracting. Cheeks defined then puffed. Musculature appearing then disappearing. Outfits that nip in at the waist, reveal arms and legs, designer jeans. Followed by muumuus and elastic waistbands.

And now my metabolism crept. I doubted my ability and desire to do it again. Perhaps it was time to give up the battle, to admit defeat and own my body as it was. Time to relax already. Then there was my younger sister, a constant reminder that I could, and should, take better care of myself. And Bob, who seemed to lose weight at the same rate as I gained it. Perhaps if he caressed my tummy rolls. Kissed the scars. Stroked the staple marks. Maybe then I could be content with who I've become. Maybe.

I snorted.

Likely I'd push him away.

I had long suspected he loves me "anyway." Even though I'm not slender. Even though I don't have big tits, though at fifty-pounds overweight, they're almost as big as when I was nursing. Even though I'm not the sort of woman he ever dreamed of ending up with. Not that I knew what kind of woman that was. Only that she couldn't be me.

I suspected his love was habitual. That he loved me because he loved me. It had become a given, not a conscious choice.

My mother used to say that men are creatures of habit. I imagined that was true of most people. I felt like a habit for Bob. Some part of me still believed there must be some higher, truer kind of love, the inspiration for centuries of stories and songs immortalizing star-crossed lovers whose devotion doesn't fade, sink with the ship or end with death. I wondered if I would be capable of recognizing love like that, if I could accept it, believe in it, if it ever found me.

Maybe there was no happily ever after. Only lives like ours, that have their flashes and gullies, that feel one way on the inside and appear another from the outside. My sisters were always gushing about how devoted Bob was to me. I was never sure if they saw something I didn't, or if I was the one who couldn't see what was in front of me.

After my last pregnancy, the veins in my inner thighs bulged. I'd run my fingertips across the rippled surface and collapse the tunnels with a fingertip, feeling my pulse there.

"You should feel this," I once said, reaching for Bob's hand.

"I'm good," he said, shivering as if he'd been struck by a sudden chill wind.

"But it feels so cool."

"I'll take your word for it."

I remember how it used to be. Learning a new lover's body. Each blemish and healed wound a story, an invitation to share a piece of private history, to deepen that sense of acceptance, of belonging. Discovering Bob's ragged appendectomy scar. A childhood burn that left a hairless, angry swath on his torso. The deep clefts in his earlobes. The balls of lint that collect in his belly button and that he used to save for me.

In the twenty-five plus years since we met, he's changed, too. His chest hair now a soft gray blanket. Knobby lumps on his calves. His own network of swollen veins. We have become more modest with one another. An erosion of daily intimacies, an increase in inhibitions. Closed bathroom doors. Dressing in the privacy of the walk-in closet.

Perhaps he felt the changes as much as I did. Yet he was still tall and fit. I envied his muscled legs, his metabolism. Last year, he jittered off twenty pounds in a month, without intending to. The doctor said it was thyroiditis, which passed. But the weight stayed off.

Men. Husbands. Bob.

When I crept back to bed, Bob was farther onto my side than before. Hands folded in prayer beneath his cheek, six-foot four frame in a fetal curl. Lost to sleep, his breath was a soft putter. Yet he roused the instant my body dented the mattress. I wondered how long I'd been cogitating on the toilet and if he was lying in wait all the while, only feigning sleep, wondering what the hell I was doing in there.

He raised up on one elbow, a wobbly shadow hovering beside me.

"Where are you? I can't find you. Ah, there you are," he said, planting the ritual goodnight kiss on my mouth.

No matter how long I stay up after he turns out his light, he wakes for that measly kiss. The rituals of which a marriage are made. Maybe that's the kind of thing my sisters are talking about when they say he's devoted to me.

Why was it so hard to see it that way?

"Good night. Hope you sleep well. Love you," he said.

"Love you too," I said. "Good night."

We hunkered into our respective pillows and gathered the covers closer. There were none of the signs that the goodnight kiss would be a prelude to anything else. Those signals are familiar, too, though far less frequent. The kiss becomes something more, ever so subtly so. An arm draped over my side. A tentative nibble at my lower lip. A shifting closer, entering one another's space.

There was only the soft pressure of the kiss, the murmured niceties, before we assumed our positions, our breath audible, tangible as puffs of smoke in the dark. As his breath evened out, relief became regret and loneliness, a sense of loss and longing that was almost unbearable. It would have been so easy to extend the kiss, to be the one to drape my arm over his side.

Now it was too late.

I couldn't sleep. My thoughts tugged me to places I didn't want to go. With my second husband, as we neared the end, I stopped playing my part. No perfunctory goodbye kiss as I left for work. No equally perfunctory goodnight peck. No "how was work?" These gestures had become incongruous, lies I couldn't sustain. My second husband was not a good person, at least not to me. Bob is.

My feelings for Bob, and about us, were more complex. I didn't think he judged me for letting myself go nearly so much as I did myself. Did he see me at all? I was wife, mother, companion. The shape I took seemed irrelevant. I was invisible.

"Look around," he would say, when I asked if I looked all right. "You look better than most women your age."

This did not have the reassuring effect I imagine he intended.

Better than most. Not bad for your age.

A friend once told me, "If you're not having sex, you're headed for divorce. He's getting it somewhere else." I wondered why she'd chosen to share this tidbit of magazine-rack wisdom with me, what she knew, or suspected. I didn't ask.

I stared into the night. Eyes wide and dry. The outline of my husband's body a mountain range under the comforter, a hump for hips and shoulders. Perhaps he was faking sleep, too. Perhaps he'd seen the glint of my eyes in the scant moonlight. I laid my hand on the cool sheet beside him, fingers splayed, reaching out. Close enough that I could have touched him. Close enough that his breath tickled my fingertips.

I wanted to be held, to feel his arms around me, to touch the smooth skin on his biceps, that one muscled spot where no hair grows. A body I knew well and yet not at all. I didn't move any closer. I couldn't. I hadn't. Not in a long time. It felt so fraught, so risky. The longer the dry spells lasted, the harder it became to breach the divide.

A cringing sea anemone, I retracted my hand, pulled in my arms, my feelings. I counted from one to ten, again and again, willing my mind to shut down for the night. Worried my shifts and turns under the covers and my noisy thoughts would wake him, I slipped from bed and crept to the couch in the front room. With a plop and the scratch of toenails on wood flooring, Mocha and Luma joined me. I was a coward. A thief in the night. Stealing from myself. I vowed to do better, to get a grip. In the morning, tomorrow.

I was awakened by my cell phone. Five AM. Aside from an emergency, Roxanne is the only person who calls so early. It's rarely for any reason, just to check in. We're both notoriously early risers.

"Hey, Bozo," I said.

"Did I interrupt you and Bob having wild sex?" she asked.

"How'd you guess?"

3

Our youngest child was far away and miserable in New York City. Stuck with a snobby, snippy Upper East Side roommate, Carolanne worried she'd made a horrible mistake, that she should have gone to UC Berkeley when she had the chance.

She phoned late on a Friday. It's never a good sign when a child has time for Mom on Friday night. I sat in the front room, beside her guinea pig's cage. I stroked the sleek patch of fur between Marmalade's eyes.

"Where are you, honey?" I asked.

"In the stairwell."

"Why?"

"Megan is in the room with some of her friends. They're talking about me like I'm not there."

My stomach muscles clenched.

"Any fun plans for the weekend?"

"Just studying." There was a hitch in her voice.

"It's a quiet one for me, too."

"They're all quiet," my daughter said. "Does it get better?"

I hesitated, remembering my own freshman year. The professor who suggested I stop writing and see a therapist. All the parties I wasn't invited to. Mean boys. Meaner girls.

"Off and on," I said.

My daughter had been so excited to leave home for college.

I'd been the same way, so sure my dreams would at last be realized, my life transformed. But I was just me. There's that adage – wherever you go, there you are. I didn't think it would help to repeat it.

"I got this from you," she said, as if loneliness were a disease or birth defect. "Half my DNA and all my mitochondria are yours, you know."

"It doesn't work that way," I said, but I do sometimes wonder if I transmitted the outsider gene to my kids.

I suggested she keep an eye out for others who looked like they could use a friend, and to take the initiative by introducing herself. I told her to join clubs to meet new people. I knew she didn't believe me when I said I was sure there were plenty of other kids who felt the same way she did. I hadn't believed it either. Like all the other lonely kids, I believed I was the only one, though I would never have thought to blame my mother's DNA and mitochondria. I'd been certain we were nothing alike.

Forty years after I graduated college, I went back to school for an MFA in Creative Writing. Even at sixty, a crowded dining hall without a pal saving me a seat was a terrifying prospect. Even though I'd paid for them, I skipped most meals. Anything not to have to walk by the popular kids' table and imagine what they were whispering about me.

⊖ ⊖ ⊖

When I was a freshman at UC Davis, the flat, rambling campus had a wholesome, rural quality, which I hated. The school drew many of its students from the small farming communities that dot the fertile Sacramento Valley. My Marin County home was less than two hours distant, but I might as well have been in Kansas.

I enrolled in a creative writing class that first quarter. The

33

professor was a mousy brunette who wore sweater sets and pearls. At least that's how I've chosen to remember her. One assignment was to journal for twenty minutes a day and turn the journal in at the end of the week. I couldn't wait for her to read mine, confident she'd see how brilliant I was. The Monday after the first hand-off, my professor gave my slim black book back to me with a deeply furrowed brow. She had underlined half the words in red ink. "These are all adjectives for how you feel. Try describing something tangible," she'd written.

Tangible. Was she serious? Obscurity was the point. Rule one of adolescent writing.

As she handed me back the black book the following week, she made sad, puppy dog eyes and asked me to come to her office after class. When I did, she said, "I think you should give personal writing a rest for a while. I don't think it's, um, good for you. Perhaps you need someone to talk to." She handed me a brochure listing various student services, with the phone number for the counseling center circled.

I was crushed, and thrilled. This ignorant, watery-eyed bitch didn't see the genius in me. That part was annoying. But she thought I needed professional help. That was cool. Lots of creative types suffer mental illness. I was in good company.

I stuffed the brochure in my backpack and rode my bicycle home, to a dorm on the edge of campus. The lobby was empty except for our RA, a chunky graduate student I'll call Rhonda, in honor of the Beach Boys song. Rhonda sat behind a collapsible card table. A banner of construction paper was tacked to the wall above her, with "Psychiatric Help: 5¢," written in runny black poster paint. There was a smaller sign taped to the front of the table, that offered, "The Doctor is IN."

I recognized the recurring gag from the *Peanuts* comic strip, where Lucy staffs a psychiatrist booth and hands out brusque, insensitive advice for a nickel. Yet what were the odds? I'd just been told I should go see a shrink, and here, right in my own dorm lobby, sat someone professing to be a mental health professional. And the price was right.

I sat down opposite her and dropped a nickel through a slot cut into the plastic lid of a coffee can. Rhonda picked the can up and shook it like a maraca.

"You're my first customer," she said. "I guess nobody else gets it. Cookie?" She nudged a plate of chocolate chip cookies towards me. "It's Dorothy, right? Or do you go by a nickname? Dot? Dottie? Dolly?"

I mumbled "no" around a mouthful of cookie.

"How's it going with the new roommate? Everything OK?"

"Yeah, she's fine," I said. Which was true, when she was there. My roommate spent every spare moment with her boyfriend, in Sacramento. It was like living with a ghost.

"Classes working out?" Rhonda asked.

I blinked to hold back tears.

"Want to talk about it?"

My lower lip trembled.

She leaned closer and whispered, "Is it, is it *drugs*?" Her gaze flit nervously around the lobby. "You can get addiction counseling at the Health Center."

Addiction. *Seriously.*

I got why she went there, sort of. It was because of what happened my first night in the dorm. We were putting our clothes away, listening to music. My roommate rolled up a towel, shoved it against the door, and lit a joint. After a few tokes, there was a knock. It was Rhonda, stern-faced, with half the girls from the floor jammed into the narrow hallway behind her, craning to see into the room. We were lucky she let us off with a warning.

"I'm sure the other girls will like you once they get to know you," she said. "You should join an intramural team."

35

Little did I know I'd be giving similar advice to my own daughter one day.

It was nearing dinnertime. In groups of twos and threes, dorm residents streamed past, through the doors and across the lawn to the dining hall.

"Got to love Snoopy," Rhonda said.

"Yeah. Lucy is great."

"You know, Dotty, there's a real counseling center on campus if you need it. I mean this was just a gag, an icebreaker, or whatever. You got that, right?"

It was my second referral to the counseling center in one day.

I went. The therapist was even more morose than me, always on the verge of tears. Or am I confusing her with the creative writing professor? Could be. She wasn't an MD, so she couldn't prescribe any drugs. She just listened, and nodded, and sniffled into a tissue. She did suggest that if I really felt like I couldn't handle things, I could admit myself to a psych ward. She offered to give me a referral. But that would have involved notifying my parents. I was depressed, but not *that* depressed.

4

The yearly sanctioned overeating season – Halloween through New Year's – was imminent. Three months packed with more obligatory social occasions than the preceding nine months combined. I was still up twenty pounds from the prior year's round of holiday gatherings. My goal was to lose at least ten for a big family wedding in early November.

I was without a child at home for the first time in 36 years. Bob wasn't around much either. He'd retired the previous December, a few years after I did, and was spending full days as a volunteer with several nonprofits. He worked longer hours as a volunteer than he had when there was a paycheck involved. Which meant I had all the time in the world to devote to my own to-do list. I'd been waiting for this kind of freedom all my adult life.

After Bob left the house in the morning, I'd make myself a cup of coffee and open my journal, setting my pen down at the top of a fresh page to enjoy a few minutes of reflection before launching the day. Then the tears would start. Some days it was all I could do to get dressed. Showering slipped from daily, to alternate days, to every three or four days. What my mother used to call a sensible "European" cleansing routine, as opposed to us hygiene-obsessed Americans.

I didn't understand what my problem was – a jumble of early

onset seasonal affective disorder, empty nest blues, belated mid-life crisis and the surreal nightmare of the presidential campaign. Add to that my mother, 94, diminished by Alzheimer's. She'd been booted out of an assisted living facility for being too aggressive and was now in a locked "memory care unit," likely her new forever home.

"People just disappear from this place," she said.

She was right. They were there one visit and gone the next, soon to be replaced with yet another mumbling, shuffling shell, what remained of a beloved spouse and parent, once a prominent doctor, professor or scientist, or, like Mom, a globe-trotting romantic and would-be archeologist, chasing her dreams until she forgot what they were.

⊖ ⊖ ⊖

Bob always bought our annual supply of Halloween candy. I reminded him to pick a kind I wouldn't be tempted to pilfer.

"Get something gummy or sour," I said.

"Why would I buy that crap?"

"Well, anything but chocolate, *please*."

"Oh, I'm getting chocolate. It's Halloween. A few pieces won't hurt."

Bob loves chocolate. But he's one of those people who can have a piece or two and be good. Not me. One taste and I can't stop until it's gone or I'm too sick to keep eating, whichever comes first. Even knowing it's likely to trigger a migraine that will knock me down for days.

"At least hide it," I said. "And not in one of the usual places."

"You'll be fine."

"I'm serious. Don't let me find it. I need to drop a few pounds before the wedding."

Most people are like my husband. They don't get it. "Oh, I have a major sweet tooth, too," they say. But do they eat an entire bag of candy or a box of cookies at one sitting, then tear the kitchen apart looking for more? Do they gain ten pounds in a month? A few years back, when I went in for my six-month dental checkup, I had eleven cavities. *Eleven.* The dentist asked if I'd been crunching hard candies in my sleep. I told him no. Which was true. Hard candies are not my Achilles heel. But I do sometimes fall asleep with chocolate melting in my mouth.

For me, sugar is a drug, one that's legal, cheap and plentiful. If you're an addict, you don't have a taste of heroin, a little bit of booze or meth. It's no different with sugar.

Two weeks before Halloween, I got home from visiting Mom. Bob's car was in the driveway. I looked for him in his office, and there they were. Two jumbo sacks of assorted chocolates, in plain sight on top of the file cabinet. 120 pieces each. 240 mini candy bars in all.

I picked up one sack, then the other, probing for holes in the plastic. I was relieved, and disappointed, not to find any.

It was possible he'd just gotten home and hadn't had time to hide the candy yet. I made a mental note to remind him to get it out of my sight.

But I didn't. As we ate dinner, watched tv, then did the dishes, I pictured all that chocolate, so close. Beckoning. Tantalizing. Inevitable. Like the secret thrill and anticipation of an inappropriate crush.

For several days, I was strong. When I laid my head down on the pillow at night, I congratulated myself on my willpower. When I woke in the morning, I resolved to remain strong.

One morning, five days into my heroic resistance campaign,

I got a text from a good friend, one of less than a handful remaining from my thirty-five-year career clawing my way up the rungs of the state civil service ladder.

"Don't forget Barbara's retirement party tonight," she texted. "How about we get some dinner after?"

"Sounds like a plan," I responded.

I set my phone down and riffled through the clothes in my closet. The last time many of the people at this event would have seen me was nearly five years earlier, when I was still taking pains to look the part of their executive director. In my head shot for the agency's website, my gaze is confident, my hair dark and sleek. I'm wearing a tailored suit with a silk blouse that highlights my green eyes. That was the version of myself I preferred my coworkers and colleagues remember.

I shucked my pajamas and tried on a favorite top, tunic length to conceal tummy and hips. I paired it with my go-to elastic waistband pants, black, of course, with a flattering straight leg. I examined myself in a full-length mirror. Front view, suck in the gut, then the sides, suck it in some more. I held a hand mirror, angling it to get a view of my backside. I tugged at the tunic's hem. Stood on tiptoes to elongate my legs. No matter the angle or pose, there was no denying the truth in the mirror.

I'd been wallowing on the couch in sweats and pajamas for weeks, avoiding mirrors and the scale. But there it was, the new me.

And my hair. Ye gads. It would be just like the first time I went gray. They'd assume I'd forgotten, or was too lazy or cheap to go to the hairdresser to get my roots done. I regretted having accepted the invitation. I regretted having responded so quickly to my friend's text. Now I *had* to go, even if it meant shopping for something new to wear in yet another size up. That, and getting my hair blown out at a salon so that, hopefully, the focus would remain above my neck.

40

I passed Bob's open office door. The two sacks of mini choco-lates were still there, resting on top of the file cabinet. No harm in having a closer look, in touching them through the plastic.

I hefted one multi-colored sack. The candies plopped to the one end, then the other. When I reached for the second bag, there it was. A tiny opening in one corner of the thick plastic. The bag had been breached. *I* hadn't done it. I was innocent. Bob had sampled the Halloween candy.

There were so many. He'd never notice if I pilfered a few more. I selected four pieces, one of each kind. If I had candy with my coffee instead of a piece of toast with peanut butter, it was close to the same number of calories. Besides, it was almost Halloween. It's tradition to sample the candy.

I plopped down on my favorite corner of the couch and set the candies on the coffee table, prepared to savor them, then get on with my day. I ate the first, forcing myself not to gobble it down in one bite, then another, then the rest. They weren't as satisfying as I'd anticipated. I hadn't taken sufficient time to savor them. I stuffed the wrappers in my pocket and returned for more. The next four went down even faster than the first. I returned to the bag again and again, taking only a few each time, telling myself they would be the last. At first I kept track, so I could account for the extra calories. Then I stopped. What was the use? There was no undoing the damage. I'd tried for years to be bulimic. Forced vomiting has never worked for me. I gag, but nothing ever comes up. My stomach is stingy that way.

I consumed the last dozen in a frenzy, fingers in constant, frantic motion, tearing and shoving, crunching and swallowing, my world reduced to the sensations in my mouth, gone too quickly, demanding more, more. I didn't stop until my stomach lurched. The couch was littered with twisted wrappers, my pajama top stained with bits of chocolate, slowly melting from the heat of my body.

Satiated, glutted, nauseous, I gathered up the wrappers and buried them deep in the kitchen trash can. I texted my friend to say that I wouldn't be able to make it after all. I wasn't feeling well.

"Sorry," I wrote. "Give Barbara my best wishes. Tell her to stay in touch."

Instead of shame, I felt only relief. I had the day to recover, to digest and pray I didn't get a migraine.

It was Bob's fault. He'd left the huge sack in plain sight, with a fucking mouse hole in it.

There was one consolation. Though I'd eaten a ton, the bag was massive. I fluffed the remaining contents, convincing myself Bob wouldn't notice. I showered and tugged on a loose pair of sweats and a t-shirt, avoiding my image in the mirror. The day was now a blank slate, no intrusions, no witnesses. There was work to be done. Editing two novel-length manuscripts for friends from graduate school.

I stretched out on the couch to ease the pressure on my stomach. My eyes were heavy. Crashing hard after the rush of all that sugar, I nodded off. The unread manuscripts slid to the floor.

⊖ ⊖ ⊖

I knew I should shove the opened sack of candy into Bob's hands and demand he get it out of the house. But my primordial self, the part of me with ultimate control over my motor functions, wouldn't let me. Three days before Halloween, the bag of 120 candy bars was more than half empty. There was no way he wouldn't notice. What the hell. I decided I might as well finish it off and replace it with a new sack.

Bloated with chocolate, I squeezed behind the steering wheel and drove to half a dozen stores searching for the same candy bar blend, finally finding one that was close enough. I

42

bought two bags. Just in case. Continuing the charade, I tore a small opening in one bag, emptied a third of the candies into my underwear drawer and put the new bag back on top of the file cabinet in Bob's office.

When I checked the next day, the candy was gone. Vanished. All of it. I searched Bob's usual hiding spots. Nothing. He'd finally done what I'd asked. Perhaps he'd known I was at it all along. Yet he never said a word. Knowing he knew was humiliating enough. I vowed to turn over a new leaf. I packed up my work and drove to our cabin in the hills of Calaveras County, to hunker down, work on my friends' manuscripts and my own, take long walks and eat wisely. There was no way I could lose ten pounds by the wedding, but even five would be an improvement. I'd be back on track. Better late than never.

The migraine hit the next morning. I was two hours from home, alone. With summer over and the ski season not yet arrived, most of the surrounding mountain cabins were vacant. We had no land line or internet, and cell service was spotty. My head was a flaming match tip. I shut the blinds and curtains, turned out the lights and sunk to the floor to wait it out. I vomited until there was nothing left to vomit, then dry heaved. My ribs ached. I wet myself with each convulsion. The floor was littered with puddles of bile, wet towels and urine-soaked clothing. If I'd been home, I would have begged Bob to drive me to the doctor. Two shots in the ass, one for pain, one for nausea, then I could sleep it off. That wasn't an option.

I passed the day on the floor, memorizing the patterns and blemishes in the laminate, the dust balls and bits of forest duff beneath the furniture. I prayed. I promised a god I only thought of at moments like these that I would be a good girl, that I would never eat an entire jumbo sack of Halloween candy again.

By the next afternoon, I felt steady enough to drive to the grocery store for soda and saltines.

I've never understood how people can drink until they're black-out drunk, how they can poison themselves like that when they know how awful they're going to feel the next day. Yet I routinely eat myself sick. I claim to fear migraine more than anything, and when I'm in the grip of one, I vow never again. Yet I forget, and so soon. Or rather, I don't forget; I'm overcome with sugar lust.

⊖ ⊖ ⊖

Thanks to the migraine, I lost five pounds. Ten pounds by the wedding was once again within the realm of possibility. Perhaps I'd even fit into one of the dresses in my closet. After that wake-up call, I kept to the program for two weeks. Then Juliet stopped by the house with her poodle mutt, Sugar. She suggested a walk.

It was a beautiful, brisk day. We climbed the hill near my house to the bike path that runs for several miles on the levee above the banks of the Sacramento River. Sugar tugged at her leash, setting the pace. I confided in Juliet that I'd been struggling to lose weight.

"You look great," she said, with that perennially chipper smile of hers.

"No, *you* look great," I said. What I wanted to say was that she'd probably kill herself if she looked like me. "I need to lose fifty pounds."

"Well, it doesn't show. You always hide weight so well."

Which was true. I've always gained weight proportionally, every square inch of me packing on just a little, so I'm up thirty pounds before I really notice.

"I'll be your life coach," she said. "It will be fun. Just like old times."

Very old times. Eighteen years ago, we'd had our youngest

children one month apart. During our maternity leaves, we walked circles around my neighborhood park, pushing our newborns in their strollers. It had been nice to have someone to go through that with. We'd been equals then. Now she could be a model on the cover of a fitness magazine. The thought of being her "project" was not appealing.

"I just eat too much," I said.

"I can help with that, too. For example, for breakfast this morning I had a scoop of plain, nonfat Greek yoghurt with a sprinkle of granola and a handful of berries. *Delicious*. And so satisfying." She patted her belly as if all that wonderful deliciousness was still in there, fueling her.

I gave her my dubious carp look, mouth an inverted crescent.

"And don't deny yourself a little treat now and then. Bill brings me a piece of See's chocolate every morning with my coffee. It's just enough to satisfy my sweet tooth and make me feel pampered. Isn't he the sweetest man?"

"I'd eat the whole box."

"No you wouldn't," she said, chuckling. "Moderation in all things; that's what Dad used to say, remember?"

It's what he would say to our mother when she groused about trying to lose weight. I used to think it was funny when he said she looked like a beached whale in her swim suit. It didn't seem so funny anymore.

I squinted at Juliet. My beautiful sister beamed back at me. Was it in my head or was her sunny expression just a tad forced? A queasy suspicion dawned. My sisters had been talking about how much weight I'd gained. I imagined Bob was in on it, too. Maybe he'd put her up to this little intervention.

"Isn't Sugar just the cutest doggie in the whole wide world?" Juliet said.

"The cutest ever," I said, deadpan. I turned to her, doubt and envy twisting my face.

"Your expressions crack me up," she said.

Juliet stopped on the path and slapped her thighs. Her eyes filled with tears.

Of course, I hadn't meant to be funny. Fuck her and her little dog, too. Fuck them all. I'd eat candy if I wanted. And not just one piece with my coffee. One piece was *not* enough. It was so not enough.

After she left, I hit the kitchen. I decimated the grandkids' snack cupboard. I was shameless. No, I was past shame.

By two the next morning, I was on the floor again, even worse than at the cabin, vomiting, crying, then hating myself for crying, because it only made the pain worse. I concentrated on moving the pain to a part of me that I could amputate in my mind, sever from the rest of my body, and still survive. A toe or finger, an entire foot or hand if I had to. Anywhere but my head, behind my eyeballs, in my temples, at the base of my skull, the places where it cut the deepest.

When Bob woke, he knelt beside me and pressed a cold rag into my hand.

"What do you think about tomorrow?" he asked, his voice thick with concern. "The wedding in Palm Springs."

"I can't get on an airplane like this."

"Yeah, that's what I thought. I'll cancel your flight."

When I woke, the worst of it was over, but I was spent, wrung out, as if I'd spent twelve hours in a washing machine. Bob kissed my cheek and left for the airport. I stayed on the couch, Mocha in his basket beside me, grateful that the pain had eased, that I had survived. I promised never again. And in that moment, I meant it.

A little voice inside me whispered. "Oh, goody, now you don't have to go to the wedding and face everyone in that massive blouse you bought at Target along with the two sacks of candy."

I was glad to have the house to myself. Misery does not love

46

company. It's too much like looking in a mirror. I see myself in others' eyes, what I've done, what I've become.

Throughout the day, Bob texted me photos and videos from the wedding and of our kids and grandkids having fun without me. He told me how sorry everyone was that I had a migraine and couldn't be there. They were full of advice. Had I tried antihistamines? It might just be sinus pressure. Had I tried acupuncture? I'd tried everything. Except for kicking my sugar addiction and, perhaps even harder, finding some other way to deal with the feelings that sent me down that path in the first place.

Bob called that night.

"Feeling better?"

I was. A lot. I'd even made it off the couch and out of the house for a walk.

"I'm worried about you," he said. "The headaches seem to be getting worse. Even worse than when you were working. This is the second bad one in just a few weeks. You should go see Dr. Wong again. Maybe there's something new you can try."

I promised him I would. Though I knew there wouldn't be anything new, no magical cure. There never is. Only more drugs to try. Ones to deal with the pain, others that *might* be preventative. I knew I just needed to do the one thing I couldn't seem to do. Detox. Stay away from sugar.

If my husband had understood it was that simple, he would have said, "Fantastic, that's easy. Problem solved!"

I wish it were.

I have never known Bob to do anything to excess. Over-indulgence to the point of feeling awful isn't logical. No. It isn't. That's never been reason enough for me.

5

December fifth was my long-awaited follow-up appointment with Paul, my hairdresser and new best friend. For an excruciating six weeks, I'd let my gray grow out so he could "see" how it was coming in. I schlepped to the salon in sweats.

Techno music pumped from the sound system. Paul beckoned me to his chair.

He parted my hair and peered at the new growth. "Good girl. This is perfect, just what I was hoping for. *Better.* Plenty for me to work with. You are going to look amazing."

"At least my hair will."

"Stop that. Don't diminish yourself, girlfriend. You are *fabulous.*"

I forced a smile.

"If you don't pump yourself up, who will?"

The plan was to circle my crown with foils, to bleach all the color from bits of my darker hair then color it gray to blend with the new growth. He covered me with more foils than I'd ever seen on one head. I was a flat-quilled porcupine. Then we waited, and waited, as he periodically peeled back the edges of a few foils to assess the progress.

"Still too brassy," he said, after the third check. "We do not want yellow or orange."

"No, definitely not," I said.

Hours later, when he finally rinsed me out in the bowl, he raised his hand beside me so I could see. A handful of whitish hair had cracked clean off.

"Are you mad at me?" he asked.

"You warned me," I said. He had. He'd said that what "we" were attempting would be tough on my hair. Besides, how could I be mad at Paul? He'd said I was fabulous. And it was only hair.

Paul still wasn't satisfied. The parts that were supposed to be gray weren't gray enough. He slathered me with leave-in conditioner and asked if I could come back the next day.

⊖ ⊖ ⊖

Paul and I spent an entire weekend together.

In the end, my hair looked good, at least it did after he styled and smoothed it with fistfuls of expensive product. Dramatic threads of silver streaked through the dark brown. He'd done it so carefully, practically counting out individual strands of hair for each foil packet, that the effect was natural looking, a subtle weaving together of colors.

"It will probably look awful for awhile," he said. "This is a *process*. It takes time. We good?"

I nodded.

I didn't think it looked awful. Even though it was dry and brittle and a hodgepodge of white, gray, brown, and, despite all his efforts, the occasional brassy streak. The following weekend, I was walking to lunch at a restaurant near the home. One of my daughters-in-law was directly behind me.

"Your hair looks great," she said. "I love the way the silver weaves down the back. It's like a reverse ombré."

"Yeah?"

"You know, instead of dark roots and blonde tips, you've got the opposite."

I loved that. I wasn't growing out my gray. I had a for-real, trend-setting hairstyle, a reverse ombré.

What a difference five years made. The last time I'd gone gray, women complete strangers, would stop me on the street to exclaim over how brave I was. They would tell me they didn't have the guts to do what I'd done, or that their husbands would never allow it, but that they admired me for being so courageous. I had to wonder. Where had bravery entered the equation? Was it because I dared to leave the house looking like that?

William Faulkner is often quoted as having said, "The only thing worth writing about is the human heart in conflict with itself." I, and many other women I know, would amend that statement to add, "and hair."

To dye or not to dye? A question I'd agonized over for at least the last ten years. Finally, I believed I'd found my answer. Just let it grow, with a little help from Paul. Even if the result was more Lily Tomlin than Helen Mirren, that was fine by me.

6

December meant the annual holiday gathering with my husband's stepmother and our extended families – siblings, children, grandchildren – at a posh restaurant on the Central California coast.

It was a seven-hour drive from Sacramento. We would stop at a hotel two hours north of our destination, to allow time the following morning to change into fancy clothes, put on our party faces and drive the remaining distance.

Deciding what to pack was easy. Only a handful of clothes in my closet still fit, the kind that come in small, medium, large and extra large, rather than numbered sizes. I'd bought a black skirt with an elastic waistband and two size large sparkly tops, intending to wear one of them at the Palm Springs wedding I missed. The new tops were now snug, the fabric taut over hips and belly. I wished I'd gone with extra-large.

My hair had looked great after Paul's skilled ministrations, but when I tried to replicate the style, it just looked fried. He couldn't fit me in before we left, so I packed my electric curlers and flat iron, along with an assortment of expensive hair products.

I'd made our hotel reservation at the same hotel where we'd stayed the previous year. Bob and I had sex that night. Something that happens so infrequently the places where it does assume mythical properties. Perhaps there was some magic to the hotel bed with its overstuffed snow-white duvet and mega thread-count sheets. There was a chance we'd break our dry spell. It was worth a try.

During the drive, I snuck sideways glances at Bob. His face in profile still handsome, despite, or perhaps enhanced by, the slight double chin, the pockets of darker skin beneath his eyes, evidence of life lived, much of it together. I was anxious, equal parts anticipation and trepidation at the prospect of intimacy. We'd been alone in the house since Carolanne left for school, but there was something about the rented room that upped the ante.

Bob concentrated on the road. There was no knowing what was on his mind and little use asking. My father used to complain that women always assume men are thinking about something, when usually, at least according to Dad, they aren't. No deep thoughts anyway, certainly no thoughts about *you*, about your *relationship*.

We ate dinner in a pub adjacent to the hotel, a busy, local hangout. Several large screens streamed ballgames. Queasy with nervous energy, I ate more than I'd intended to. All my burger and fries and half of his. My gut was tight as a watermelon as I waddled back to the room. We changed for bed. I donned my slinkier, travel PJS, and we slid into our respective sides, mirroring our positions at home.

Within minutes, Bob set his *Time* magazine down and turned out his bedside light. I did the same. We kissed, the habitual goodnight touch of the lips, soft, no lingering pressure.

"Night, love you," he said.

"Love you, too."

As his breath evened out and lost its self-consciousness, I was relieved, then regretful. We were in the magic hotel room. I'd wasted the opportunity by overeating and losing any confidence I might otherwise have mustered. Worse than that. It had been pure self-sabotage. In the light of day, I pretended otherwise, but I was deathly afraid of intimacy, of what it might reveal about me, about us. The extra pounds had become my suit of protective armor, shielding me from pain, and pleasure.

⊖ ⊖ ⊖

I woke early and closeted myself in the bathroom to begin the beautification process. Electric curlers to tame the worst of the frizz. Flat iron to smooth the roots. Foundation and powder to cover the brown splotches on my face. Lipstick to lend some color to flesh-toned lips. Eye shadow and mascara. Assessing the results under the yellowy bathroom lights, I was pleased.

I have always obsessed over my hair. Like Samson, it's a source of both strength and weakness. An otherwise awful day can be borne with equanimity if my hair looks good. That day, it did. If I could protect it from the ocean mist until I'd made my grand entrance at the luncheon, I could face the relatives who hadn't seen me in a year with a confident smile and my head held high. All eyes would be drawn upwards, away from my body. Such is my faith in the power of good hair.

On the natural, I'm a cup half-empty kind of person, always have been, despite my sisters' efforts to drag me into the light. That morning, they would have been proud of me. I smiled at my reflection in the hotel mirror. If I'd known how, I would have winked at myself.

I pulled on the formless black skirt and tried on both tops, choosing the golden tunic over the pebbly blue one. It had a gauzy under blouse that extended beyond the hem, adding additional cover for the crucial bust to hips region.

We drove south on Highway 101, the wide Pacific to our right, condominiums clinging to steep hillsides on the left. Once the windows were safely closed, I flipped the visor down and primped my hair in the mirror. So far, so good. I fiddled with the radio dial.

"God, I'm anxious about today," I said.

I waited for him to say something, but only the swell of classic rock on the radio broke the silence.

"I always feel like this party is a big deal, an annual moment of judgment," I said. "As if they are all checking us out. Seeing how we look compared to last year. You know? And what we've accomplished. Like it's a competition to see which side of the family has done better for themselves."

Our relationships with his stepmother and her children have always felt complicated. But perhaps that's always the case. It's been several years since my father-in-law, Bob's father, passed. His widow has kept up the family holiday traditions and been loving and generous. Perhaps the anxiety was no different than what I would feel facing any group of people I hadn't seen in a while. There's the hope that they will be impressed. That they will say, "Wow, you look amazing. You haven't aged a bit."

I didn't expect that to happen. All I really hoped was not to be the afternoon's topic of whispered conversations for the opposite reasons, because I'd let myself go, because I'd aged a decade in the few years since retirement, because they felt sorry for my husband for being saddled with me. I tugged at my top, yanking it out from between my tummy rolls.

"I've gained so much weight. I wish I felt better about how I look," I said.

My fit and trim husband, handsome in suit and tie, turned to me with a sympathetic nod. "Yeah, I know what you mean," he said.

Silence stretched as the road unfurled, the white center line an endless ribbon. I slouched against the passenger door and pressed my forehead to the cool, hard window. Bob must have known I was fishing for complements. Instead, he'd validated and echoed my insecurities. I couldn't even be angry with him. Bob is an engineer, a literal kind of guy. I *had* gained weight. I *didn't* look my best. He hummed along to the tune on the radio, hands loose on the wheel, steering with the heel of one hand, at ease, the car a fluid extension of his body, with no inkling he'd struck a tender nerve, again.

Sometimes it seems as if, despite the obvious biological attributes – boobs, reproductive organs – my husband doesn't see me as a woman, one who needs, at least every once in awhile, to feel desirable, beautiful, if only to him.

I knew from many years' experience that there was no point explaining how I felt or getting upset. He'd never responded with anything approaching what I hoped to hear, and there was always the chance he'd say something I *really* didn't want to hear. That, too, had happened.

⊖ ⊖ ⊖

In the early days, back when we were "dating," Bob had said "I love you" before he'd ever said anything about finding me beautiful or even attractive. I assumed he *thought* those things about me, that he must, that the reason he stuck around involved some level of physical attraction. It became a challenge to get him to say something. I'd spend extra time on my hair. Buy new outfits. Pose provocatively. I made a middle-aged fool of myself.

One night, in bed, basking in the afterglow, I batted my lashes and hunched my shoulders so my breasts pressed together.

"Do you think I'm beautiful?" I asked.

He stared into my eyes and smiled. The quiet clamored against my bedroom walls.

"Well, maybe not *beautiful*," I said, thinking I'd shot too high for his prosaic mind, that he was clicking through the standard conventions of beauty, perhaps calculating my face geometry. "But, well, pretty, attractive? Do you think I'm attractive?"

His smile broadened. He pulled me close and kissed my forehead. With fervor. Really mashed his lips into it.

"It doesn't matter how you look. I'm already in love with you," he said.

"Yeah, I know, I love you, too, but..."

"I really don't even think about what you look like anymore. I just see the woman I love."

"Meaning you used to think about it, before you loved me?"

I disentangled myself from his arms and pulled the covers up to my chin.

"Well, you know," he said, "Like you do with anyone new."

"You notice flaws?"

"Well, sure. I mean I've got plenty," he said, with a self-deprecating chuckle.

"I think you're handsome," I said, not sounding particularly pleased about it.

"*Right.*"

"No, I mean it. I do. Because you are."

He moved back into my space. Closed his eyes and kissed me again. I kept mine open and noticed how his lashes rested on his cheeks.

"So," I said, not willing to let the wound scab over, "What stuck out for you when we met?"

He shrugged.

"What?" I said. "My mole? Did my mole bug you?" I tapped the dark lump beneath my bottom lip. It wasn't massive, not pencil eraser sized, but big enough that I wished it weren't there, big enough that it was the first thing *I* saw when I looked in the mirror.

The slight hunch of his shoulders, the downward turn of his mouth, let me know the mole had bothered him.

"What? You couldn't get past it at first. You couldn't *not* notice it."

"Yeah, something like that," he said. "But then, you know, I fell in love with you. Now I hardly notice it all. It's just part of your face."

"You hardly notice it?"

"Yeah."

"That's big of you."

"Jesus," he said, "you sound like my ex-wife."

I had the mole removed, along with another, much bigger protuberance on the back of neck. Roxanne used to affectionately call that one my "muffin," as in "How's the muffin today? Lift your hair so I can say, 'Hi.'" When the doctor lopped off the muffin and my facial mole, she said the one beneath my lip was deep. She'd had to dig it out. After the stitches were removed, I was left with a divot, that, at least to me, was more noticeable than the mole had been. There's no mistaking a gouge in your face for a beauty mark.

Sometimes a girl just wants her guy to tell her she's pretty. Even if she suspects it's bullshit, even if it's a stretch. It's nice when sisters, friends, even other men, tell me I look good. But it's not the same. And yeah, if it's so damn important to me, why didn't I find a partner who could give me what I needed?

This whole, seemingly trivial, "do you think I'm beautiful?" fixation came up in marriage counseling years ago, during the tough years, when Carolanne was a toddler and the teenagers were all behaving like teenagers.

I remember the therapist asking, "Bob, can you see that your wife needs to hear that you find her attractive?"

"Yes," Bob had said, brow deeply rutted, as if he were trying with all his might to grasp this difficult concept.

"And do you think that's something you can do?" the therapist asked.

"Well, I'm insecure about my looks, too," Bob said.

"Meaning?" the counselor asked, with a coaxing lilt.

"That she doesn't give me many compliments either."

"Yes, but can you hear it's something that she needs to hear from you?"

"Yes."

"And do you think you can do that for her?"

Bob nodded, lips compressed, as if it wouldn't be easy, but he would give it his best effort.

Maybe he said it a few times, maybe he didn't. It didn't become a habit.

Eighteen years into this marriage, with my looks significantly diminished from what they were when we met, it was past time to concede it wasn't going to happen.

$\ominus \ominus \ominus$

We survived the holiday party. The other wives said nice things about my hair, and I said nice things in return. Back home, when I groused to Roxanne about what Bob hadn't said in the car, she wasn't any help.

"I bet he thought you were the most beautiful woman in that room," she said.

I sneered at her.

"He adores you. You know that, right?" Roxanne said.

I suppose he must. Why else would he put up with me? But would it be so hard to throw me the occasional bone? Maybe he doesn't want it to go to my head.

Yeah, that must be it.

7

What is it about Christmas?

Jesus had no role in my childhood, aside from our Catholic neighbors in San Francisco who tried to save my soul by taking me to catechism classes. I only went twice and never told my parents. They would not have approved.

Christmas was always a time when miracles could happen. There was the year my sisters and I got the first Super Skates on our block, spring-loaded roller skates that stayed on without straps or keys. And the mini dress I got when I was twelve. One magical dress and becoming Mick Jagger's next girlfriend seemed within reach.

What is it about Christmas?

Even as an adult, my chest aches with anticipation, of wants that might finally be fulfilled, and now, as a mother, with the hope that the children and grandchildren won't be disappointed.

Christmas has not been good to Bob and me. Whatever is festering beneath the covers tends to choose Christmas day to erupt.

There was Christmas the year before we got married. Both in our forties by then, we'd been together for three years and had established a routine that included shared summer vacations with all the kids and Bob spending his two weekly non-custody nights and days – he had primary custody of his boys – with my family. We were in love. Life was good. I assumed we'd likely marry, that it was just a matter of time.

Christmas day, he arrived at my house late, after dropping his boys off with their mother, an ordeal that had taken longer than anticipated. Their divorce became final the year we met, but the wounds hadn't healed. I didn't know it then, but they never would.

We kissed in the foyer, just inside the front door.

"What's that?" Bob said, staring over my right shoulder.

I looked right.

"And what's that over there?" he said, this time staring over my left shoulder.

I twisted to the left.

He stooped to my height so that we were eye to eye, and kissed me. Between kisses, he murmured, "What's that, over there, no over there," glancing over one shoulder then the other.

Back then, the what's-over-there game was still endearing. I blushed and played along. Over time, it was just Bob, one of those things he had likely done with every girlfriend he'd ever had. He does the same thing with the grandkids now. At two and four, they still fell for it. Now, our five-year-old grandson, Elliott, still looks, the first time, then he rolls his eyes and says, "You're not for real, right, Grandpa? I know there's nothing there."

I felt the stiff outlines of a box in Bob's pants pocket and assumed it was my surprise, his special gift. I traced the shape with a finger.

"Don't get ahead of yourself there, girl," he said.

I retrieved my gift to him from under the decorated tree in front of the dining room window. I'd had a "glamour girl" photo portrait done at the mall. I looked all right, but not the way I'd hoped. Too much makeup. My hair a curly whoop. The pose pure cheese, head thrown back, a big lipsticked grin, as if

I believed I was all that and then some. I'd hoped for something subtle and sexy. Not this. It wasn't me.

"I love it," he said. "It's you."

He extracted a small jeweler's box from his pocket. His eyes twinkled. He held it overhead. I reached for it. He hid it behind his back. I grabbed for it, playing along, until he let me have it.

"Open it," he said. "I hope you like it."

I cracked open the box, hinged the lid up. A delicate ring nestled in ivory satin. I lifted it from its slot.

"Does it fit?" he asked.

"What finger should I put it on?"

He took the ring from me and began with my pinky, trying it on each finger in turn as if searching for the one that was just right. After trying them all, he slid it back onto my second finger. I held out my hand and wriggled my fingers. I hadn't paid too much attention to the actual ring, a gold band with three small stones of equal size. Each a different color. Diamond. Green. Red.

"It's so pretty," I said, holding my hand out in front of me. "What are the stones?"

"Diamond, ruby and sapphire."

"Beautiful," I said. "I love it."

"You know what it is, right?"

I hesitated. My smile coy around the edges. He hadn't said anything about it being an engagement ring. He hadn't proposed.

"They're birthstones," he said, beaming. "For you and your two kids. It's a mother's ring."

"Oh."

I studied it more closely, buying a few seconds to compose my face. It *was* a lovely ring, a lovely gesture. One I might have expected years ago, from one of my children's fathers. From my boyfriend, my lover, I'd expected something else. If not an engagement ring, something that bespoke our commitment to one another. I didn't need any reminders that I was a mother. A single mother at that. What I needed, or thought I needed, what I wanted, or thought I wanted, was a partner to raise a family with.

For weeks after, family members and friends would ask what Bob had given me for Christmas. When I said, "a ring," their faces lit up with excitement. My sisters hopped up and down and clasped my hands. Before it went much further, before they began asking how long the engagement would be, if we'd set a date, if he'd gone down on one knee, what poetic words he'd used to propose, I held out my hand.

"It's a mother's ring," I said.

"How thoughtful of him. How sweet," they said.

It was sweet. Just not particularly intuitive. I honestly don't believe he meant to disappoint me. How's that for having a cup half full?

There's a coda to the ring story.

A few years later, early days in our marriage, Bob's ex-wife was making our lives more difficult, adding to an already rough transition as we struggled with a headstrong toddler and three disgruntled teens – my eldest was away at college. Alimony and child support were never enough. She moved frequently, and each time she'd run short of cash. She wanted to negotiate for more but not through the courts. She and Bob couldn't occupy the same space without hurling insults and accusations at one another. Hoping to move the "discussion" out of our kitchen, our living room and the driveway, all the raised voices, slammed doors and screeching brakes, I offered to mediate on neutral ground.

"Good luck with that," Bob said.

One evening after work, his ex and I met at a Denny's. We ordered an appetizer to split, the fried assortment basket, chicken strips, cheese sticks and onion rings. I was nibbling the casing from an onion ring, thinking we just might find common ground over greasy finger foods, when she leaned across the table.

"Nice ring," she said, reaching for my hand. "I have one just like it."

I glanced at her hand.

"Oh, I don't wear it anymore. It's identical, though. Except, of course, the stones are for me and *our* boys. Same jeweler. He used to buy all my gifts there."

It had stung when he gave it to me, after I'd hoped for a different kind of ring. It was a scab ripped off to realize he'd given the same gift to his children's birth mother. Sitting across from her in that Denny's booth, the roar of rush-hour traffic beyond the plate glass, she knew exactly how I felt, how she'd meant me to feel. It was there in her eyes as she pushed the basket closer, offering me the last onion ring.

"You take it," I said.

"Let's split it," she said, sawing it in half with a butter knife.

I tucked the ring away in my jewelry box. Bob never asked about it or suggested adding a gemstone for our daughter.

What is it about Christmas?

Thankfully, this past year's celebration was peaceful. With the kids all grown and flown, they usually are. New Year's Eve was likewise uneventful, a quiet end to a year that, for me, had wound down with months of depression, a hole I was just starting to clamber out of. I saw no point in staying awake for the TV countdown or toasting the new year with champagne and a kiss.

That night, as I pulled on my pajama pants, I believed the annual last day of the year bout of unearned, unfounded optimism, of proclaiming lofty resolutions for the next 365 days, was a thing of the past. No sense wishing and hoping for the same things I'd wished and hoped for as far back as I could remember. To lose twenty, thirty, forty pounds. To be a better wife and mother. To finally write that damned mystery novel.

I decided 2017 would be the year of accepting myself as I am. Grudging heart, double chins, chaffing thighs, practiced procrastinator, all that and more. The whole full-fat enchilada. Such were my thoughts as I bedded down to dream in the new year.

I was resolved not to resolve.

8

New Year's Day, I woke before the sun. Coming back into my body, I took stock. No aching head bone. My eyeballs weren't hot embers. No vise gripping the back of my neck or squeezing my temples. Flat on my back, I stretched my legs, pointed my toes and gave thanks. My year of self acceptance and diminished expectations was off to a good start.

That evening, I babysat the grandkids. Elliott and Eva sat at the dining room table while I retrieved tubs of Play-Doh and assorted accessories from the hutch. Elliott wanted me to make cars, like the ones from the Disney movie. I wasn't very good at it, but he always seemed satisfied with the results. It was a familiar ritual, one that Bob and I had entertained Carolanne with and the others before her.

The dining room is the one room in the house that's decorated with family photographs. Our five children through the years. Awkward group photos of those first Christmases together, when we struggled to "blend." Weddings and graduations. My sisters. Our parents, three of the four deceased. Only my mother is still with us, though she scarcely knows it. The grandchildren get the most real estate.

"There's us," Eva said, pointing at matching photos of the two of them on ponies, wearing cowboy hats.

"And Mommy and Daddy," Elliott said, pointing at one of the photos from their wedding. "I'm not there, right?" he said.

"You weren't born yet," I said.

"And not me?" Eva said.

"And not you."

I set the photograph on the table. It's one I love, because it was a wonderful day, but also because of the way I look, standing between my son and Bob, beaming at the camera, thin and full of life. I look so happy and in the moment. Elliott tapped my image.

"Who's that lady, Grandma?" he asked.

"That's me."

"No, it isn't."

"Yes, it is."

"You're not being for real, right?"

Elliott hopped down from the chair. He dashed to the hutch and pointed up at a photo from my wedding to Bob. "There you are," he said, pointing at my mother, dumpling-shaped and white haired in her frowsy mother-of-the-bride dress.

"That's Grandma June. Here I am," I said, pointing at myself standing beside Bob.

"That's Aunt Juliet," he said, laughing at my joke.

My son, Elliot's father, got married a little over ten years ago. I was in my early fifties. Carolanne was a flower girl. Only ten years. Back when strangers still sometimes mistook me for my younger sister. Yet my grandson didn't know me. He couldn't imagine that version of me.

I remember being disappointed with how I looked on my son's wedding day. I'd struggled to lose weight before the big day and still considered myself twenty pounds too heavy. I was self-conscious of my upper arms in the sleeveless dress. And I was envious of the bride's mother, petite and elegant in a traditional Vietnamese tunic and fitted pants. If only I could have appreciated how lovely I was.

While they dug through the Play-Doh tub, I studied the old photographs. The gray hair sprouting at my temples wasn't the only reason Elliott didn't recognize me. In ten years, I'd aged over twenty.

After Play-Doh, we moved into the living room. Elliott got the Legos down from a shelf and dumped them out onto the floor.

"Help me build a garage for my cars, Grandma," he said.

I hesitated, gauging the distance to the ground, the proximity of chairs and walls, props I'd need to lower myself down, and to get back up again.

Elliott gathered several throw pillows from the couch and made me a cushy throne.

"There you go, Grandma."

He knew the drill.

When my son returned to fetch the kids, I grasped the arm of a chair and hoisted myself to standing.

"You okay down there, Mom?" my son said. "Need a hand?"

"I'm just fine," I said, glaring at him.

I *had* become my mother, struggling with the simplest tasks.

I used to consider people who were the age I am now, old. Now that I was over 60, I didn't feel old, not on the inside. It wasn't age that made it hard to get up and down, that sapped my energy, that left me wheezing after climbing a flight of stairs. I'd done that to myself. One mini candy bar at a time.

If I felt this way in my sixties, what condition would I be in ten years from now? My two grandchildren would still be in their teens. Perhaps they would have cousins. Would I even be around to be part of their lives? What was more important than that? What else was any of this about?

On New Year's Eve, I'd been ready to throw in the towel. The headaches and bouts of depression, my depleted marriage, avoiding friends and family because I was ashamed of how I looked, helping other people with their writing instead of focusing on my own. None of that had been enough to trigger the desire for change. Yet out of the mouths of babes. Elliott had only said what he saw, what I hadn't wanted to face. I wanted to be a grandma he could count on, a grandma he could learn from and have fun with. Hell, I wanted to be able to sit on the ground without it being a major production.

I needed to figure this out. I needed a plan. Like every other year. But this time I meant it. I was too old to keep backsliding, to put things off another year. It only got harder.

2017 would be the year to give it my all and not give up. To get healthy and make peace with my body and my marriage. To take pride in my accomplishments and to live life as if it mattered, as if *I* mattered. As if this might be my only chance.

If not now, when?

Part Two

9

The new year brings the annual barrage of ads for the latest weight loss miracle. I'm not immune to their allure, especially those that make the most preposterous claims – if the price is low enough that I won't have to explain the charge on our credit card bill. With each passing year, it's harder to find one I haven't already tried and failed at.

I do realize that the only real "secret" to weight loss is to eat fewer calories than you burn, a seemingly straightforward equation. Except that it isn't, not for me, and, apparently, not for the millions of others who hope this year's magic pill or program will be the one.

2017's enticing diet miracle comes via a quarter page ad in *The Sacramento Bee*. It ran every day for weeks, beginning back in December, promising "at least" a 15–35-pound weight loss in 30 days "or less," or your money back, and, of course, "no rigorous dietary restrictions or exercise required." Maximum results for minimal effort. Perfect. To learn the details, including the cost, you have to attend a consultation with a "licensed" physician at one of their many area locations.

I haven't stepped on a scale in months. Why invite misery? But I imagine I have 30 to 40 pounds to lose. I do the math. Assuming the minimum guaranteed weight loss of 15 pounds per month, I'll reach my goal in a little over two months. If I stick with it for three months, by spring I'll be back in dresses and skirts, pants with zippers instead of elastic. By summer, I'll be wearing a bikini. It's all simple math.

⊖ ⊖ ⊖

I find the miracle weight loss center in an unassuming strip mall off Laguna Boulevard. There's no permanent sign out front, just a flimsy banner that flaps in the wind.

"Is this place new?" I ask the receptionist.

"Oh, no, we've been at this location several years."

"I just wondered because of the sign."

"Yeah, I don't know why they haven't gotten around to that."

I do, too. I remember the Fen-Phen clinics that popped up in strip malls in the mid-90s. I got skinny on those pills–before they were banned by the FDA.

The chubby-cheeked blonde receptionist hands me a pen and clipboard with a questionnaire attached. She motions me to take a seat. A dozen folding chairs face a podium and screen, as if they expect a crowd, though I'm the only customer that morning. There are several chiropractic beds beside the podium. I wonder how spinal alignment factors into the program. Stretching perhaps. I wouldn't mind growing a few inches taller. If nothing else, it would help spread the weight around.

After I've filled out the questionnaire, I'm directed to a private office, one of several along a drab corridor. The doctor behind an institutional metal desk is a plump brunette in her early thirties, casually dressed in slacks and t-shirt, and sporting a bouncy pony tail.

At the Fen-Phen clinic, the doctor at least wore a white lab coat over her clothes. After she'd completed the cursory physical exam and we'd discussed my goals, she whispered, "You really don't need to lose that much weight. You sure you want to do this?"

I should have seen the FDA action coming.

I've been to a lot of diet centers. So many of the staff are heavy. They must offer an employee discount. But it does undermine my confidence, like taking an aerobics class with an instructor in worse shape than I am.

"This is an amazing program," the young, pony-tailed doctor says. "I lost close to one hundred pounds on it."

I blink, thinking she must have been very overweight indeed.

"Then I had another child, and I let the weight creep back on. You know how it is."

Having gained upwards of 50 pounds with each of my three pregnancies, I do know.

"Life gets busy. Priorities shift. My daughter is older now. I've already lost thirty-five pounds. In just six weeks."

"That's fantastic," I say, perking up.

She's pretty, in a nonthreatening way. I decide I like her. I can picture the two of us on the journey together, more peers than doctor and patient. At a rate of 35 pounds in six weeks, I'll be done in a blink.

"So how does the diet work?" I ask.

"Oh, it's not a diet. It's a lifestyle change."

"Right."

"We'll get to that," she says. "But first, let's have a look at your numbers."

I shuck my shoes and coat and stand on the electronic scale, while she taps the computer keys.

"I'll just retrieve the print-out," she says. "Then we'll go over your information and see where we stand."

I already know where I stand. I just want their magic pills or potion so I can get on with losing my belly in six weeks without diet or strenuous exercise.

According to the fancy scale, I'm obese, up fifteen pounds since the last time I weighed myself. Disappointing, but no big surprise. My body is fifty percent fat. Not good, but still, no huge surprise. It's the next statistic that makes me choke. Metabolic age, 84, over twenty years past my chronological age.

"Scary, right?" she says. "But that's just tied to your weight and percentage of fat. The number will drop dramatically as soon as the pounds begin melting away. I promise."

By 84, Mom's mind had begun converting to Swiss cheese. I'm 62, still wondering what to be when I grow up. 84 is not acceptable. I need those 22 years back.

"The good news is, you have a surprisingly high number for muscle," the lady doc says. "Once you start, the weight will come off quickly. I'm betting you'll lose more than fifteen pounds in thirty days. At least twenty-five. You'll be down to 165 by March 1. How does that sound?"

It sounds perfect. She's my new best friend.

"So," I say, "What's the diet? How does it work?"

"Well, as I said, it's not a diet."

I nod, impatient to get on with it.

She flips through a thick binder. Shows me charts and graphs and lists of allowed foods. Lean proteins. Chicken, fish, nonfat dairy. Low carbohydrate vegetables. Proprietary smoothies based on my "unique metabolic and hormonal factors." A fat-burning cocktail that will recalibrate my metabolism and re-ignite my body's natural furnace. There isn't any fat-burning going on in my furnace. Recalibration sounds like just the ticket.

I don't believe in miracles. There's no Santa Claus, and you don't lose weight without hard work and discipline, and even then, there's no guarantee. Engrained habits must be broken. Behaviors rooted in conditioned responses to emotional pain, insecurity and loneliness must be redirected. What she describes isn't magic either, despite the intriguing customized smoothie concoctions. I've done this diet before.

"This sounds like ketosis," I say.

"You've heard of it?" she asks, visibly tensing.

"I've done it. It works, but it's really hard."

"Not the way we do it," she says, loosening her smile. "The daily smoothie is the key. It resets your metabolism, which is what's been preventing you from losing the weight."

I'd thought it was couch-sitting and binging on crap, like an entire sack of Halloween candy. But I prefer her explanation.

She explains that for one flat fee, the center will support me 24/7, for the rest of my life, as in forever. Weekly weigh-ins. The patented drink for the duration of my "active" period. Extensions beyond the first 30 days at a lesser rate. Doctor supervision. Educational classes. A hotline.

By significantly reducing sugars in the diet – including ones normally considered healthful, such as those found in fruits and carbohydrate-rich vegetables like peas and carrots – the body is forced to burn fat, rather than sugar, for energy. It has no choice.

I'd eaten like this on my last successful diet and gotten down into the low 130s, my high school weight. In the years since, I've tried to replicate those results, but haven't been able to summon the discipline. Maybe she's right, and this is what I need. The accountability created by plunking over a chunk of cash and standing on a scale every week, with her rooting me on, plus those magic drinks. For fifty bucks a week, even one hundred, I'll do it.

"So what does it cost?"

She turns to a page in her binder. I try to read the tiny, upside down type, but her hand covers the bottom half of the page. She reiterates the services, running down the list. Then, finally, she moves her hand and turns the binder so I can see for myself.

$3,000 for thirty days.

"Wow," I say, slumping in the chair, knees splayed.

It's just another weight-loss clinic, with a few more bells and whistles. No energy shots or pills, no surgical procedures. I might pay three grand for some serious drugs, the kind that ratchet up your metabolism so you *can't* eat, but this?

"I know it's a lot," she says, "but this is the only program of its kind."

"I'll have to think about it."

⊖ ⊖ ⊖

Back in the gritty parking lot, the flapping sign taunts me. Yes, D, it's true. Despite the ads, the guarantees and pronouncements by licensed doctors and experts, the testimonials and tantalizing before-and-after photos, it comes down to simple math. It would just be so nice, so damned convenient, to stumble upon a bona fide shortcut, an easy quick fix.

I won't return to the strip mall clinic. I can't bring myself to shell out three grand for thirty milkshakes. I could probably have liposuction for that price and be done with it. Bob even suggested it.

We were in the car. I was grousing about my weight, again, about how shitty my sister, Juliet, makes me feel when she bounces in my front door looking like a teenager. One of those ads came on the radio, for a clinic where they "melt" away your fat, painlessly and effortlessly.

"Maybe you should give that a try," he'd said.

"Are you serious?"

"Sure. If it bothers you so much."

My left-brain husband, always with the logic. It stung that he went there, that he saw nothing hurtful in the suggestion.

Is it unrealistic, is it unfair, to expect him to defend how I look, when I don't?

Pulling out of the parking lot, merging onto Laguna, I can't get my metabolic age, 84, out of my head. I've lost weight before. I know how to do it. I decide to try ketosis again, on my own. I just need to get serious about it.

I drive straight to the drug store to buy "keto sticks," these little plastic strips you swipe through your pee to measure the level of ketones in your urine. If the stick turns the right color, it's proof you've shifted into the magical fat-burning zone. Next stop, the grocery store, to stock up on zero carb proteins and super low-carb veggies. Bring on the lettuce and cucumbers, the broccoli and cauliflower.

Yum.

Next, I tackle my closet. I gather up all the jeans that don't fit me. Which means all the jeans I own. I organize them in descending order, by size, with the largest pair on top. A lonely pair of size eights rests at the bottom. I will work my way back into all of them, one size, one pair, at a time.

I can do this. I *will* do this. 2017 is my year.

I say I'm a diehard pessimist, the family Eeyore and all that. It's my shtick. Truth is, I'm a closet optimist. Standing in my literal closet, my inner optimist flickers to life. I won't only lose weight, I'll transform every aspect of my life. I'll be super wife, mom, daughter, sister, friend. I'll be more productive, creative and generous of spirit than I've ever been before. I will eat to live, not live to eat. I will live life to the fullest, rather than waiting for it to begin.

I will experience a total renaissance of mind, body and spirit.

This is another tendency of mine. All in or all out. Euphoria or depression. The going for broke phase feels so good, like the first twenty mini candy bars. When it sputters out, not so much. But that won't happen. Not this time.

I make a neat stack of the jeans and set it on a prominent shelf as a daily visible reminder.

Passing the dining room on my way outside for a walk, I pause to study the photograph of me at my son's wedding. I want my grandson to know *that* me. I want to feel closer to forty than sixty. I want to be mistaken for my younger sister again.

My 63rd birthday, January 17, will be my official start date. I won't set crazy, unrealistic goals this time. No fifteen pounds a month. I will give myself a full year, birthday to birthday. Phase one of my year of transformation. Lower my metabolic age. Regain those twenty years, then go for twenty more.

All that wisdom from a $37 visit to a strip-mall diet center.

10

Launching the new year coincides with a class I signed up for with a good friend, Shelley, an English professor I met at a conference for aspiring writers. She lives in Sacramento, and we've been meeting for coffee once a week ever since. Shelley is that rare friend. No matter how down on myself I am when I walk in the coffee house door, her sincere support turns me around, makes me realize I'm lucky. I say rare, because usually uplifting people drive me nuts. I want to shake the senseless optimism right out of them.

The class, under the tutelage of a respected author, was designed to provide support and a framework for completing the first draft of a book in one year. January to January. It was Shelley's idea to give ourselves this structure. The class will meet six times over the next twelve months. The due date for submitting the full manuscript for critique is a day after my next birthday.

I signed up for this before my New Year's Day revelations, yet it jibes perfectly. The class will be the framework for phase two of my year of transformation. Be productive and creative. Take concrete steps to realize those childhood dreams of being a writer. Not unlike losing weight, writing doesn't take magic, but rather diligence and persistence.

You just do it. And keep doing it.

Twelve aspiring authors show up for the first book-in-a-year class, all women, ranging in age from their thirties, some with young children at home, to a few like me, retired from challenging careers, our offspring grown. We meet in the author's home in Northern California's verdant wine country. My new eating regime is underway, so I bring my own food for the weekend. Hard boiled eggs, celery sticks and portion-controlled packets of almonds. We lounge in nubbly oatmeal-colored chairs and sofas around a large glass-topped coffee table. As we introduce ourselves and go over logistics for the year ahead, I am suffused with a warm, supportive glow, further empowered as the clock advances, and I resist the platters of fresh pastries offered by our host. Mid-morning, when the first pangs of hunger strike, I dip into my stash and nibble on a peeled egg.

I am doing this. I am strong.

Most of the other participants began the class knowing what they planned to write. A young adult novel, historical fiction, literary suspense, a few memoirs. I am a blank slate. I consider fixing the hackneyed murder mystery I wrote in graduate school. Or the thinly veiled memoir I wrote at twenty-two. As the morning's exercises progress – writing prompts to help us identify the stories and characters we keep coming back to – I scribble in my notebook, incidents from my life, moments remembered. The ones that keep me from falling asleep at night and that wake me up with a start long before sunrise. Bad relationships. Friends I miss. Firsts and lasts. Grudges. Moments that, while in the past, are still causing trouble in my head, with a sense of having been left undone, unresolved. Moments I can't shake, that make me flush with shame, and that send me to the refrigerator.

I've already determined that 2017 will be the year I crack the code for living my life in the now, for making peace with the past and embracing the present. There are the pounds I hope to shed. No, the pounds I *will* shed. My metabolic age to fix. My gray roots to grow out and embrace.

Whether I have one year left or twenty-one, or even if I live past 100 as my mother seems likely to do, I hope to keep growing and learning. I want peace, happiness, love. I want to feel alive.

That's what I need to write about. I will chronicle my year of self-discovery. A year to get my shit together. A year to write about it. I have no clue where the coming months will take me, where the journey will end. But I'm determined to give it my best shot and to tell the truth, regardless the outcome.

The price tag for the book-in-a-year course is about what I would have shelled out for the thirty-day weight-loss miracle. This feels serendipitous, a twofer for my investment. A new me and a completed book. Truth is, I have more confidence that I will finish a book than I do about being successful with the rest of it. I've written all my life. I can produce words, lots of them. Mostly drivel, but still, getting words onto the page isn't usually my problem.

Our instructor suggests we just write, get it all out there, a complete first draft, without second guessing or stopping to edit. I like the sound of that. I'll spill all the uneasy memories, like upchucking a bad meal. Down the road, I can arrange and rearrange them, search for patterns, stitch them back together in a way that makes something whole and worthwhile out of it all. I will write my way back into my life, one word, one page, one memory at a time.

11

I've been on my self-designed program a week. I wake and squint at the clock on the bedside table. 4:30 AM. Perfect. Plenty of early morning privacy for my first weigh-in. For seven days, I've avoided sugar like the plague and stuck with lean proteins and low-carb veggies, squeezing carbohydrate intake down to under twenty grams per day. As my body adjusted and shifted from burning glucose to fat for fuel, I'd weathered the dreaded "keto flu," several days of headaches, diarrhea and fatigue. Now that those symptoms have subsided, my energy is the best it's been in months. While eating like this may constitute a "lifestyle change," it's also a diet, a tough one.

I extricate myself from the covers, careful not to disturb Bob or the cat, and slip out of the bedroom. I skip upstairs to the scale, taking the carpeted steps two at a time. My starting weight was 182 and change, rounded down. A friend lost fifteen pounds her first two weeks doing ketosis. I've been good. I, too, could watch the pounds melt away, my new shape emerging in weeks rather than months. Even if I only lose five pounds, or four, I'll be halfway to my first ten, rounding up this time. If it's only three pounds, I'll still be into the 170s. Progress is progress. What matters is sticking with it, discipline, consistency, determination. What matters is how I feel. Hell, what matters is how long before that topmost pair of jeans fits.

I click on the bathroom light, drop my robe to the linoleum, kick off my slippers and strip to my underwear. I pee first, holding the little plastic dip stick in the stream. The tab at the end turns a satisfying maroon, the same as the last two days. I'm in the zone, a fat-burning furnace.

I nudge the button on the electronic scale with my big toe, cross my fingers and step on. The numbers scroll, calibrating, then settle on 180. It doesn't seem possible. Not given how good I've been. Two pounds is a normal day-to-day fluctuation, a blip. I see better results after a migraine.

My shoulders slump. I'm not halfway to my first ten. I'm not half way to anything. I won't be fitting into a pair of my old jeans any time soon. I take a deep breath. Step off the scale, kick the button and step back up, exhaling forcefully this time to empty my lungs. I rock onto my heels, then up on my toes, once, twice, then again, chin pinned to my chest, intent on the scale's flickering decimals. When I rock forward, putting more weight on the balls of my feet, the scale registers 180.7, 180.8. When I rock back, shifting my weight onto my heels, I hit 180, then 179.9. 179.8. I freeze, not breathing, every muscle taut. Higher, lower, finally settling on 179.7, not rounding up this time, no way am I rounding up. I know I won't be able to replicate the number once I step off the scale, so I don't try.

I'm in the 170s, barely.

I suck in a few deep breaths, pull my PJs back on and, with considerably less bounce in my step, stumble downstairs to record the number.

Despite the paltry progress on the scale, I remain committed. The first ten is always the hardest. And it only gets harder with age. I need to accept responsibility for my own health. I've been putting my body through this cycle of yo-yo dieting all my adult life. I've lost the same 20 to 50 pounds at least a dozen times. I need to approach it differently this time, holistically, body *and* mind.

College was the first time I gained enough that I couldn't fit into my clothes, enough that I was uncomfortable in my body. Being overweight didn't only change what I saw in the mirror, but how the world reacted to me too. Boys didn't hit on me. Even girls didn't strike up conversations so readily. I became instantly less interesting. Amazing what a little extra padding can do.

Sophomore year, I went on my first real diet. Weight Watcher's. I lost the weight. To reward myself, I bought a pair of electric blue, corduroy bell bottoms and a skin-tight sweater, white with little confetti flecks of color. I got asked out that same weekend, to a cheesy Monte Carlo night in the recreation room of one of the large dormitories. I wasn't even attracted to the guy, but I'd gotten my body back and been asked out. People wanted to be seen with me again. They found me interesting, intriguing, appealing. At least that's how it felt. I now imagine it was just that I was noticeably more confident and outgoing.

That was the first of many diets. Sometimes I had a partner. My mother, a sister or a friend. Pills, juice fasts, cabbage soup. Even one I made up – the "feast and fast" plan – to mimic how it must have been for prehistoric man, when food was scarce so you stuffed yourself after a kill, insurance against future famine, then went for weeks subsisting on twigs and berries. It worked, until I couldn't stop feasting.

So I'm at it again. Two pounds down, almost three, albeit with a little fancy footwork on the scale. It's time to stop snickering about lifestyle changes, because that's exactly what I need to change my life.

I'm 5'8" and shrinking. I weighed 132 in high school. That may not be a realistic goal. But 135, 140. Why not? Bottom line,

I need to lose 40 to 45 pounds. I count out the weeks on a calendar. At a reasonable two to three pounds a week, I'll be there in four or five months. Well within my year, and with a six-month cushion to accommodate the inevitable setbacks. I just need to stick with the plan.

You got this, D.

12

This sensation is frighteningly familiar. Lying in bed beside my sleeping husband. Wide awake, lonely, frustrated with myself. I used to bitch about our lackluster sex life. Not anymore. I can't. I'm to blame.

Bob and I met at 40 and married at 45, each of us already bearing our battle scars. For a few years, infatuation buoyed us. But with time, marriage, and kids, we reopened old wounds and added new ones. Past hurts keep me from trusting, from letting my guard down. It all feels so risky. I have become my memories, what's been said, and done, and weathered. I've always been a person who dwells, one who moves on but doesn't forget, who never really lets it go. At 63, that's a lot of baggage to cart around.

Bob is a decent guy. Sometimes the things he doesn't say or do hurt me. Which I suppose means it's about me, at least as much as it is him, and that I can choose to change how I feel.

Food and men are a lot alike. I have a lifelong love/hate relationship with both. They bring pleasure and pain, escape and servitude, joy and regret.

My mother was a lifelong dieter, never happy with her post-baby body, yet boastful about her perfect figure in younger days. She was a great flirt, too, a skill that intrigued and embarrassed me, and one I never acquired. Perhaps I chose boyfriends she'd disapprove of on purpose. I imagine that's what she thought.

"Don't you think you can do better?" she used to ask, after meeting one, and, "Why do you think so little of yourself?" Not great tactics to use on a headstrong teenage girl, and what teenage girl isn't headstrong? She accused me of picking the "low-hanging fruit," and the "bird with a broken wing." Not exactly flattering analogies. I imagined that, in her eyes, I was a bottom feeder. And perhaps I was.

But why? What is it with me and men?

I can't sleep.

I slip out of bed, snatch my reading glasses from the bedside table and retreat to the couch.

I pick up the morning's paper and scan the headlines. More allegations of previously unreported sexual harassment and abuse. The juggernaut of the "me too" movement continues. I'm not surprised so many women have had these experiences. Among my circle of acquaintances, most women have a rape story, at least one. Mine happened nearly 50 years ago. Sometimes it still feels like yesterday. I've relived it so many times, often on nights like this, when I can't sleep. I wonder how much is still true to what happened and how much time has altered my memories, eroding the edges or perhaps sharpening them to points.

Would my rapist tell it the same? Does Ron even remember me? Yes, I knew his name.

While my husband sleeps and the animals snuffle and purr beside me, I reach for my computer to get Ron out of my head, to put words to what happened, words I can then parse and examine with older eyes. I've tried to write about him before, but I've always told it as fiction, pretending it was only a story. Now I'll tell it straight, everything I can remember, before I forget. Maybe some good will come from finally telling the truth, the whole truth.

The time has come to rout out old ghosts.

13

I was 14 when my family moved from San Francisco's Sunset district into a three-story A-frame at the toe of a suburban cul-de-sac across the bay in Marin County. From the back of our house we enjoyed a panoramic view of Tamalpais Valley, the next community up Highway One from Mill Valley proper. Over the summer of '69, I became friends with Liz, a girl who lived in another peaky house at the top of our street. That fall, as an incoming ninth grader at Tamalpais High, I had my first real boyfriend, after years of imaginary ones. But Michael disappeared, literally vanished without a trace, at the start of sophomore year. I wondered what awful thing I'd done to make him go without telling me. Or – and this seemed the most likely explanation to my fevered teenage mind – I suspected Mom had scared him away or paid him to leave. I imagined the whole school knew the truth and that they were all hiding it from me. Even Liz's soft gray eyes brought no relief. I was convinced she knew more than she was telling me and wanted to spare my feelings.

My first boyfriend's mystifying disappearance and getting into Ron's car are forever linked in my mind, as if one were the inevitable consequence of the other.

The events of that day have acquired the permanence of an old movie, the past captured and frozen. What the two of us wore, and said, all of it, stamped on my brain, frame after frame. But it was a long time ago. The version I've held on to all these years may be as fictional as any film. Or it may have happened just like this.

I was walking home from school, alone.

The high school faces the main road out of town, the road that joins up with Highway One. I usually took the back-way home, over the hills behind campus. That way I could avoid having to pass the girls waiting for their boyfriends at the curb and all the other kids hanging out in clumps, hitchhiking to the coast or whatever it was that groups of friends did together after school. Everyone, seemingly, had somewhere to go and friends to go there with.

I was just past the gymnasium, on the wide shoulder beside the football field, when a black Mustang crunched onto the gravel in front of me and stopped, engine idling, brake lights flashing red. The car and the guy behind the wheel, seemed familiar. I thought I remembered having once seen a girl I knew from classes – Crystal, with the chunky blonde hair and wide-set blue eyes – climb into the passenger seat beside him.

I had this inchoate notion that he wasn't a total stranger. He was friends with Crystal, maybe, and she was my friend, sort of. All that was clunking around inside my head as I came up alongside the car, and he leaned across the seat to roll the window down.

"Need a ride?" he asked, though I hadn't had my thumb out.

Here the line between what happened and what I want to think happened, gets muddy. I remember bending over, peering into that car and knowing I'd never seen him before, not in town, not at a dance or concert, not anywhere. Because if I had, I would already have concocted a fairytale in which we were together. He was that kind of guy, older, how much older, I don't know. Twenty would have seemed old to me. Dark stubble shadowed his cut cheeks. His hair was very black, shorter on top, shaggy in back and on the sides, like an English rock star. The air inside the car was musty with patchouli and pot. There were guitars in the backseat.

I would have touched my own hair and hoped the gathering mist hadn't turned my curls to frizz. I was always hoping my hair hadn't frizzed.

"I'm headed up Highway One, to the beach," he said. "I can give you a lift, if you're going that way."

The wet had begun to wick through my faded denim jacket, not that the weather was the reason I considered getting into his car. He'd pass right by my street on his way to the coast, if that was really where he was headed. That wasn't the reason either, though it lent logic to the impulse. The guitars factored into it. A couple of local bands lived on the coast. I connected the loose dots and figured that's where he must be headed. I'd never hitchhiked alone, only with Liz or Michael, but I imagined most any other girl in my position, any cool girl, would get in the car. I reached for the handle. He pushed the door open from the inside.

I sunk into the low seat, set my pack between my legs and shut the door. His arm shot out, grazing the front of my jacket. I sucked in my breath as he tugged on the door handle then pushed the lock down with a firm thwack.

"Door don't always close all the way," he said.

"I live just off the highway, about two miles up," I said, trying to force the wobble from my voice. "You can drop me at the top of my street. That would be great."

"Cool. I'm Ron."

I told him my name, hating the sound of it, Dorothy, a fifties housewife at the beauty salon kind of name. I wished I'd made something up, but I wasn't thinking that fast. At least he didn't ask where Toto was, or why I wasn't wearing my ruby slippers. I got that enough from kids at school. When he punched the gas, the rear wheels sprayed gravel as the car spun onto the damp road.

"You go to that school?" he asked.

"Yeah."

"I know some chicks that go there."

I pictured Crystal, the blonde from biology class. She was pretty, in a gawky, regular teenage girl kind of way. That it was her, and not one of the super hip and popular girls, made me think he wasn't too far out of my league.

"You have a horse?" he asked.

I shook my head, wishing I did.

"Then what's with the cowboy boots?"

I shrugged, embarrassed. He wasn't the first person to ask. I'd bought the boots with Michael, at a Western store in San Rafael. Michael had the exact same pair of tan, suede Frye boots. We'd dressed alike, had the same curly hair and snub noses. People used to say we looked like twins. He'd been gone several months, but most days I still wore our uniform.

Ron occupied the low bucket seat, black corduroy trousers, one knee canted my way, jittering against the gear shift. My legs looked too thick in comparison. I raised my heels off the floorboards, flexed my calves and lifted my thighs off the seat to give them some definition.

"You play guitar?" I asked.

"Yeah. I write songs, too."

"Far out." We actually said things like that back then, and not in an ironic way.

"Right now, I'm just hauling and setting up equipment for this band. I'm their fucking gopher."

He hunched his shoulders and smirked. I nodded to show I got it. I liked that he hadn't bragged about being in a band, having a record deal or whatever. Later, I would think that was the moment the hook set. He was an underdog. Talented, under appreciated, unrecognized. I imagined I knew how that felt.

Ron dredged a half-smoked joint from the ashtray, set it between his lips and dug in his pocket for a lighter. Our fingertips touched as I took the lit joint from him. I struggled to hold the sticky smoke in my lungs without coughing.

"You sixteen?" he asked.

"Fifteen."

I'd heard some girls at school, popular girls, the ones who always had the coolest boyfriends, say that older guys liked their chicks to be thirteen and innocent or sixteen and experienced and that the years in between were nothing special. At fourteen, before Michael, I'd believed I was the only virgin left in the entire ninth grade. I wished I'd told Ron I was sixteen, or thirteen, anything but the truth, but as with my name, I couldn't think that fast. This wasn't some fantasy in my head. I couldn't stop the scene so I could get it right.

"What bands you like?" he asked.

"Lots," I said, unsure what the right answer was.

"Bunch of fucking half-assed hippy bands out here," he said.

I was glad I hadn't named any of the local bands. Truth was, I lived for the dances in town Friday and Saturday nights. Everybody was friendly, even if at school on Monday kids I'd smoked dope with, guys I made out with in the dark lot behind the hall, looked right past me as if I wasn't there.

"They have no fucking clue about music or about this business," Ron said. "That's what music is, you know, a fucking business."

I blinked, unnerved by his vehemence, but kind of digging it, too. He cared about something. Enough to be passionate about it. He bristled with energy, a halo of static all around him. He was different. Most people I'd met since moving to Marin were so mellow they might have been sleepwalking.

"Where are you from?" I asked.

"What, you don't think I'm from around here?"

I didn't. I figured New York, or maybe New Jersey, not really knowing why, likely from some gangster movie I'd seen.

"There's a tape in there." He jerked his chin at the glove compartment. "Grab it for me."

I popped the glove compartment open, groped around, held up an unlabeled tape.

He stuck the cassette into the deck. Turned up the volume on a scratchy live recording. The smoky car filled with sound. I recognized it, a San Francisco group I'd heard play at the Fillmore one time.

"You like this?"

"I guess I liked them better without the new singer," I said. "He sounds too AM."

"That's total fucking bullshit. This song is the best thing they've ever done. It's not just some stoned, rambling bullshit. Listen."

I'd only been parroting what I'd heard a late-night DJ say, that the lead vocalist was taking the band away from its psychedelic roots with a more mainstream, pop sound. Most nights I fell asleep with the headphones on, radio tuned to the FM stations from San Francisco. Now I did what Ron said. I listened. The song, the voice and words, wormed their way inside my head.

The song ended, replaced by tires wicking wet asphalt, the back and forth slap of windshield wipers. I hadn't noticed them before, and thought, whoa, when did the mist become rain?

"Am I right?" he said, with a knowing nod.

"For sure."

Ron sped past the 7-11 where Liz and I bought snacks with our babysitting money and the thrift store next door where we found most of our clothes. The road began to climb, a series of tight, hairpin curves. This was the last stretch before my street, a sharp left that plunged off the main road and down the side of the hill. Nauseous, I cracked the window. The car filled with the medicinal, camphor odor of wet eucalyptus.

He hadn't asked for my number, hadn't said anything about seeing me again. No one from school had seen us together. It would be like it never happened.

"Dora Court is around the next bend. There's no good place to pull over. You can just drop me at the next right." I hefted my pack onto my lap.

If he'd heard, he made no sign. The car crested the hill. The street sign for Dora Court was silhouetted against a gray sky.

"This is it," I said.

Ron didn't slow, didn't pull into the next turnout, or the next. He leaned into the curves and ground through the gears. Sarah Court snaked off the next ridge. After that it was open country until the coast.

"The next street is cool, too," I said, louder, in case he hadn't heard over the throttling engine. "You can just drop me anywhere. This is fine."

Sarah Court disappeared in the rearview mirror. I gripped my backpack. I could yank the door open and tumble out. I studied the shoulder. Red dirt. Rocks. I pictured myself there, outside the car, rolling to safety.

"You need to get home?" he said. "There's something I want to show you. You cool with that?"

His smile was lazy, neutral, as if it was no big deal that he hadn't stopped, as if this had been the plan all along. Adrenalin constricted my heart. Maybe I'd overreacted. Maybe he wasn't some crazed psycho-killer like on the TV news. Just a little high, his words a few curves in the road behind his thoughts. Besides. I already knew him, sort of. This was *Ron*. He was with a band, one with songs on the radio. And he knew Crystal from biology.

If it were today, I would have had a phone. I wouldn't have

felt so much like we were on our own private planet hurtling through uncharted space. I would have texted Liz. She'd have been primed, waiting to hear all the details. But back then, all the trivia that gets typed back and forth in snippets and fragments got saved up to be savored later. Whenever anything real was happening, half my mind was busy recording it, getting ready for the replay.

"You have a boyfriend?" he asked.

"Not anymore. He split."

"That sucks. The band is playing Friday night. At this place in San Rafael."

He hadn't said I should come or even that it would be cool to see me there. But why else would he have mentioned it? I pictured myself there. He'd invite me backstage. Introduce me to his friends. Kids from school would see us together. Maybe he would have a friend for Liz.

I wriggled my toes inside my boots. As the blood began to flow, they tingled like tiny needles all over.

"Bet you'll go to college," he said.

"Maybe." I pretended not to know, though both my parents were Berkeley grads and college was presumed.

"You're quiet, so I figured you must be smart."

"I'm not super smart, just average."

The eucalyptus had thinned, replaced by clusters of boulders and scrubby brush on the hillsides. I was miles from home. There were long lulls between the lights of oncoming cars. No more houses. There wouldn't be any for miles, until the windswept beach towns on the coast. Muir Beach. Stinson. The hills flattened on the rise before the final descent to the coast, but the road still twisted and turned, rising and falling with the unsettled land.

Approaching lands end, the road angled to the right. The sky was dark, a lighter shade of gray up high that became thick and murky, then almost black down low. The highway hugged the coast. On our left, beyond the narrow shoulder, the cliffs were sheer. If a car careened off the edge, there would be nothing to break its fall until it hit the jagged, white-tipped rocks below.

Ron shifted, accelerating and decelerating, weaving between the two lanes, slurring the white line, hewing a straighter path between curves. An oncoming driver flicked his high beams and leaned on the horn. I gripped the seat, toes bunched tight inside my boots. Around the next bend, the Mustang crossed over into the opposite lane. We were headed straight for the cliff. I opened my mouth to scream. The sound that came out, a desperate, constricted squawk, seemed to have come from someone else. I closed my eyes, anticipating impact, praying to lose consciousness before we hit.

My stomach heaved as the car swerved then stopped. I opened my eyes.

Ron had executed a tight u-turn and slipped into a turnout on the cliff's edge, its footprint inches longer than the car, which was now perched on a precipice facing south, the ocean beyond the passenger door, the highway on the driver's side. Rain pinged the roof. The wind gusted. The car shook. I made another sound, the squeak of a balloon deflating, as I loosened my grip on the seat cushion. It was like when a friend dared me to ride a bike down our stretch of Highway One, from the top of our street to the valley below, without tamping the breaks. I was terrified as the bike gathered speed, tears wicking from my eyes and the wind a deafening roar in my ears. Then, gradually losing speed at the bottom, coasting, regaining control of my senses, it was over. I was alive.

Ron turned off the engine.

Without the wipers, the world beyond the windows was a slipping curtain of water. I shivered. The cooling engine ticked and popped.

Ron plucked another joint from his shirt pocket, lit it with a deep inhale, one eye shut in concentration as the tip glowed red. I'd had enough. I was ready for this to be over, to be at Liz's kitchen table, waiting for the toaster to pop.

He slumped in the seat, eyes half shuttered.

"This is my favorite place in the world," he said. "I come out here to get my head straight. Fucking band. Fucking ignorant hippies."

Ron set the joint in the ashtray. He clasped me by the neck and pulled me to him. His cheeks were abrasive, not softly fuzzed like Michael's, his tongue and teeth insistent, his breath hot in my mouth. I fought for air. I'd known something like this would happen. Maybe I'd even wanted it. Now I felt detached from my body, me watching me with this man. I imagined what was happening was supposed to feel good. Maybe it did. I was just too tense, too freaked out. Maybe this was how it was with older guys, harder, more insistent, closer to pain than pleasure.

Ron moaned, or it might have been the wind, an eerie sound that slithered up my backbone. My legs shook. I couldn't make them stop. His grip on my neck tightened. His nails dug in to my throat. There was no question now. It hurt. I didn't want this. I groped for the door lock, the handle, then froze. Beyond the door was the sheer cliff. My breath came in desperate chuffs.

Ron grabbed hold of my hair and yanked, pulling it tight. My eyes stretched wide. A car approached. Yellow headlights swept the roadway. A fantail of water hit the side of the car. Then nothing. With one hand, Ron held me by the hair. With the other he undid his pants. Two rows of buttons and a flop-down front, no underwear, nothing to yank or shift. His penis stared up at me from a nest of dark hair. With Michael, I'd kept my eyes on his face or closed. Now there was nowhere else to look.

"Just do what I say," he said.

His fingers pressed into my windpipe. I opened my mouth,

gasping for breath. His hands were on my head, pushing, pressing.

"Like that," he said. "Yeah, that. No, not that."

I fought for air, sucking it in through my nose.

When he'd finished, his grip loosened. I pulled away, gagging, rolled down the window and spat. The rain had slackened to a drizzle. My head lolled out the window, a thing detached. The ocean below was shrouded in mist.

"Swallow next time," he said. "That's pure life force there. Best food there is. You shouldn't waste it."

It was a line from a story, a bad one, so awful I committed it to memory, word for word.

He gripped my thigh above the knee.

"Got it?" he said.

He squeezed harder.

"You hear me?"

I nodded.

I knew he'd said it before, just like that. Pure life force. Swallow next time. He'd done all of it before, just like this. I wasn't the first girl he'd picked up past the high school. He'd been trolling for someone like me, a girl on the periphery, one he could cut from the pack and no one would notice. I wondered if it had been the same with Crystal. Picturing her gave me hope. She was alive. I wanted to hug her, to be her friend.

I watched the sea below, tugged by its cold gravity. I had thought I was prepared for whatever might happen. I was no baby, no virgin. I was desperate for a new boyfriend. Someone to make me feel I belonged and was special. But this wasn't about me. I was just the girl on the side of the road that afternoon, the one who fit the profile.

Ron turned the key in the ignition and pulled back onto the highway. I believed there was more, that he wasn't done with me and that whatever was to come would be worse. Deflated, detached, my body rocked with the motion of the car. While we were moving, I was safe, I was alive.

He swerved off the road and came to an abrupt stop in another tight turnout. The scent of eucalyptus crept through the open window. The sign for Dora Court was visible just around the bend. He'd brought me to the top of my street.

Relieved, I snatched at the door handle. His arm shot out, like the restraining bar on a midway ride, hard beneath my breasts, pinning me to the seat.

"We cool?" he said.

I wanted him to be ugly now, older, harder, different than before. But he still looked like a guy up on stage, a guy on an album cover. The kind of guy I should have known would never really be interested in a girl like me.

I pressed against the door.

"Look at me," he said. "We cool?"

"Yeah."

"Yeah what?"

"We're cool."

His arm dropped. I reached for my pack.

"Hang on a minute," he said. "Give me your number."

Ron retrieved a tattered address book and pen from the glove compartment. He opened the book, thumbed the pages.

I recited seven numbers. Later, I would wonder why I gave him my real number. Maybe I was afraid it was a test, that he would have known if I lied and he wouldn't have let me out of the car. Maybe I didn't have the presence of mind to pull a number out of my head. Maybe I wanted him to have it.

I waited until his car disappeared around the first sharp bend in the road before I headed down the steep hill. My street was slick with matted leaves. I didn't stop at Liz's house. I didn't want to tell her, or anyone, about Ron. I stooped over the gutter and gagged.

Nothing came up.

I saved what I'd written in a file named "Ron," closed my computer and stretched out on the couch to rest my eyes.

The cell phone on the coffee table buzzed. Beyond the arched front window, the sun was rising. I picked up the phone, saw her name on the screen: Roxanne.

"Hey, Bozo," I said.

"Did I interrupt you two having wild sex again?"

"You know it. But it's good you called, I'm exhausted."

"Oh, you crazy kids. Just can't keep your hands off each other."

"You know us so well," I said.

14

I've been good, at least in terms of what I put in my mouth and burning more calories. I feel good, too, with fewer headaches and more energy. Sex has begun to cross my mind, as something I might conceivably want to do with my body. It happens in dreams. Surreal montages from past and imagined lives. In real terms, though, in bed with my husband at night, it still feels way too risky, considering the possible outcomes. Rejection. Disappointment. Embarrassment.

Bob lingers over the goodnight kiss. His lips are soft beneath that bristly mustache. This always surprises me. It shouldn't. He doesn't pull away when our lips part, doesn't retreat to his edge of the bed. He drapes an arm over my hip. I think of all the things I might do, the ways I might react. Thoughts are loud inside my head. My fingers tingle with blood. But I can't move. I'm frozen.

His arm grows heavier. It's leaden, oppressive. I sink into the mattress, pinned by its weight, fighting the urge to shrug him off. That would be rude.

"It's so cold," he says, pretend-shivering under the covers. Bob wears shorts and sandals all winter. He's never cold.

His arm grows heavier with each breath. It's an anvil, weighing me down.

He doesn't want me, not really. He never has. How could he? How could anyone? I am vile and disgusting.

It's pity. That's all it is. He can keep his pity. I won't make him suffer like that. He must be picturing some other woman beside him. No other explanation makes sense.

We are a lie. No, I am a lie. He is oblivious. He doesn't know me. I can't let him know me.

In my previous marriages, I reached a point where my husband's touch repulsed me, where each time felt like a violation. It's not like that with Bob. I still love him, even, sometimes, desire him. But it's usually in the abstract, when he isn't there, when closeness isn't an actual possibility.

I know this is bad, that I am bad, and that he'd have no trouble finding a less brittle woman. Perhaps he's flirted with that possibility and will take the bait one day. Perhaps he already has. I wouldn't blame him. I've been pushing him away for years, willing him to just get on with it and leave me, so I can stop feeling bad about being such an awful wife, such a gluttonous pig woman. It would be easier that way. I could stop anticipating the inevitable end. This, too, could be in the past, another memory to replay when I can't sleep.

His breath catches in a ragged, unselfconscious snore. I ease out from under his arm.

I am a coward, an awful wife. I deserve whatever he might choose to do, whatever fate is in store for our marriage, my longest by over fifteen years, my best, by miles. I hate how miserly and isolated I've become.

He tried.

I pretended not to notice.

Sleep is impossible.

I slip from the bed and retreat to the couch. The past is more real than the present. The plot holds fewer surprises. I know how it ends.

Mocha's nails clatter on the wood floor. He settles into his basket at my feet. I pat his head and straighten his floppy, inside out ears. I am safe, safe from my own life.

15

I met Michael in art class my first semester of high school, 1968, one year post Summer of Love. He was one of a handful of kids seated around a wide table gouging squares of linoleum with fluted knives, while the teacher, the cool one everybody liked, the one with longish hair who wore black high tops and jeans instead of a suit, fiddled with the FM dial on a paint-spattered radio and told us pretty much anything was okay by him, so long as we were mellow and didn't throw things or get so loud we drew attention to his classroom.

Like me, Michael was new to the school and town, so he didn't have any friends yet. His parents were divorced, and he had just moved up from L.A. to live with his mom. Which, as my mother later pointed out, made him easy pickings, a safer bet than most of the other kids, who already belonged to some teenage posse.

Michael was cute, tall and lanky, which meant he didn't make me feel like an Amazon. Brown eyes, curly dark hair. That's how I remember him, though I don't have any photos. Just the movies in my head. He fit my idea of what a hippie boyfriend should look like. Maybe I did the same for him. I couldn't wait to tell Liz about him, to recount the minute details of how he looked and dressed and smelled, musty like the bins of old clothes at our favorite thrift stores.

Michael and his mother lived on a rundown houseboat moored at Sausalito's Gate Five. Everybody knew Gate Five – a haven for artists, or those who self-identified as artists. Even my dad, an artist, whose day job was as a public-school art teacher, was impressed when I mentioned the place.

From Tam High down to the junction with Highway One, about half a mile along the busy road out of town, the route to Sausalito and my house was the same. One afternoon, we made plans to meet up after classes and walk there together.

It was a chilly fall day. I wore a big poncho I'd made from a plaid wool blanket by cutting a hole for my head in the middle, then crocheting a band around the opening to keep the fabric from fraying and to make it look intentional and not just like a blanket with a hole in it. The wind whipped at his light blue work shirt, the cotton worn to transparency, buttons open to mid-way down his thin chest. He thrust a hand in his pants pocket, pulled it out, palming a joint.

We were on the narrow shoulder facing oncoming traffic, just past the football field – across the road from the spot where, less than a year later, I would climb into Ron's car.

"Let's find a place out of the wind," Michael said.

We clambered off the narrow foot path and over the side, sliding several feet down to the crusty salt flats, a tidal wetland, the muddy bottom dry and cracked in a pattern like giraffe hide. A wood catwalk on stilts led to a weathered, locked utility shed twenty feet from the road. We walked the balance beam out to the shed and hunkered down beside it for shelter from the wind. In that sea of dried mud, the peaty scent of vegetative decay filling our nostrils, Michael cupped the match flame in the hollow of his hand. In the near distance, Highway 101 arched across the sky, traffic thickening as commuters – my parents would soon be among them – fled the city for Marin, for bigger, newer houses and the belief that their children were safer in the "country," away from all the hippies and degenerates in San Francisco.

We kissed. My first unimagined kiss with my first real boyfriend. In my memory, it was his, too. The distant hum of the highway rode the breeze. I held his cold hands and brought them under the scratchy wool poncho, under my loose peasant top, and laid them on my bare breasts. A light mist dripped from the sky, beading on the blanket, on our hair as we kissed, smoky tongues and warm fingers. I worried I wasn't doing the kissing right. I hoped some of the cool girls would walk past on the road and recognize us by my poncho. If no one else saw, only Liz would believe me.

That moment, marooned on the mud flats, perched on a splintery plank, our hands beneath the tee-pee of my poncho, and that feeling, half my mind, my senses, there with him, aware this was momentous, that this was finally happening to me, the other part of me hanging above us, outside, me watching me, wondering, is this it, is this what it is, is this how its supposed to be, supposed to feel. That moment, that first and only, etched in my memory, half lived, half recorded for replay.

Those were the years when, like for most teenagers, I believed my "real" life was separate and apart from my parents, and that my family couldn't possibly understand or appreciate what was happening to me, what I thought and felt and dreamed of. No one could. Only Liz. And now Michael. These friends of our youth who become our universe, later only memories.

That stretch of road is now nothing like it was then. There's a smooth, two-lane paved trail for bikes and pedestrians that connects Sausalito and Mill Valley. Young mothers in expensive workout clothes trot behind jogging strollers. Couples in biking spandex zip past. The unkempt wetland is partially developed. They must have filled it with soil, reclaiming the land to build on it. What remains is prettier than I remember, or perhaps only more intentional, less wild and forlorn. No parched giraffe hide, no reek of decay.

○ ⊖ ⊖

Despite the undisputed hipness of Gate Five, Michael and I often wound up at my house after school. My parents wouldn't get home from work until six, and there was always food in the refrigerator, a washer and drier, a flush toilet and shower. Amenities I took for granted, but Michael didn't.

If Mom was in a decent mood, he stayed for dinner. When it was time, I'd walk with him back down to the highway to hitch a ride. We'd take our time, making out alongside the creek bed at the bottom of the hill. Cars were more likely to stop for a girl, so he liked me to stay with him until one pulled over. As soon as that happened, I'd disappear back the way I'd come, wending my way uphill in the dark, startling at every sound.

I remember feeling constrained and controlled by my parents. Now it seems as if my generation had incredible freedom compared to the next. As grade school kids in San Francisco my friends and I roamed the avenues for miles in all directions, from the zoo to the ocean and clear across to Golden Gate Park. From the age of eight or nine, a friend and I would take the streetcar downtown to Market Street to go shopping at the Emporium with my mother's credit card and eat a slice of pizza or a dish of French fries at the Woolworth's counter.

After we moved to Marin, I was on my own for hours after school, until dinnertime. The high school was two miles from our house. After the first day, when Mom dropped me off, I don't recall my parents ever asking how I got there and back. They wouldn't have wanted me to hitchhike, but they never arranged for rides. It was presumed I would walk. Until my daughters could drive, I participated in carpools or drove them to school and back. It would have been unthinkable to me to leave them to figure it out on their own.

Michael and I must have said the words, "I love you." But I don't remember that, nor do I have memories of staring lovingly into one another's eyes like movie sweethearts, him touching my face tenderly and telling me how beautiful I was. What I remember is feeling like half of a matched pair, and how we stumbled down the road together, our arms wrapped round one another's waists so that we moved as one body, like clumsy contestants in a three-legged race.

His mother was a free spirit who dabbled in art. She had no job, no visible means of support. Alimony and child support, I now imagine, though that wouldn't have occurred to me then. She was nothing like my parents, which I thought was amazing, and she would have condoned and facilitated anything we wanted to do. She and Michael lived in close quarters on that houseboat, and she often had male visitors for the night. When that happened, Michael would drag his sleeping bag up onto the flat roof. She offered to supply us with birth control. He opted to shop-lift a box of contraceptive foam from the drug store at the junction.

I wasn't on the pill yet, and nobody, at least nobody I knew, used condoms back then. I sewed a corduroy draw-string purse to keep our contraceptive stash in, decorating it with a beaded sun medallion and dangling bead fringe. Likely I spent more time making that pouch than we ever did putting it to use.

We planned the day we would do it.

Fire trails crisscrossed the grassy hills on the other side of the highway from my house. There was an outcropping of rocks surrounded by compact bushes that had been rounded by the wind, creating a low hideout big enough for the two of us to wriggle under the bushes and lie down, protected from the wind and prying eyes. That's the spot we chose.

We took off our matching boots, leaving our socks on. I asked him to look away while I wriggled out of my jeans. Not because I didn't want him to see me, but because I was on my period and had to hide the ugly belt and pad I wore. This was before the handy adhesive pads of today and Mom wouldn't let me use tampons. She said they rubbed calluses inside you and that I shouldn't be putting anything up there anyway.

We spread our jean jackets over the dusty earth, then fumbled with the foam and plunger, making a whipped cream mess.

I remember it hurting some, not a lot, and then it was over.

"Is that all it is?" he said after.

I don't think he said it to be mean. We were friends. We shared everything. I think he really wondered. I did, too, though I would never have been the one to say the words. I blamed myself. I must have done something wrong, or not done something right.

"So why do my mom and her asshole friends make so much noise? I mean, how is it any different than jacking off?" he asked.

It wasn't awful. It just wasn't as exciting as what had come before, the kissing, the necking. But we'd done it, we'd crossed the threshold, together. Losing our virginity, that odd phrase, came without any of the fanfare we'd anticipated, no musical score, no epiphanies, no deeper connection.

After years of fantasizing, of gleaning the mystique and romance of sex and love from books, movies and fan magazines, I suppose it was bound to be anti-climatic, literally and figuratively. Perhaps, and this was my greatest fear, Michael knew it wasn't all there was, that I wasn't all there was, and that sex would be better, much better, with another girl.

Romeo and Juliet love. Pride and Prejudice love. Bah, humbug.

If those moments with Michael on a windswept hillside, red

Marin clay beneath my ass, ratty sanitary pad peaking out from under my jeans, had been my one chance at love, it wouldn't have sustained me for very long or inspired much of a story. It's his question during the tepid afterglow that stuck with me, and that acquired the weary ring of truth.

"Is that all it is?" became my life's subtext.

16

Over the years, I've told a handful of people that I was raped when I was in high school. Some version of my story has happened to so many that the topic tends to come up, particularly with women friends. What happened with Ron, up to the point when I got out of his car and stumbled home, has always been the easier part to tell. It seemed containable within boundaries most people could understand and empathize with. Teenage girl makes a bad decision and becomes the victim of sexual assault. Teenage girl is arguably lucky it wasn't worse. A sad story. An unfortunate story. But familiar.

I never shared what happened next. I didn't want to think about it, let alone talk about it or write about it. If the assault was muddy, if I was complicit, even to blame, as some people, usually men, would eventually tell me, if I'd gotten what I deserved that wet afternoon, then I'd really deserved what happened after that.

Ron hadn't written my number down wrong.

I was home alone, still in my nightgown at noon, waiting for a steamy bowl of macaroni and cheese to cool when the phone rang. I picked up, expecting it to be Liz.

It was Ron.

It had been over a week. I'd already relived the rape a hundred times. Standing under the hot shower until my skin turned red. Faking sick for two days after, so I could stay home from school and not have to see anyone. I hadn't thought I'd ever hear from him again. At the sound of his voice through the line, I shrunk from the kitchen window and tucked my knees up under my gown to make myself small, to hide, as if he were out there and could see what a grubby slob I was.

"You still there?" he said.

"Yeah."

"What, you didn't think I would call?"

"I don't know."

"Why wouldn't I?"

He wasn't flirtatious or insinuating. It wasn't like that. He was blunt, declarative, like he was inside my head and could hear my thoughts then spout them back at me.

"You want to hang out?" he said.

"How'd you know I'd be home?"

"Lucky guess."

It was an in-service day at the high school, not a regular holiday. My younger sister was at school and my parents at work. I figured Ron must have driven by the campus and seen how deserted it was. I pictured that little black book he'd pulled from the glove compartment.

"How many numbers did you call before mine?"

"You home alone?"

"Yeah."

"Give me the address. I'll pick you up."

Whether it was what I wanted or not, he was coming.

I didn't know how long I had before Ron arrived. No time to shower. I changed into pretty panties, threw on pants and a t-shirt and struggled with my hair. I wished I'd curled it the night before to tame the frizz and that my favorite jeans were clean. I must have known this wasn't a date. Even so, I was excited. He'd called. He'd called *me*. I was ashamed, too, for feeling giddy after what he'd done, a queasy stew of emotions that would soon become familiar territory.

Ron pulled up to the curb fifteen minutes later, the same car, rumbling and black. I ran from the house, jean jacket slung over my shoulder. Before I stooped to climb in, I squinted across the cul-de-sac, hoping my perky neighbor was at her window. I'd watched her climb in and out of so many cars and pick-up trucks, listened to my mother tsk about Brenda this and Brenda that, about how popular she was and that it was a shame we weren't friends because she could probably introduce me to some nice boys. Mom couldn't understand why I spent time with Liz when such a nice girl lived right across the street. But the curtains were drawn. Brenda wouldn't see me climb into a car with Ron a boy—no, a man—better looking and way cooler than any of the jocks she dated.

"I thought we'd go to this place I know," he said. "It's nice, private."

"You mean like a restaurant?"

He accelerated up the steep hill, leaving my stomach below. Ron didn't drive clear to the coast that second time. He didn't say he had something to show me. He didn't tell me I looked good, that he'd missed me or that he'd been thinking about me. I don't think he told me anything at all. We hadn't gone far when he pulled off the highway and down a deserted fire road, just far enough that we couldn't be seen. We never left the front seat.

I knew what was coming. I tried to swallow.

"You'll get used to it," he said.

Less than half an hour after he picked me up, I was home. The cheese on my noodles hadn't even congealed.

⊖ ⊖ ⊖

The rest of high school, Ron was my secret boyfriend. One who called and arranged to pick me up on days when school was out or when I was home "sick." He must have guessed I was the kind of girl who looked for excuses to stay home alone. Or maybe he just worked his way through his book and sometimes I picked up. I never believed I was the only girl like me. I never asked how high or low I was on the call list. The less I knew, the fewer questions I asked, the easier it was to pretend it was something other than what it was.

In between his calls, I fabricated an elaborate fiction where he, we, were whatever I wanted us to be. He took me to hear music. We danced. I met his friends and hung out backstage. I wore the coolest clothes, had long straight hair, was ten pounds thinner, had larger breasts. All the kids from school saw me with him and wanted to be my friend. Making believe I already had a boyfriend, it didn't bother me as much when the boys at school snubbed me or other girls flaunted their boyfriends and their perfect, pretty lives.

I was ashamed, too, enough not to consider telling anyone about him and what we did. Lonely and desperate enough to have someone, anyone, that I never told him no. Grateful that he remembered me from week to week, even if it was only in half-hour increments in the middle of the day.

⊖ ⊖ ⊖

At school, I was drawn to Crystal. I once chose an empty seat beside her in the back row of biology class. Her cowboy boots were the real thing, scuffed, caked with mud and sprigs of hay. I decided that while she was prettier than me – in my book, any girl with straight hair had something over me – she was kind of goofy and tomboyish, too.

Crystal was hunched over her notebook, hair falling forward to cover her face.

"What are you drawing?" I asked her.

She turned her notebook so I could see. Prancing ponies filled the margins, ones with oversized eyes and lashes, their long tails and manes elaborate curlicues.

"Cool," I said. "You have a horse?"

"Yeah."

There was something about her toothy smile, the way her cheeks dimpled, that made my insides ache.

⊖ ⊖ ⊖

I did eventually tell Liz about Ron. I had to tell someone, or else what was the point? I didn't tell her what we did together. Only his first name, how cool he was, what he looked like and about the band he worked for. He was older, I told her, busy with his music.

Liz probably knew there was less to Ron than what I made him out to be, but she was a good friend. She didn't press me for details.

One weekend, we hitched down to the record store in town to search for any sign of him on record album covers. There was one cryptic mention of "Ron, *El Raton*," on a record by the band he'd said he worked for, and a grainy, black and white photo in a jumbled collage that could have been him.

"He's really cute," she said, both of us squinting at the fuzzed image that might or might not have been Ron.

Since pre-teen days, I'd had this thing. I imagine many girls do – boys too, for all I know. The belief that unless I had a guy in my life, some guy, no matter how nebulous – a secret crush would do – someone to hitch my daydreams to, I was adrift, I was nowhere, I wasn't real. For much of my high school years, Ron filled that role. It's awful that he did, that the thing about which I was most ashamed, allowed me to walk the halls each day with a swagger in my step and a knowing gleam in my eye.

It's not as if I really believed it. I may have been consciously deluded, but I wasn't deranged or simple-minded. I knew he didn't care about me or maybe even like me. I knew he saw other girls, maybe even ones he did care about. I never tried to stalk Ron or get closer to him. I understood there was no "closer" to get, that what he did with me was all it would ever be.

At least I wasn't alone. I wasn't some total misfit loser. I had a boyfriend. One who'd picked me up at the side of the road. One who called.

17

Bob wakes and shuffles into the kitchen. I've been up for hours, scribbling in the front room. I join him for a coffee refill.

"I remembered a dream," he says, with a proud smile.

He can never remember dreams.

"Very cool," I say. "Tell me."

The dream is a convoluted jumble, as dreams tend to be. He was out on a lake with a group of random guys. They held a tarp between them to capture hot water and keep it separate from the lake water. They wore special suits and used instruments of some kind to separate the hot water from the rest.

"What do you think it means?"

"That you had to pee," I say. "All the technical stuff was your engineer's way of processing the urge."

He laughs. I laugh. It's relaxed, easy, despite my silent rejection the night before. It's a small thing, yet I'm grateful. Relieved. His ungrudging ease gives me hope. It's a new day. Another chance to be a better me.

He gets dressed for the day, in his railroad museum garb, complete with lanyard, buttons and insignia marking his accomplishments as number one, star docent of the year. When he returns to the kitchen, I'm making myself a virtuous egg white omelet.

"What's that, over there?" he says.

I tuck my chin to my chest like a balky child, but I can't not smile, just a little.

He leans in to kiss me goodbye. "Look, over there," he says, his voice softer now, our faces close.

I blush and can almost imagine it's twenty years ago, that we are still the way we used to be. The drought isn't over, but this small moment makes it seem possible, a trickle of affection that could gain momentum if I let it.

That night in bed, after the good night kiss, we lie facing one another. He rests an arm on the slope between my hip and belly. I put an arm around him.

"How was the museum?" I ask, my voice hushed, though we have the house to ourselves. "You go out to lunch with your crusty old friends?" A reference to the advanced age of most of his fellow volunteers. Still in his sixties, he's the youngster.

He laughs. He always laughs when I call them that.

Our kisses deepen. Our hands move over one another's bodies. I feel the shift inside me. Rusty at first, a neglected gear. My breath slows. Becomes audible. Sensed through the skin, the body's shield, its largest organ. Oh, this, yes, I remember now.

We break the fast. It's good, easy too, crazy easy considering all my anticipatory angst. I wonder why we don't do it more often. I always wonder why we don't do it more often.

⊖ ⊖ ⊖

I wake to the sound of rain pelting the windows. Another good omen. In California, rain is almost always cause for celebration. I putter to the toilet and hold a plastic stick in the stream of pee. The tip turns that lovely maroon color. *Yes.* I am still in full fat-burning mode, I had sex and there's rain. The year is looking up.

Time for my second weekly weigh-in.

I creep upstairs. Kick off my slippers and drop my pajama bottom. It's too chilly to take off my top. Before stepping onto the scale, I close my eyes and make a wish. Under 180, please, into the 170s, please. I haven't touched the scale since the prior week, when I'd rocked back and forth to earn that measly, fraudulent, 179.7.

I step up, expel all the air from my lungs and stare down at the number. 176.6. Three pounds. That's more like it. I am now legitimately into the 170s, no fudging necessary.

I record the number in my journal and on the calendar. I've lost a tad over six pounds in two weeks. A few more pounds and I'll be sliding into those size fourteen jeans. I do the math. I could be fifteen pounds down in another five weeks. I keep doing the math. Ten weeks. Fifteen weeks. Twenty weeks. At this rate, I'll be down a size in another week or two, then another size, and another, working my way back into that stack of jeans. Reaping complements from friends and family. In no time at all, my thighs will stop slapping together. I'll be wearing dresses without leggings, purging the fat clothes from my wardrobe, donating the extra-large elastic waistband skirts and pants, then the size fourteens, the size twelves, and, and… stop.

The last time I lost forty-plus pounds, I got rid of all my big-girl clothes. Within a year, I'd gained all the weight back and had to buy new clothes, new "fat" clothes. This time I'll put them into storage bins. I won't get rid of them for at least five years. That's the smart thing to do.

I am over the initial hump. Two weeks in and seeing progress.

I need a concrete incentive, a marker out in the future to work towards. Something sooner than next January.

Two years ago, the three of us – me, Bob and Carolanne – spent a week in Hawaii, our first time there. Caught up in the beauty of the islands, I'd been suckered into a timeshare presentation, then into purchasing one. I log onto the website to verify our available points. We have just enough for a week on the Big Island in a small condo, perfect for the two of us.

I can't remember the last time Bob and I had a vacation without at least one of the children along. On our brief "honeymoon" on the Northern California coast, I was nauseous, the baby growing in my belly a lumpy reminder of the reason we'd gotten married in the first place.

I book the Hawaii condo for the first week of October. Eight months to lose forty pounds, to get in shape and feel comfortable in a bathing suit, something besides baggy shorts and a tank top.

My sister Juliet and her boyfriend vacation in Hawaii several times a year. She posts tropical paradise photos to Facebook. Juliet in a bikini on a paddle board. Juliet sipping a fruity, umbrella cocktail, skin glowing, a white blossom behind her ear, impossibly young, impossibly gorgeous.

I gulp down envy and bile. I am not my sister. I will never be my sister. I wasn't blessed with flawless skin and perpetual youth. But I can be a better me. I picture myself in a flattering, curve-hugging one-piece, more glamorous 1940s film siren than *Sports Illustrated* cover girl.

It will be romantic, our first real honeymoon. A week to bring us back to the way we were.

2017 is unfolding according to plan. I'm proud of myself. Exorcising my demons is part of it. Facing up to the ghosts of past selves. Turning it into story, events that happened to me, yes, but a different me, my fifteen-year-old self, my twenty-six-year-old self, my forty-year-old self. I'm not those girls, those women, anymore. It is time to forgive them, to forgive myself, and to accept their stories, my stories, for what they are. Things that happened a long, long time ago, to a different me.

I open my computer and reread what I've written so far.

There's more to Ron. It doesn't get better. *I* don't get better. Just write it, our teacher says. Don't worry about what people will say or think. You may even decide not to share it with anyone. My younger sister says she doesn't believe in hanging onto the bad things that have happened. She's gotten so good at letting go of the past, that it's as if it never happened at all, as if she's been washed clean by the force of her own will. That, or she's a very good actress. Either way, I envy her the ability to shed the past like a worn-out coat.

I'm wired differently.

18

I won't pretend to remember every time I saw Ron. From the handful of times that remain most vivid, because they stood out as milestone moments for one awful reason or another, it now seems that, though the relationship wasn't "real" in the ways I sometimes pretended, there was an arc to it, a beginning, a middle and an end. The beginning, that first time, remains the most vivid. It's one of my stories, central to the mythology of my life. That moment, in a black car hugging the rugged coast, has a power over me, one I want to unpack, to dismantle so that I can tuck the pieces away in some safer corner of my mind, so that I can forgive myself for my part, for thinking so little of myself, for not believing I had a choice.

I don't want to be that girl anymore. Which seems ludicrous to concede at sixty-three. But there it is. We carry some memories around for so long they become subliminal snowballs, gathering weight with time's passing, becoming anchors to the spirit without our even knowing. But more than that girl, the one who made a foolish mistake, I don't want to be the girl who for over two years kept getting into that car.

For a while, I let myself believe that I was one of his favorites. His calls became more frequent. In the car to and from whatever field or back road was his destination that afternoon, he talked more easily.

"You don't give me any shit like most chicks do," he said, one afternoon. This must have been after, when he was driving me home.

"Yeah?"

"Like Crystal. Chick with a horse. You know her?"

"Kind of."

"She told her old man. I could have gone to jail."

That's how I learned I'd been right about Crystal, that she had been like me for awhile.

I was proud that Ron confided in me. Perhaps I even let myself believe I mattered to him, that he knew me at least a little, enough to like me for me. I don't think I understood about statutory rape. Or if I did, I thought it was lame. Most of the girls I looked up to weren't with high school boys.

Believing I lacked good hair, a pretty face, or impressive boobs, I considered age my strongest asset. One that was fast dwindling in value. At least I could scratch Crystal off the list of my imagined competition. Once I knew it was over, I wanted to talk to her about Ron, to know if he'd been the same with her, whether she had resisted more than me that first time, whether he'd hurt her and if that was why she told her dad. I never had the nerve.

I still picture Crystal as she was then, a big-boned farm girl with a gap-toothed smile. I hope life's been good to her and that whatever happened between her and Ron didn't haunt her like it did me. I imagined I saw it in her eyes back then, the weight of it, the bruise. But perhaps I was only seeing myself. Even now, I have these crazy questions. Why did he pick her up in front of the school, like a real girlfriend, when with me it was always someplace else, where no one would see us together? Was I different than other girls? Was he ashamed of me?

There was a time when I wanted more than anything for the popular kids to see me with him. But maybe it was good that never happened. I doubt I was the only one who knew about Ron.

"You can drop me in front of the house," I said to Ron, late one afternoon.

"Won't your parents be home?"

"They don't care."

I wanted my mother to see me with him. According to her, by my age, she'd already had multiple marriage proposals. To hear her tell it, she'd been the belle of the ball at Shasta High.

"If you just paid more attention to your appearance," she would say, "if you wore your hair in a more flattering style, dressed in something besides jeans, if you would just smile and take an interest in other people, you might get asked out some time. Going on dates is fun, you know. It's what you should be doing at your age."

As I climbed out of his car, Mom was standing at the kitchen sink, with a clear view of the street. Hunched low in the seat, a blur of longish dark hair and a leather-jacketed arm, Ron spun the car around and accelerated back up the hill. No wave, no last look my way.

I dropped my pack at the bottom of the stairs to my bedroom and kicked off my boots.

"Who was that?" Mom said.

"A guy."

"He looked older."

"Not much," I said.

"You know, honey, in my experience, the boys who seem the most exciting are usually not very nice."

I snatched up my book bag and closeted myself in my room. Whatever reaction I had hoped for, that wasn't it. Besides, what could my mother, any mother, possibly know about exciting guys?

⊖ ⊖ ⊖

One time Ron broke the pattern. He called me on a school night. Mom answered the phone. I took it on the extension upstairs. I would have yelled at her to hang up. I would have listened for the disconnect. Then I would have worried that she hadn't really hung up, that she'd only pressed the button down and was still on the line, masking her breathing with a hand over the receiver. I'd gotten away with eavesdropping enough times to know it wasn't that hard to do, not on an old-school landline.

Ever since Ron dropped me off, Mom had been acting weird. She would turn my pockets inside out and sniff my jeans. She asked more questions about where I was going and where I'd been. Where vague answers about being with a friend used to suffice, she now wanted last names and phone numbers. If I said I was spending the night with a friend, she asked for a parent she could call.

Ron gave me his address and asked me to come see him after school the next day. Even if it was just doing what we always did, in a house instead of the car, it was the closest we'd come to a real date. I'd never seen him naked, only the one part of him. He'd never tried to take off my shirt or pants, never once tussled with the buttons on my jeans. I didn't wear a bra, none of the cool girls did, so there were no fasteners to fuss with. Even so, I don't think he ever touched my breasts. Aside from kissing, rough kissing, and his hands on my head, Ron never touched me at all.

After school the next day, I walked to the address he'd given me. The house was directly across the street from the high school, on the road that ran along the side with the amphitheater, parking lot and playing fields. From the front picture window, he had an unobstructed view of the kids who hung out along the chain-link fence, the greasers and stoners, sneaking a smoke, making out between classes and at lunchtime.

Approaching the house, I was reminded of the first time he'd called. I'd wondered then how he'd known I would be at home. Mystery solved. The high school was his front yard. Dozens of underage girls parading past most every day of the week.

I saw him from the road, watching the street, strumming an acoustic guitar. With the guitar grasped in one hand, he opened the front door. I wondered how this would go, if I'd crouch in front of the chair or he would take off his boots and pants, maybe even take me into the bedroom. I would have worn my favorite jeans, a top that showed my boobs. They weren't big and bouncy, but at fifteen they were at least perky, with neat, compact nipples, not big, sloppy discs like some I'd seen showering after PE. I would have worn my sexiest underwear, even knowing they'd likely go unseen.

He lit a joint, took a hit, passed it to me.

"Sit," he said. "I want to play something for you."

I perched on an armrest. The moment felt huge. He wanted me to hear his music. That must have been why he asked me to come to his place. I didn't know what to do with my hands, my face. Ron had never been like this before. He messed around with the guitar, as if he were finding his place, warming up. We were just hanging out. It seemed like a good thing, but without the usual script, I didn't know my part. I was anxious, dry mouthed, feet jittering on the floor.

He had just gotten into what I figured was the song he wanted me to hear, singing along with the chords, when the front door banged open. A girl in a tiny mini dress and high heels stood there, skinny legs planted apart, one hip cocked. She had long, strawberry blonde hair, a pretty, made-up face, eyes rimmed with mascara. Her gaze darted from him to me.

"Who the fuck is she?" she asked.

Ron kept strumming.

"I work all day so you can do your music and you pull this

shit?" She looked me up and down. I registered her quick assessment and dismissal in my gut.

Ron just sat there, as if this was between me and the strawberry blonde. She was older than me, but not old, old, maybe nineteen. Model thin. The kind of girl I imagined would be with a guy like Ron. She hiked her dress up, twisting the fabric in her hands.

"He did this," she said. "Look at my legs. Look."

I didn't want to look. But I couldn't help it. Her legs were so thin I could see the front door through her thighs, so thin her pantyhose sagged at the crotch.

"You see these bruises? He did that. He beats the shit out of me. He'll do the same to you."

She pulled the dress up even higher. Her pelvic bones jutted like wings above lace panties. I sucked in my stomach. I was an Amazon in comparison. Ron just sat there with the guitar resting on one crossed leg, nonchalant, as if this kind of thing happened all the time.

"So, what, she your girlfriend now? This little chick your new girlfriend?"

He just smirked, as if the question didn't deserve an answer. I stood and backed towards the door.

"No," I said. "No, I'm not."

"Then what the fuck are you doing here?" she said.

"Nothing," I said. "I was just leaving."

"You don't have to go." Ron must have meant me, but his eyes were on her. "You got no right to insult my friends. Apologize."

"Who the fuck is she?"

"I'm nobody," I said. "I'm not anything."

Ron didn't correct me.

Through the shut door I heard a crash, a high-pitched scream, then sobs. He didn't come after me. I hadn't expected him to.

It wouldn't occur to me until years later, when another guy used me the same way, that Ron must have set it up on purpose, that he'd wanted me there when his real girlfriend, the one he lived with, likely the one who paid the bills, got home from work. To make her jealous. Or to put her in her place. Whatever it was about, it had nothing to do with me. I was just a prop, someone he knew would show up when he called.

Even though he'd asked me to come, I felt as if I were the one who'd done something wrong, as if what happened was my fault. I'd seen her. Those bruises taunted me. He must have cared about her for real, enough to hit her, enough that they fought, then made up. I trudged home, thinking I'd blown it, that Ron and I were over, that he'd scratch my name from his book.

⊖ ⊖ ⊖

He didn't.

Things went back to the way they were before. Daytime phone calls. Quick hookups. Weeks passed. He gave me another address. Said he'd moved, that the blonde bitch was history, and this place was cool.

When school let out, I tripped up the street to the address he'd given me. It was a few blocks farther from the high school, on a street of older, ramshackle wood homes, ones with overgrown bushes and shaggy lawns. I was still a sophomore, but I'd turned sixteen, which I only remember because that was the semester I took choir, and I was carrying my choir jacket over my arm that day, taking it home with me for an evening performance. The jacket hung on a wire hanger, protected by a plastic dry cleaner bag. My backpack was overloaded with books to study for exams over the weekend. I wore my favorite dress, a clingy mini, lavender background with a psychedelic pattern and a soft ruffle around the neckline. My mother called it "a real butt scraper," with a satisfied nod and smile. She'd picked it out, said it showed off my legs, which, according to her, were my best asset. I'd done my hair up in rags the night before so my head that day was a mass of thick sausage curls, held back from my face with flowered ribbons, my sexy Little-Bo-Peep look.

It was spring. Sun sprinkled the pavement through the overhang of tree branches. A light wind fluttered the front of my dress, the short skirt around my bare thighs.

I knocked at the door.

Ron waved me inside. It was nothing like the other house. If there was a front room, I never saw it. He pulled me into a bedroom, said it was his. He opened the closet door. It was empty, except for two kimonos on hangers, silk with glossy embroidery. He hung my choir jacket on the rod.

"This one's yours," he said, sliding one of the kimonos off its hanger and handing it to me.

"Mine?"

"Yeah, take off your clothes, put it on."

"*Mine*, mine?"

"Why wouldn't it be?"

I didn't want to put the kimono on. It didn't feel right. He was acting funny. Different. It was cheesy. Of all the things I'd done with Ron, the pretense of the kimono in the empty closet, that he'd thought I would believe he'd bought it for me, made me feel cheap, underestimated. What we had wasn't much, but I'd never felt like he outright lied to me. I'd done that part myself.

"It's a beautiful day. Let's go outside," he said, giving up on the kimonos. He led the way through the kitchen and out the back door.

The yard was narrow, with one big tree at the back and a bare mattress in the middle of a weedy lawn. He pulled me down onto the mattress and leaned back on his elbows. My dress inched up so my patterned underpants showed. I kicked off my shoes.

He undid his pants. I stared at the fences on either side of the yard. High enough that no neighbors could see in. Yet the dark upstairs windows seemed to glare down at us. I missed the safe confines of the car.

"It's cool," he said. "We're alone."

He tugged at my dress, lifted it over my head. The breeze grazed my bare nipples. I'd wanted him to see my body, to touch my body. Now that it was happening, I felt exposed and goose pimply. I couldn't get the kimono and the unlived-in bedroom out of my head. I shifted onto my side, a half fetal curl. With my back to the house, I felt less vulnerable. He tugged at me, positioning my limbs and torso as if I were a mannequin, until I faced the house again. I covered my bare breasts with my arms. He peeled them back and held me by the wrists.

Those blackened windows stared down. He loosened his grip to pull off his shirt. I inhaled, willing myself to relax, anticipating the moment when he covered me with his body. Finally, we'd be close in a way we never had. Up on one elbow, angled away from me, he slid his fingers beneath my panties and tugged.

At that moment, I sensed movement in one of the upper story windows. A flutter. A shadow where it was once only black. I scooted away from Ron. Readjusted the scant cover of my underpants.

"Relax," he said, reaching, again, for my wrists. "We're alone. I swear."

But I'd seen it. Ron's jerky over-the-shoulder look, up, at the window where I'd seen movement. I clambered to the edge of the mattress and grabbed my dress, struggling to wriggle back into it, as Ron snatched at my hands, my legs. I grabbed my shoes from the grass and sprinted for the back door. Ron bolted upright and ran in front of me to get there first. There was a window in the top half of the back door. Ron tried to block it with his body, but I saw the shirtless guy standing there.

"You freaked her out, man," Ron said, shouting. "You fucking blew it."

I pushed past Ron and through the door, through the kitchen and back the way I'd come. For a moment, the three of us were close in a narrow hallway. The other guy loomed over me, a full head taller than Ron. He leered down, bloodshot eyes, long, fright-show blonde hair, low-slung jeans, dog tags on a chain on his bare chest. Maybe Ron had looked the same that first time, all the other times, too, but I hadn't seen it. His eyes were so black and expressionless. He'd had more practice. I knew what Ron wanted. But with this guy it was different, scary different. He lurched towards me.

"Leave her alone," Ron said. "Seriously man, it's over."

I ran to the bedroom for my things. The tall one followed me. I felt his breath. Smelt his sweat. He was laughing, cackling, pawing at my arms. He didn't follow me out the front door. I felt his eyes as I stumbled down the street, hugging my pack and shoes, dragging my choir jacket in the dust, afraid to look back, only wanting to get away. At the bottom of the hill, I stopped to pick gravel from the soles of my feet.

I must have understood that it had been a set up, that Ron didn't really live there. Maybe he'd been bragging about what a dumb fuck I was, about this high school chick who would do anything he wanted. His friend wanted to watch. Maybe he'd paid for the show. Maybe he'd planned to join us on the mattress, or film us from the upstairs window. And there I was in my ribbons and curls, my favorite party dress.

131

The choir recital was that night. My family came. Maybe Liz did, too. It was in a big church with stained glass windows, the one where my older sister would soon be married. The choir teacher arranged us in rows up on the altar. He stood behind me and whispered in my ear, "How about you just mouth the words to the songs. You can sing in class, but it's better if you don't here. Just this once, okay?"

Before he said that, I'd thought I had a good voice, an amazing voice. I'd been carried away with the classroom harmonies, fantasized myself clear into a rocking girl band. Ron would see me sing. Everybody who mattered would. I'd be amazing and beautiful and popular. Before that afternoon on the mattress, I'd thought Ron sort of liked me, not that he loved me or anything, but that I was at least a real person, not just some stupid chick. Even so, I knew it could have been much worse, that I'd been "lucky." Ron used me, degraded me, allowed me to degrade myself, but in that moment, when he could have let his friend hurt me, he didn't. Maybe he cared enough to not let that happen, maybe he didn't want to blow what he had, maybe he saw what I saw in that guy's eyes, and it freaked him out, too. More likely he was afraid of pushing it too far, to the point where I told someone, as Crystal had. I don't know that I would have. Not if the only scars they left on my body were the kind my parents couldn't see, the kind no one could see.

I did what choir director said. I opened my mouth, but no sound came out.

19

There is a curated group of life events that have made it onto my emotional "hit parade." Like the set buttons on a car radio, these are the ones I push the most. I've replayed some of them so many times, they haven't been allowed to fade.

My boyfriend's prophetic words after we lost our virginity together made my top ten. As did getting into Ron's car. What my mother said to me around that same time made the list, too.

It was a Sunday morning. I'd been out late the night before, at a dance in town. Awake, blinking up at the ceiling. I reached overhead and grabbed hold of the bed frame with both hands to get a good stretch and a whiff of my stale underarms, finding reassurance, familiarity, in my own smell. Something shiny poked out from beneath the pillow, its surface hard and dappled brown. I shifted onto my side and pulled out a hand mirror, one I kept in the bathroom I shared with my younger sister.

I stared into its crackled surface. My hair was a matted mess, eyelids pooched with sleep. I frowned, positive I hadn't put the mirror under my pillow. I climbed out of bed and stumbled down the stairs in my nightgown, bare toes digging into the shag, holding the mirror out in front of me like a candlestick.

Mom was in the kitchen, emptying the avocado-colored dishwasher. I hovered in the doorway. She straightened, arched her back, and glared at a spot below my navel. I knew what she was looking at, a smudge, the size of a fat finger, crotch level on the front of my gown. I wished I'd put on a robe.

"What is that?" she said, wrinkling her nose.

I'd had an itch and scratched myself through my gown, through my underwear. I knew it looked gross. Her expression made me feel like I was, too. The hand mirror drooped at my side. I hunched my shoulders so the brown circles of my nipples didn't poke through the thin fabric and give her something else to mock.

"I see you found the mirror," she said.

"*You* put it there?"

I pictured her, a malevolent crone hovering over me as I slept. Goosebumps pricked my bare arms.

"Well?" she said.

"Well, what?"

"Did you look at yourself?"

"Excuse me?"

"Did you look at yourself in the mirror?"

"*Yeah.* It's a mirror."

"And?" She sighed, the beleaguered, long-suffering sigh of the mother of a teenage girl. "I had hoped you'd be compelled to take a good, hard look at yourself."

"I get it," I said. "I'm a mess. I'll shower."

"No, child. I had hoped you would gaze into the mirror and ask yourself a question."

"Jesus, Mom. I can't read your mind."

"You can't guess the question?"

It was my turn to sigh, the beleaguered sigh of a teenage girl with a clueless and relentlessly irritating mother.

"I had hoped you would ask your mirror, 'Why, *why* do I hate myself?'"

"God, Mom, I don't hate myself. Do you?"

"I'm making you an appointment to see a psychologist."

"I don't ask my mirror why I hate myself, so I have to see a shrink."

"Oh, *honey*. You need to talk to someone."

My grimy toes gripped the linoleum. I repeated the question, mouthing her words, determined to commit them to memory. *Why, why do I hate myself?* Classic Mom. I couldn't wait to repeat it to Liz, imitating Mom's delivery, the way she lingered over *why, why*. It was practically Shakespearean.

I was a pretty good mimic. I still am. Some of my best material has always come from my mother.

What I was meant to ask my hand mirror became one of my stories, a scene I loved to hate. Which I suppose says as much about me as it does about her. My mother's question, the twisted truth of it, struck a deep chord. And there was the way she said it. Accusatory, as if I were the embodiment of the disgusting stain on my nightgown.

She did take me to a therapist. I refused to speak to him. After a few visits, he told Mom she was wasting her money.

All parents have their shortcomings. God knows I do. One of hers was a lack of empathy. I now believe she was honestly worried about me, yet she only succeeded in making me feel like a leper. Perhaps there wasn't anything she could have said or done that would have penetrated my shell.

Now, as a mother, a grandmother, I think back to some of our conversations. I was struggling. I was unhappy. I needed help, but like many, if not most, teenagers, I didn't perceive her as having one single thing to offer me. Nor did I believe she was on my side. I cast her as the villain, my adversary, the one who stood in the way of my freedom and happiness.

Relationships between mothers and daughters are often

strained. I wouldn't lighten up on her or consider that she'd likely done the best she knew how, until many years later, when I left my first husband with nothing but a quarter for a pay phone and our toddler son in my arms. She came for me. She took us in. No questions, no I told you so.

All these years later, and I'm still struggling with the question my mother wanted me to ask my mirror.

Mom nailed it, as mothers often do. I hated myself. Sometimes I still do. Writing, remembering, sends me to the kitchen. What an idiot I was. What a fool. A homely, ill-kempt, stupid, stupid girl. I grab a box of ice cream sandwiches from the freezer. There are four left, I eat them all, too fast to really taste them. When I pull the wrapper from the last one, the vanilla ice cream is still hard.

I'm not sated. I need more. I can still think. I need more. I feel sick. I need to lie down.

My parents didn't put the self loathing in me.

No one man put the hate in me, though most didn't do me any favors, either. They were symptoms, manifestations, not the disease.

63 might be kind of late in life to go searching for a better way to be, to cope, but better late than never. I come from good genes on both sides. I could live past 100. That's a lot more years.

Half a century of shame is a lot to shed. Harder than dropping 50 pounds. It would be a neat trick to slough them off simultaneously. Drop a size, let loose a decade of remorse at the same time.

Even if I only succeed in losing the shame and not the pounds, I'll consider it a success. I already know that the other way around isn't sustainable.

20

I knew the moment my last child was conceived. It was a few days after Thanksgiving 1997. Bob's mother, Carol, had died in her sleep a few weeks earlier. She was the age I am now, a sweet woman who looked as if she'd lived hard and suffered the consequences. I accompanied Bob to the coastal Southern California mobile home park where she'd spent her last years. He drove his old pickup truck with a wobbly trailer attached.

I'd met his mother a few times over the years we'd been together. She had a lumbering side-to-side gait, wore bright rouge and lipstick, hair dyed yellow blonde and styled the way she'd always worn it. From photos, I know that she was once a very beautiful woman.

My daughter, Grace, was five or six when we first visited Bob's mom.

"I always wanted a girl," his mother said, when she met Grace.

Bob and I had been together several years when she died. We'd fallen into the patterns of an established relationship, yet it seemed increasingly unlikely Bob would want to remarry. His divorce had been awful, and tension with his ex, fights about money and the kids, were ongoing. It was hard on his boys, and he didn't want to put them through any more change. I understood, though I thought he was short-sighted, unwilling to move forward, to even consider altering a status quo that didn't seem to me to be anything worth clinging to. I'd decided that once I'd helped him through the loss of his mother, I should move on. Perhaps I contemplated some sort of ultimatum. I know I didn't want to continue the way we were, half of me enjoying what we had, half of me bitter than it wasn't more, the bitter half spoiling the good times, turning me into someone I didn't want to be.

We spent a long, fall day loading the material remnants of his mother's life into plastic trash bags and cardboard boxes. We stripped the sheets from the bed where she'd drawn her last breath, a moment tinged with uncomfortable intimacy. I sifted through the clothes neatly folded and hung in her dresser and closet, while he emptied the kitchen cabinets. He'd told me to keep anything I thought I might use. A row of cheap, unworn tennis shoes was lined up neatly on the carpeted closet floor. A half dozen cheerful pairs – red, turquoise, yellow and pink, black and white – as if she'd intended to start a new walking routine, but never had the chance. There were multiple sets of identical tops, too, each a different shade, many with the tags still on. I imagined she ordered in bulk from mail order catalogs, finding an item she liked and getting it in every color, a habit my own mother acquired in her senior years.

The sad irony of all those stiff new shoes and clothes slowed the task of filling the trash bags. It felt wrong. Even if I'd wanted to keep some of her things for myself, everything was several sizes too small. We boxed up her china to keep in the family, nothing valuable, but a pretty rose pattern I still bring out on special occasions. And I kept her sewing machine. There were a handful of oil paintings and prints that Bob remembered from his childhood. One, a portrait of him as a tow-headed boy of six or seven, a dog alongside him who could be a great, great grandfather of our shaggy mutt, Mocha. In the end, it didn't amount to much. Most of her things went to charity, odd bits of silver to a consignment shop, a few gifts for the neighbors she'd become friends with.

We talked while we worked. Or rather, for once, Bob talked and I listened. Memories from childhood. Reflections on mortality, loss, the ephemeral and precious nature of life, hung in the stuffy mobile home, as we touched her things, handing them to one another, burying them away in sacks and boxes.

Bob reminisces so rarely that when he does, it feels momentous, a rare act of candor and trust. Each time I imagine a door has opened, and I'll finally meet him. He seems a man separated from his past, as if his life hasn't been a continuum, but rather there was then and there is now. Chameleon-like, Bob appears to assume whatever role he's occupying in the moment. Perhaps it's a symptom of having been an only child, raised by emotionally distant parents. Sometimes I suspect his history and any attendant emotional underpinnings, all the remnants of other lives, have been sloughed off like so many withered snake skins.

"This is it," he often says. "What you see is what you get." I find both statements comforting and terrifying. So much of who I am lurks beneath the surface, deepening, complicating, tormenting, enriching. I can't imagine life without my hidden icebergs. I love and hate them. I learn more about myself and the world around me by reflecting on where I've been. Bob never speaks of his first wife or any past loves or heartbreaks. He rarely shares his disappointments and triumphs. Perhaps he holds his memories close. Perhaps they've all been let go, as no longer relevant, no longer consequential. I doubt I'll ever know.

In his mother's stuffy double-wide, I grasped at these snippets of his past, realizing how little I knew him, despite our years together. His parents were unhappily divorced when he was young. As one of four children in a messy, crowded, two-bedroom home, his childhood, in comparison, seemed to me to have been a lonely one, despite the advantages of his father's relative wealth. Now that we are adults, my sisters are my best friends, my context. They know me as others never will. Bob doesn't have anyone who knows him like that.

We drove the loaded trailer to his father's oceanfront home, where we would spend the night. Tired, dusty and heavy limbed, we showered off the grit of his mother's belongings and climbed between crisp, clean sheets in the spare room downstairs. Salty sea air pushed at the cotton curtains through tall, open windows.

On the recommendation of my doctor, I'd gone off the pill a few months earlier. He thought clearing out my system might lessen my migraines. It hadn't. This was the same doctor who had previously recommended that I take the pill continuously, to stop my periods and even out my hormones, with the idea that hormonal fluctuations might be a root cause of the headaches. That hadn't helped either.

Bob and I held one another and kissed, our bodies close.

"It's okay," he said. "You're safe."

"You sure?"

Bob believes in the veracity of facts and logic. He'd taken responsibility for tracking my cycle. Even though I'd never believed it was so clear cut as that, I'd let him. Fertility, in my experience, isn't always predictable. I might have raised objections. I chose not to. I don't know that I actively wanted to get pregnant. But I knew it was a possibility, that for me it was always a possibility, no matter what he, or anyone, said.

It felt different that night, hurting in some deep, tender part of me. I sensed that the pain meant something, perhaps the end of us. I imagined it might be our last time, so close and yet so far apart, sharing sorrow, then letting go.

Within weeks, I was nauseous. Bob said it was the flu. I recognized this flu.

After sifting through the remains of his mother's life, we'd created the granddaughter, the little girl she'd hoped for. Carol didn't live to see us married, didn't meet the baby girl who bears the names of her three grandmothers. Carolanne June would prove to be the bond between Bob and me, between my two older children and his. Carol for his mother. Anne for his stepmother. June for mine. An unanticipated new life that forced our hodgepodge family together.

Without her, I doubt we would have married. I doubt we would be together today, nearly 20 years later.

⊖ ⊖ ⊖

I was 44, in a high-profile, demanding job, when a pregnancy test confirmed what I'd already known.

"It's not possible," Bob said. "Your cycle. I counted."

Yeah, well, these things happen. Looking back, it seems I'd known all along. Perhaps, on some level, I'd thought, what the hell, nothing else is moving us off the dime, let's throw a baby into the mix. For whatever combination of reasons and distractions, I'd let it happen, knowing what the possible outcome could be.

Bob came to my house on the Sunday before Christmas, as he had every Sunday for years. I was four weeks along. It was decision time. My body. My decision. That's how I saw it. He planted himself on the hard bench at the oak dining nook that filled half of my kitchen, one side of it wedged beneath the sill of the large front window with a view of my suburban street.

"We need to go over the options," he said, elbows planted, hands clasped.

Intellectually, I got it. Perhaps if I hadn't already been nauseous and flooded with hormones, I might have seen the logic in a sensible discussion.

"What options?" I said.

"You know, the options."

"Well, what are they, these *options*?" I said, spitting the words at him.

"I'm just saying, we should list the pros and cons."

"The pros and cons of..."

I was already a mother, twice over. There is no magic list of options. You have the baby or you don't. If you have a baby, you keep it or you don't. What else is there?

The cons were obvious. I didn't need a yellow legal pad and number two pencil to remind me:

· We weren't married or planning to get married.
· We were both too old.
· Life was already plenty complicated.
· Neither of us had planned to have more children.

The pro list was short, yet deep, at least it was for me. Not with the kinds of quandaries posed by moral or religious doctrine. I strongly believe in a woman's right to choose. This time, having the child *was* my choice. As soon as I'd suspected I was pregnant, I'd known I would have this child. In my mind, that surety reduced the options discussion to whether we'd raise her together, or I'd be on my own.

A legislator I once worked for used to say, "Don't confuse me with the facts. I've already made up my mind." That was me. Every word out of Bob's mouth maddened me. So much so that I'd begun to believe it would better for all of us, and far simpler, just to end the relationship, even knowing that Bob was the kind of man who would want a role in the child's life. I could more easily picture a future where he would be her father than I could one where he was also my husband.

When I put myself in his shoes and considered how the

ample list of cons, it seemed improbable there would ever be a good time for a baby, or for us. I had to decide based on what was right for me and my unborn child. I knew how to go it on my own. I'd done it for years before I met Bob. Tough years in which I'd made plenty of mistakes. I doubt there's a parent, single or otherwise, who can claim otherwise. Still, I'd done my best and hoped my son and daughter knew they were loved.

Christmas arrived. Nothing was resolved.

Bob's boys were supposed to join my family later that day, but there was some squabble with their mother, and they couldn't come. Bob arrived, late and alone. He carried gifts from his truck into the house, arranging them under the tree in my family room. He'd gone overboard. A bicycle for me. Toys for my son and daughter. Gifts weren't what I wanted.

When I allowed myself to fantasize, I concocted scenarios where he showed up with a black velvet box in his pocket. The real thing this time. He'd tell me he'd realized he wanted the baby and for us to be a family. He'd ask me to marry him. He'd tell me he wanted to spend the rest of his life with me, that I was the one he'd been waiting for, the perfect antidote after his awful first marriage. In daydreams, I sometimes accepted. I threw my arms around him, all weepy and relieved, just like in the movies.

Other times, I turned him down.

"I don't need your pity," I'd say. "You don't have to worry about all the reasons why this is a shitty idea. I got this."

I looked like crap. I felt worse. I didn't really blame him when there was no magic moment, no proposal, no looking ahead to our happily ever after. The lights twinkled on the tree and reflected in the glass ornaments. The wrapped gifts mocked me. I didn't want any of them. I just wanted peace of mind and for the nausea to stop.

"You're still in the first trimester," he said.

"I'm aware."

I would not, could not, allow the reason to abort this baby be that Bob wasn't ready. I had a reasonably secure job. One that paid the bills. I owned the home we lived in, had a reliable car and good health insurance.

The outcome was a stalemate. We each stuck to our guns. He was kind and solicitous. He felt bad for me. Which only pissed me off more.

"I love you so much," he said. "I'm sorry this is so hard for you. I wish I could help. I wish I knew what to do."

Yeah, whatever. Merry Christmas.

"I need to go pick up the boys. I hate to leave you like this. Should we come back?"

"Better not," I said. "Take their presents to them."

"Talk to you later?"

"Sure," I said. "Talk to you later."

"I love you."

"Love you, too."

If I hadn't been so nauseated, I might have taken the initiative and put us both out of our misery by breaking up with him. Instead, I picked up a book and took to the bed.

I believed we'd seen our last Christmas.

⊖ ⊖ ⊖

On the eve of my 44th birthday, my mother called Bob and scheduled a meeting for the three of us. I let him know it hadn't been my idea, that it was none of her business, and that he didn't have to come. I half-hoped he wouldn't show. But he did.

We sat in my kitchen, awkward as a pair of naughty children waiting to see the principal. My oak dinette had become the favored spot for bad news and tough conversations. Bob and I sat side by side on the hard bench. Mother took the chair facing us.

A smile played at the corners of her censorious lips. We'd been very, very bad. But even as she sat in judgment, I got the impression she was secretly pleased at this turn of events. Perhaps she suspected I'd played the oldest card in the book, getting knocked up to force my reluctant boyfriend to marry me.

She pulled calendar, pencil and notebook from her big handbag.

"Bob," she said, narrowing her eyes at him.

"Yes, June." He clasped his hands on the tabletop.

Mother cleared her throat. She tapped the calendar, counting the weeks since mid-November, flipping the pages to December, then January.

"There isn't a lot of time," she said.

Bob studied his hands.

"It should be before March. Sometime in February." Her gaze moved down to my belly. "You'll be showing, but that can't be helped."

She hadn't mentioned marriage or weddings, but there was no question what she was talking about.

"How about February 28? It's a Saturday." She poked her chin at Bob as if daring him to raise any objection.

I couldn't read his expression.

"You'd never forget your anniversary," she said, to him, as if he were the only one who required a sales pitch. "It's a memorable date. Last day of the month, except for leap year."

"There is that," he said, raising a finger as if she'd just scored a point.

Mother beamed. Bob nodded, a slow, thoughtful dip, chin up then down. She put out her hand. He clasped it. They'd come to an agreement. It was as if I wasn't there.

"This isn't necessary," I said. If Bob wouldn't put a stop to her meddling, I intended to. I was not about to have my mother broker a marriage for me. "I'm super busy at work. I don't have time right now."

"Don't be an idiot," Mom said. "You've worked hard to get where you are. This could cost you your job. I won't let that happen."

Bob nodded solemnly, as if she were right, as if public opinion, as if not losing my job, were valid reasons for us to marry.

It was still the nineties, not yet the era when it became fashionable for couples to tie the knot years after the children were born, if ever. But it wasn't unheard of, and there were laws about wrongful grounds for termination. She was being ridiculous. Wasn't she?

As it turned out, I lost my job anyway, while I was out on maternity leave. Perhaps if I'd had the baby as a single mom, the boss wouldn't have dared. There's no knowing. Nor does it matter. None of that was on my mind that afternoon in my kitchen.

"And there will be a wedding," Mom said. "Agreed?"

"Excuse me?" I said.

"A real wedding. We don't want this to look like some frantic, rushed affair, some cover-up."

"But it is, Mom. It will be."

"We'll see about that." She had that determined, just-watch-me glint in her eye. "I'll take care of everything. The venue, food, flowers, music, photographer. All of it."

She turned to Bob.

"And *you*, young man, will buy a nice suit for the occasion. The two of you will take care of invitations and who will officiate. Write vows if you like. I'll handle everything else. Just show up, appropriately attired."

"Yes, ma'am," Bob said.

A wave of nausea hit. I pushed away from the table and hurried to the bathroom. When I returned to the kitchen, Mom was making a list of all the tasks that needed to be completed to pull off a wedding in a little over one month.

I was going to have a real wedding, my first, without a proposal, without an engagement or a ring. I'd never been one of those girls who fantasized about her dream wedding and all the attendant trappings. But true, ever-lasting love? That's another story.

I'll never know how things would have gone down if my mother hadn't meddled, if we hadn't let her. Some things can't be fixed. You let them fester or you move on.

⊖ ⊖ ⊖

There were no family meetings, no counseling about what this union of our two families would mean for us or our kids, all children of divorce.

My birth son, my eldest, was seventeen the drizzly afternoon I married for the third time. It was his last semester of high school. He hadn't heard yet, but by that fall we would be moving him into a dorm at uc Davis, my alma mater. His roommates would retreat to the doorway as I changed his newborn baby sister's diaper on one of their unmade single beds. We'd been on our own together since before his second birthday. I wasn't proud of the mother I'd been. I could say I'd done my best, but I knew it hadn't always been good enough. That afternoon, in our motel room, as I stood before the mirror preparing to get married, tears streaked my mascara. My son stood beside me.

"Don't cry, Mom," he said. "If this thing with Bob doesn't work out, I'll always take care of you."

His words both hurt and swelled my heart. Despite all the times I hadn't been there for him, my baby, who'd weighed less than five pounds at birth, was whole in the ways that mattered.

My father, an often taciturn man, with whom I'd always had an uneasy relationship, deposited me beside my soon-to-be husband and disappeared into the small crowd. Nothing felt real. Up until that moment, I'd expected and perhaps even wanted Bob to have a change of heart and call the whole thing off. Yet there he was. Tall and handsome in his new suit.

I was none of those things. Temples throbbing with migraine, makeup a runny mess, uncomfortable in control undergarments to contain my baby bump. Doubt was a rough stone chafing inside me. He didn't want this chaotic life. He couldn't want me. No one in their right mind would. This would end badly. I was sure of it.

Perhaps I was the one, more than he, who'd been swept along by the current of events, who was there against my natural instincts. Perhaps he'd moved on and now embraced this next step. Yet I couldn't believe he had changed so profoundly in a matter of weeks. I assumed he'd accepted a burden, made a compromise, because we'd made a baby, and because my mother said so. I wasn't the love of his life.

We'd labored over our vows, expressions of hope and happiness at blending our two families into one, words that had many of the friends and family we'd invited to witness our marriage, wet eyed. After the customary "I do's," and the kiss, there was a family hug, the four children – nine, eleven, fifteen and seventeen – beneath a white wicker arch stitched with fresh flowers, courtesy of my mother.

$$\ominus \ominus \ominus$$

For an "arranged" marriage, ours has worked out reasonably well. Yet, because I'm me, I find myself speculating. What kind of woman would he have chosen if he'd had a choice? I picture an outdoorsy, petite blonde, twenty years younger than me, with a sweet disposition and nice tits.

It's stupid. And degrading. And I can't stop. It's the emotional equivalent of eating an entire tube of cookie dough. Soothing going down, but the aftermath isn't pretty – and often involves more cookie dough.

Bob and I didn't immediately live together after the marriage. We both had houses to sell, and the kids were all mid-semester, in schools at opposite ends of Sacramento. As the pregnancy progressed, and in preparation for the big merger, I sifted through my belongings, preparing to combine households. We wouldn't need two washers, two toasters, two dining room tables and all the rest. When we finally did share a house, it was a mash-up of his and hers, from the children to the furniture and the contents of the hastily filled kitchen cabinets.

Over a lifetime, I'd accumulated two cardboard boxes filled with diaries and journals. I revisited them in the wreckage of our family room, my belly so big I had to hold the notebooks off to the side. I was reluctant to drag all this ancient history with me into our new home, our new life. What if I was hit by a bus and died? Would I really want my new husband, or my children, to read this stuff?

I tried to skim through the old journals page by page, ripping out the embarrassing parts. But it was slow going. Besides, the stuff I didn't want anyone to see was the interesting part. The rest was boring. I wouldn't want anyone to read those bits either. After flipping through several of the notebooks, I considered the piles that remained. It was a pointless exercise.

I dumped all of them into the recycle bin. It was time for a fresh start.

⊖ ⊖ ⊖

We eventually found a five-bedroom house to accommodate our brood. One with decent schools and a great system of walking trails. It's the home where we still live. There was nothing wrong with the house or the new neighborhood. Except that it meant a complete upheaval for my kids, new schools, the loss of old friends and all that was familiar to them. This proved especially hard on my daughter, Grace. She'd already been through a lot with the divorce from her dad. But Bob had been adamant that we live near his former home. He didn't want his boys to have to change schools. My daughter didn't have a choice.

I was nine months pregnant when my house finally sold and we moved in together. It was summer and very hot in Sacramento. The only shoes I could squeeze onto my swollen feet were sandals.

"Just set up the bed," I told Bob, "That's all I care about."

Three weeks later, surrounded by packing boxes and disgruntled children, I went into labor.

Then things got tough.

21

It's the last Sunday in February, my weigh-in day. Our nineteenth anniversary is in two days. That doesn't sound like a huge accomplishment for someone my age, except that I didn't make it to a second anniversary with either of my previous marriages.

I slip from bed before dawn and tiptoe upstairs to visit the scale. 174.2 and holding. For the third week in a row, the number won't budge, no matter how much I fidget on the scale. My body is making me work hard for the first ten pounds.

It's the five-week mark. The point at which the expensive diet plan promised "at least" a fifteen-pound weight loss or my money back. I need to stay positive. Eight pounds is eight pounds. It means almost fitting into the size fourteen jeans. Almost. I hold onto that thought. Do some chores. Eat a sensible lunch, which makes me sleepy. I just need a little something to pick me up. A slice of toast with a light smear of peanut butter, sliced banana instead of jam. Healthy. Satisfying. Except that when I finish the one slice, I want, no, I *need*, another.

Maybe I just need to switch things up. My body is convinced I'm starving and has shifted into conservation mode. That's why my weight won't budge. Yeah, that's what it is. I need to jog my metabolism by treating myself to a day of indulgence. It's worked before.

Two bowls of cereal. Four more slices of toast. Two with

peanut butter, two with butter and jam. One binge day, and I'll hop right back on the program. It's the old "feast and fast" plan from years ago, only this time, I won't get stuck in feasting mode.

Mellowed out on carbs, I retreat to the couch.

I'm stuck on Ron. I wonder what his life was like, how many more years he spent trolling the high school. Maybe he's dead. Or in prison. I picture him gaunt and toothless. But what if he's happily married, with grown kids and grandkids? I don't want that. He doesn't deserve that.

I open my laptop. I don't have a lot to go on. A first name. A band. The years he worked for them. That song he played for me in his car. I type search terms into my browser. I scrutinize album covers and old photos from the sixties and seventies. I follow tenuous leads, lost in the sinkhole that is the Internet.

I return to the kitchen for a handful of Wheat Thins. I bring the whole box and set it on the couch beside me as I scroll and click. It's my binge day, after all.

Minutes become hours.

I wonder what happened to Crystal and all the other girls in his little black book. I crunch Wheat Thins as if the answer might be in the next cracker. I return to the kitchen for the graham crackers I bought for the grandkids. I finish off one wax paper sleeve, then open another. I set the computer aside and stretch out on the couch.

I wake to find my husband hovering over me.

"You okay?" he asks.

"Not feeling so good."

"Poor baby."

His forehead and mouth are puckered with concern. Poor baby because I don't feel good? Poor baby because he knows I've been a pig and made myself sick again? Poor baby because I never learn?

Babies can't help but be what they are. I can. Can't I?

⊖ ⊖ ⊖

As my mother predicted, neither of us can ever forget our anniversary. Bob gives me a card. It's a Valentine's Day card that he says perfectly captures his feelings for me. I can picture him standing in the greeting card aisle at Rite-Aid, reading all the canned sentiments, searching for the perfect one. He's taped a sticky note over "Valentine's Day" and penciled in "Anniversary." I give him a pair of socks with train engines on them, and I cook his favorite dinner, salmon. I assume we'll make love that night. It's been over a month, or only a month, depending how you look at it. We aren't "due." But it's our anniversary.

We don't.

My binge day becomes the rest of the week. Sunday arrives, but there's no use getting on the scale.

On Monday, I cancel my "mandatory" doctor's appointment, even though the doctor threatened to not renew my prescriptions for anti-depressants and migraine medications without a follow-up appointment. Every checkup he tells me to lose weight. I hate that I'm such a predictable stereotype: older white woman, sedentary lifestyle, sluggish metabolism and libido, suffers depression and migraine. I'd been looking forward to impressing him with my progress. Yet here I am, another year gone by, and still proving him right.

So much for my big plans for 2017. My resolve didn't last two months.

22

It's hard now to understand why I kept seeing Ron, why I didn't stop. I do know that even as I came when he called and did what he asked, I desperately wanted a real boyfriend. I knew that what I did with him was nothing to be proud of. I didn't tell anyone about it. I didn't even like to think about it. Nor did I enjoy it or look forward to the next time. How could I have? It was never about me, or even about sex, but rather power, control, domination. I didn't get this intellectually, but I knew it in my bones. I'd surrendered free will. The battle was over the first time I answered his call, or even before, when I didn't tell.

I met Mark in my junior year of high school. He had chestnut hair that he sometimes pulled into a ponytail longer than any I could ever muster. His clothes weren't the typical Northern California hippie uniform. Fitted bell bottoms instead of loose 501s. Loose button-down shirts with the tails out, instead of ironic t-shirts. I figured that was how hippies dressed in L.A., which to me might as well have been a foreign country. He was on his own, living in an old van he'd driven up from Southern California. He wasn't a runaway, exactly. His dad knew where he was and was likely sending him money, though such practical considerations didn't concern me then. Mark told me he'd enrolled in high school to keep his father from reporting him missing. At the time, his situation didn't seem so strange.

Teenagers ran away all the time. They'd flocked to San Francisco by the thousands. Many never went home.

Mark was new to town, with few acquaintances and in occasional need of the amenities of a real house. No doubt my mom noticed the similarities to Michael's situation. More low hanging fruit.

We began to hang out. The next time Ron called, I told him I couldn't see him anymore, that I had a real boyfriend. Ron didn't act disappointed or upset. He didn't try to argue with me. Still, he called every few weeks to check if I still had the boyfriend.

One afternoon, Mark and I were sitting in the back of the van. I asked if he could drive me to a convenience store for tampons.

"Can't you wait until you get home?"

"I can't," I said. "I have to pee super bad."

"So?"

"So I'll need a fresh one." I hunched my shoulders, uncomfortable with having to explain.

"What do you mean?" he said.

"It'll get all soggy. I'll have to take it out."

He busted up laughing. The jar he used to pee in toppled onto the blankets. Fortunately, the lid was screwed on tight.

"What's so funny?" I asked.

"You know you don't menstruate through your pee hole, right?"

"Where else would it come out?" I asked, not meeting his eyes.

"Didn't your mother teach you anything?"

She hadn't, and I'd slept through biology. I was eleven, in the sixth grade, when my period started. Dad was on a sabbatical leave from teaching, and we were living in Mexico that year. I didn't know what was happening to me and was too embarrassed to ask. I thought I had some horrible disease and that I would probably bleed to death. I stuffed my dresser drawers with bloodied rags and underwear.

"Ask your big sister where the supplies are," Mom said, when she found my mess. "She'll tell you what to do, for next time."

That's how I'd learned there would be a next time.

I hated that Mark had said "menstruate," that awful, clinical word. I wanted to argue with him, to say that he was wrong and how would he know more about my body than I did? But as soon as he'd said it, it seemed so obvious. Of course, it didn't come out the same hole.

If my parents weren't home, I'd make Mark a snack and run his clothes through the washer while he showered. My older sister, Roxanne, was working part time at a fancy bakery café and going to the College of Marin. She would bring home these amazing chocolate toffee bars from the bakery. Sometimes she sat with Mark while he lounged at our kitchen table in my robe and slippers, his long hair wet and shiny. He was different with her. Funnier. More animated. She got his puns and literary references, which often went over my head.

Once, he was still there when my parents got home. I invited him to dinner, assured him they would be cool. We crowded around the kitchen table.

"So Mark," my dad said, "how are you managing on your own, aside from availing yourself of our facilities?"

"I manage."

"Indeed," my father said.

I hoped Mark wasn't picking up on Dad's sarcasm.

I moved the food around on my plate and wished my parents could just be cool like I'd promised him they would be.

Finding a safe place to park the van overnight was a constant worry. I asked Dad if Mark could just stay on the street in front of our house. He was a softer touch than Mom, or at least he was less direct with his answers. I could plausibly pretend I hadn't understood.

"I suppose that would be convenient," Dad said with a bland smile. "That way your friend can shower in the morning. Perhaps have some breakfast."

"Indeed," I said, stealing a word from his lexicon.

The next morning, when I came downstairs, Dad was already at the kitchen window. I stood beside him. The Indian bedspread covering the van's side windows shifted. I poured a mug of coffee for Mark and doctored it the way he liked, with lots of milk and sugar.

"Why don't you whip him up some eggs and toast while you're at it?" Dad said.

Mom wasn't so oblique. She said we weren't an RV park.

"Where's he supposed to go?" I asked.

"That's not our problem, is it?" she said.

"It's mine."

"I guess I have to admire you," she said, laying on the sarcasm, so I understood it was opposite speak. "When I was your age, I wasn't interested in being anyone's hand maiden. I just wanted to have fun, to wear pretty clothes and go to dances."

"I go to dances."

"You know what I mean."

"You're always after me to have a boyfriend. So now I have one. I thought you'd be happy."

"Oh, honey," she said. "Are you giving him money?"

I probably was. The van didn't run on daisies.

⊖ ⊖ ⊖

Mom was a decent cook. Porcupine meatballs. Stews. Casseroles. One night she made a huge pot of chicken and vegetable soup. After the rest of the family had gone to bed, I lifted the pot from the fridge, set it on the stovetop to reheat, then ladled out heaping bowlfuls for Mark and me. I got sidetracked and forgot to turn the burner off. In the morning, all that was left was a ring of dried up bits at the bottom of the pan.

"That would have been supper for at least two more nights," Mom said.

"At least the pan didn't melt," I said.

"Oh, child," she said, with that long-suffering sigh. "Such a waste."

I knew she wasn't only talking about the pot of soup.

⊖ ⊖ ⊖

Mark found a decent place to park, on a side road that didn't see a lot of through traffic. It was just down the road from our house. I passed it on my morning walk to school. I'd knock on the side panel and call out so he'd know I wasn't some asshole come to harass him. I'd sit with him while he woke up, peed in the jar or out the door, and ate the breakfast I'd brought, still warm from our kitchen. He was never in a hurry to get to school, if he went at all.

I don't remember the first time we had sex. I'd been on birth control since after Michael. When months would go by without anything going on in that department, or only Ron, I felt foolish popping that pill every morning, but not enough to stop. I assumed every other girl at school was on it. Stopping would have been an admission I didn't want to make.

I do remember times in that turnout between my house and the high school. In the back of the van, on his unzipped sleeping bag and musty comforters. There was always something wrong, something I wasn't doing right. He would complain that I moved too fast, too slow, or that I made too much noise.

"Come on," Mark would say, rolling off me. "I know it doesn't feel that good. I am not that great."

I was acting, attempting to be sexy, thinking if I did it right, if I pleased him, it would bring us closer, it would make him love me. Looking back, it seems likely we just weren't that attracted to one another. While it may have been a relationship of convenience for him, it was one of desperation and need for me.

Mark never took his shirt off. He didn't want anyone to see his chest. He'd been teased for being "husky" when he was a kid. He was insecure. About his weight and appearance, and, perhaps, his sexuality. Maybe even more than I was. I see that now. I don't think I was the only one who had to fake it.

After a few months roughing it on the side roads, Mark sold the van and bought a small motorbike. He said he'd rented a room. But he didn't take me there. He was missing more school. Days would go by that I didn't see him.

"Your Mom's crazy," he said, when I asked why he didn't come over any more. "She hates me. I bet she's got security cameras in every room."

Sometimes—I never knew when—he'd pick me up, take me for a ride on the motorbike. Winding through the hills, my hands on his soft belly, wind pressing my eyelids shut. While we were together, bodies touching, I could pretend nothing had changed, nothing was wrong.

⊖ ⊖ ⊖

One Friday night, I told my parents I was spending the night with my new best friend, Mandy, a smart, cynical redhead, whose divorced, alcoholic mother didn't much care what she did. I wasn't close with Liz anymore. Mandy and I hitched to Sausalito, to the coffee shop where Mark worked as a busboy. I wanted to see where he lived. I told him I had all night, that I could stay with him.

"Nice," he said. "But don't judge."

"Why would I?"

Mandy got home on her own.

Mark's apartment was just off Highway 101, on the outskirts of San Rafael. The complex looked like an old motel. Mark's unit was on the second floor, up a concrete stairwell. He shared the place with a couple. They had the one bedroom. Mark slept on a couch in the drab living room.

When we got there, his roommates were watching an old black and white movie. The girl, Natalie, sat on the guy's lap with her arms around his neck. Natalie's eyes were huge in a pale face. She was Olive Oil thin, with the coltish look of a girl not yet fully grown, aside from the taut basketball-sized bump under her t-shirt. She was giddy and chatty, excited to have female company.

Natalie was thirteen, from Florida. She'd run away from home, with her best friend after they watched a TV show about hippies in California. Her friend chickened out at a truck stop somewhere halfway across the country and called home.

"She's pregnant," I whispered to Mark, when the two of them got up to get something from the kitchen.

"I knew you'd judge," he said.

The boy carried her back to the couch, cradling her in his arms as if she were an invalid.

"Do you miss home?" I asked her.

Mark glared at me.

"I miss my little sister," she said. "Sometimes I wonder what she's doing. And my bedroom. It was cool, all black and orange, like Halloween. That's my favorite holiday. Momma sewed a bedspread, matching pillow shams and curtains out of this fabric from the craft store. It had black cats and witches and all that."

"Sounds cool, babe," her boyfriend said.

"When you turned out the lights, these little star and moon decals on the ceiling glowed," she said.

"Maybe we can do something like that when we get our own place," he said.

"Yeah?"

"Totally."

Natalie was my younger sister's age. Her childhood over because of a dare. Her boyfriend was nineteen. He worked while she stuck close to the apartment. They were afraid she'd get picked up. I imagined he'd found her in some worse situation. Now they had each other.

She'd be close to sixty now, if she survived the sixties, her baby close to fifty.

⊖ ⊖ ⊖

With Michael, I remembered how we met, the first time we kissed and had sex in the dirt. With Mark, I don't remember the firsts. I do remember the last time I saw him.

I didn't like hitching alone, especially not on the freeway, but none of my friends had cars, and it was days since I'd spent the night with him in San Rafael. The need to see him again consumed me. A creepy older guy stopped for me, a ride I would usually have passed on, even if I was with a friend.

"What you got in there?" the driver asked, staring down at the foil-wrapped package I held in my lap.

"Zucchini bread."

"Smells great. Who's it for?"

"My boyfriend."

"Pretty young thing baking him bread. Bringing it right up to his door. Dude doesn't even have to leave the house. What'd he do to deserve the royal treatment?"

"It's a surprise," I said.

"Want to give me some of that surprise?"

When he dropped me at the exit nearest the apartment building, I was so relieved, I broke him off a big chunk of the zucchini loaf.

The door to the apartment hung open. The place looked ransacked. Kitchen drawers pulled open. Cupboards bare.

Nothing but the worn furniture it came with, trash on the carpet. I was sure I'd gotten there too late. Then the toilet flushed. Mark came out of the bathroom.

"I brought you something." I handed him the mangled bread. He left it on the sticky kitchen countertop.

"What's going on?" I asked.

"They had to split. I can't afford the place on my own. Rent's not due for a couple days. Just hanging out until then."

"And then what?"

"Guess I'll have to figure that out, won't I?"

I didn't ask *what about me?* If I'd had a different family, I might have suggested he crash with us. I had nothing to offer, not even money. Just the lame bread that hours before I'd convinced myself was a plausible excuse to show up uninvited.

We smoked some weed, snorted some cocaine. Had sex on the bare mattress in the bare bedroom and in the bathtub. He didn't critique my technique or compare me with anyone else. He was focused. The world reduced to our slick bodies. Without having experienced it before, I understood this was goodbye sex. I felt as if I'd never known him at all, and he didn't know me. None of it had mattered, and now this was it. One last time before he hit the road.

He gave me a ride after, but not all the way home.

"I can't go near your house," he said. "Not even close. Your old lady has it in for me."

As soon as we left the freeway and entered the streets of Mill Valley, he was jumpy, hunched into his collar, scanning cars and faces. He dropped me near the high school.

I never saw Mark again. The next time Ron called to ask if I still had the boyfriend, I said no, the boyfriend was gone.

⊖ ⊖ ⊖

Sophomore year of college, I heard bits and pieces of a story that confirmed my suspicions about Mark's disappearance. I was living in a two-bedroom apartment with three other girls. One of them, a psychology major, had a paper to write, a case study. Jan chose me as her subject. I don't remember what the point of the assignment was. I do remember having mixed emotions that she'd chosen me. Flattered she found me complex and intriguing. Worried she thought I was fucked up. In addition to interviewing me, she drove to Marin to talk to Mom.

Jan never let me read her paper, but she did tease me with a few bits of information. Mom had told her that she'd found Mark tampering with the brakes on her car and that if she hadn't caught him at it, if my mother had gotten into her car and driven down our steep, windy stretch of Highway One, she would likely have crashed the car, perhaps been badly injured, even killed as the car plunged off the road. She told Jan that she threatened Mark with the police unless he disappeared and never saw me again. She gave him money, too, as an added incentive.

I don't know if that crazy story was true. My mother wasn't past stretching the truth when it suited her, and perhaps she meant for Jan to tell me. Whatever reason he left, he would have gone eventually. He was unhappy and insecure. Being with me didn't help. Or maybe it did, for a while. He lived an unrooted, dangerous life. I don't know that I even asked why he'd left home, that he would have told me if I had, or that I would have understood. I'd envied him his freedom from parents and school. Perhaps he envied my life, too.

What I remember most is Mark's hair, long and brown with gold strands that caught the sunlight, and his big luminous eyes. Doe eyes, Mom once called them, with lashes and brows darker than the hair on his head, adding the kind of drama to his face that girls hope for and guys seem to get.

Long after Mark disappeared, I clung to the fantasy of him, of us as star-crossed lovers kept apart by cruel fate, in the form of Mom. I concocted elaborate scenarios where he showed up at college to whisk me away from the doldrums of Davis. My classmates would watch us drive into the sunset. They would envy our love, our carefree hippie life. We'd live happily ever after, moving from town to town, selling homemade baked goods and crafts.

Mom was right. Even in dreams I didn't demand much. Just someone to love, someone to love me back, a loaf of zucchini bread.

⊖ ⊖ ⊖

Ron didn't ask what happened with the boyfriend. He didn't ask me anything. It was like before, and it wasn't. I was seventeen, two years older than I'd been the afternoon he first picked me up. He was driving a different car, smaller than the Mustang, a sports car.

"Could we have regular sex for once?" I asked, the first time after Mark.

Ron stared at me, eyes narrowed, as if he didn't understand what I meant.

"Don't you want to?" I asked.

Ron frowned. He eyeballed the car's interior, seeming to grapple with the logistics of how this could possibly work. He described the complicated and awkward physical contortions required to match up our private parts within the confines of the tiny car. I don't remember the details, except that he said it could be done, technically, and that it might hurt. As if we couldn't just get out of the car or drive to his place. As if our universe consisted of two bucket seats with a gear shift between us. I was embarrassed for asking, which I guess was what he'd intended.

I did what I'd always done. And the routine resumed.

Another time, I asked him, "Why don't we ever go anywhere?"

"Like where?"

"I don't know. To hear music. Get something to eat. Hang out. Anything."

He pulled onto a deserted road. Before dropping me off that time, he stopped at the 7-11, the same store where, in more carefree days, me and Liz bought junk food.

"Come on," he said. "I'll get you a drink, a candy bar or something."

I followed him into the convenience store, which, in my memory, was packed. Two years in, and we'd never been in a public place together. Ever. Ron's shirt was rumpled, the top buttons on his pants still undone. He swaggered towards the refrigerated glass case for two sodas. The rounded mirrors in the corners of the store and the harsh overhead fluorescent lights, magnified my humiliation. I imagined everyone saw, everyone knew.

I never asked him to take me anyplace again.

⊖ ⊖ ⊖

With Mark gone, there was nothing left for me in Mill Valley. I just wanted to get away, to be around people who knew nothing about me. I completed the units required for graduation and was done with high school the summer after junior year. But I hadn't applied to college in time for the fall quarter. The soonest I could start, the soonest I could escape, was January.

That December, I told Ron I was going away to college. He said he wanted to see me before I left, to say goodbye.

For years, I'd carried a spiral-bound sketch book with me wherever I went. That way, I always had something to do with my hands, somewhere to look. It was my security blanket.

I'd never brought it when I saw Ron. Anything in my hands would have been superfluous. But I carried it that day. Set it in my lap after I got into the car, a last-ditch effort to assert my individuality, to show, if only to myself, that I was somebody, a girl who drew, a girl who wrote cryptic poetry, a girl who was going away to college, a girl with a head on her shoulders.

It was different that day. And it wasn't.

He parked. We got out of the car, a first. Still clutching my sketchpad, clinging to that proof of me, I followed him down a trail through the woods and out onto a clearing on a hillside with a view of the valley. The day was clear and bright. Though there was no basket of goodies, no blanket, I could almost pretend we were going to have a picnic. We sat down. He took the sketch book from me, turned the pages, touched some of my drawings, said it was cool that I did something like that.

Then he opened his pants.

⊖ ⊖ ⊖

I came home for spring break and hung out with Mandy, when I could find her. When she was sixteen, her mom had changed the locks on their house and not given Mandy a key. She'd been on her own ever since. It was impossible to pay rent and buy the kind of clothes and shoes she liked earning minimum wage. She had a personal ad in the *Berkeley Barb*, offering euphemistic "massage" services.

I'd never told her about Ron. Mandy would have pressed for details and told me I should at least make him pay.

We sat on a bench in town, people watching. A sports car approached. Mandy buried her face in my neck and angled her body away from the traffic. I recognized the car—and Ron. He hadn't looked our way.

"Is he gone?" she asked.

"You know that guy?"

"Total asshole," she said. "He picked me up hitchhiking one time, then he wouldn't leave me alone."

"Like how?"

"Like when I wouldn't have sex with him, he said he'd rent me a house, fill it with clothes and jewelry, silk kimonos and shit."

The mention of kimonos put me back in that house with Ron and his horny friend, me a dolled-up choir girl in my butterfly dress.

"You didn't consider it?" I struggled to keep the rising interest out of my voice.

"You kidding? He doesn't have that kind of money. Even if he did, he said he'd set me up, but then I couldn't see anyone else. He wanted me all to himself." She threw her head back and laughed. "Me. His devoted concubine. As if. I'd lose my mind."

"Was he at least cute?" I asked.

"Just another loser. I can't believe anyone would ever fall for his bullshit."

I didn't see Ron after that. Maybe it was because of what Mandy said. Maybe I just aged out, and he stopped calling. I prefer to believe I made a choice, that I was done sinking so low for so little. Truth is, I don't remember, and the fact that I don't makes me suspect there was no final phone call, no opportunity for me to tell him no thanks, not anymore, not ever again. If anything like that had happened, I'd likely have memorized my words and his responses. But I have no such moment to replay and relive with pride.

23

I've only reached early college days with this reminiscing binge, and already I've seen enough. Like Scrooge, I want it to stop, to not be true. I want to have been a different, kinder, happier girl.

I'm not a weak person in most regards. I work hard. I'm responsible. I try to do right by others. I've made and continue to make mistakes. I can't undo them, can't take them back or poof them away, but I don't have to relive them in perpetuity.

Do I?

I've given some of my memories so much power, embracing them, clinging to them like a second skin. I want to stop being a malingerer, a victim. I'm sick of hating myself, then hating myself for hating myself.

The meaning ascribed to past events is mutable. I captured these film clips, these traumatic and hurtful moments, with the sensibilities of a child, a teenager, a young woman. I didn't speculate, reflect or let perspective seep in. Would the events I recall so vividly differ from another's point of view? No one – not even Ron – could be so clear cut, so one-dimensional, as the version of him I preserved in mothballs.

He was a predator. He exploited my vulnerability.

And I let him.

Intellectually, I get that I should move on, let it all go. I've had a full life, a good life by so many measures. What it comes down to, what I just can't seem to shake, is the bedrock belief that nobody – no, let's be honest here, no man – has ever, will ever, could ever, choose me.

Men fascinate and terrify me. In relationships, any attributes I may have seem irrelevant. I am a girl. I am ashamed. I am stupid. I am never good enough. I will be rejected.

My expectations permeate every relationship, from the subconscious reasons I'm attracted to someone in the first place, to my surety that it will end badly, because I forced it, because how could I possibly be what he wants?

I cling to the belief that my husband, Bob, "settled." I expect him to leave. And when he doesn't, I take that as further proof that he doesn't really know me, because if he did, he would already be gone. Yet it's been nearly twenty years, for God's sake, two decades. A real marriage. The other two were blips, counted in months.

I don't really believe he'll leave me, and that's saying something. But I twist that around, too, by conceding that eventually I'll have to be the one to end it, not because he loves me more than I love him, but because he fears change so much, that, regardless how miserable he is, no matter how badly he wants out, he'd do most anything to retain the status quo.

Despite all the books, movies and fairy tales, perhaps most people settle. It's the rarity of the arrow straight to the heart that makes it a compelling, immortal story.

⊖ ⊖ ⊖

This year was going to be different. I was going to get my head straight. Lose forty pounds. Fit back into a closet full of tight jeans, at least the size twelves, no, get real, at least the fucking size fourteens. Yet it's March, and I'm shopping for size sixteen pants. The fall trip to Hawaii looms ever closer. I'd planned to be in swim suits and hiking shorts by then. That possibility now feels improbable.

I'm not just treading water; I'm moving backwards.

24

March brings the second meeting with the group of twelve women who signed up to complete a draft of a book in a year. In less than two months, I spewed out well over 100,000 words. I'm already past the outer limit of what our professor committed to read and critique next January. I don't usually stick with book ideas. 50 to 100 pages in, the well runs dry. I question the premise. I'm convinced the writing's crap. I can't conceive anyone will give a damn, that I give a damn anymore. I stop, futz around for a while, then start up on the next glimmer of an idea.

This time I'm sticking with it.

The money is part of it, though I've already spent a small fortune on writing conferences and workshops, and I went back to school after retirement, earning that expensive MFA in Creative Writing at 60. The influence of my fellow writers and our leader is another reason it feels different this time. We're in this together, rooting for one another. Shelley, my writing partner, is a constant reminder to keep at it. If she can remain energized about completing a book while still working full-time, juggling caring for her elderly parents and all the other things on her plate, then I have no excuse.

I retired to write. This is my job.

Age is a factor, too. With each passing year, I adjust my expectations. 65 is just around the corner. It feels like now or never time. Time to write a damn book or stop yammering about it, already.

The other elements of the plan – the whole lose weight and appreciate my marriage part – aren't happening, at least not yet. There's no point in exercising moderation. No hard-boiled eggs and celery sticks for me this time. I dive for the pastries on the coffee table. I reason it's all part of the "process." Binge eating and binge writing go hand in hand. Before I retired, a deadline at work always meant a quick trip to the vending machine for a candy bar, or two, to stoke the mental furnace. Writing projects have always entailed multiple trips to the kitchen, grazing the price of getting the job done.

This time is no different, except for the fact that my thoughts, actions and words were meant to be focused on ending the addictive behaviors that are eroding my health and peace of mind. This phase is the necessary prelude. The spitting it all out phase. Once I'm done spewing, I'll be able to see my way clear to make the other stuff an equal priority.

At the writing group we all give status reports on our progress. When I share my impressive word count, trying not to sound too boastful, the other women's eyes bug.

"You know I'll only read the first 100,000 words," our leader reminds me.

I assure her I do, that I'm just following her instructions and getting it all down. Which is true. What is also true is that I have no clue how I'll shape this stream of emotional diarrhea when I'm done. I only know I've tapped into a vein and that I couldn't stop now if I wanted to. Truth is, I don't want to stop. Unlike binge eating, binge writing isn't something that happens to me every day. I'm not about to pinch the spigot prematurely. Dredging up the past, turning all those slimy rocks over, is like scratching an itch I've been warned not to, or eating an entire sack of Halloween candy.

I'm a bad, bad girl, and it feels good.

When it's someone else's turn to share, I rouse myself from the couch to heap more moist coffee cake onto my plate.

Back in high school, I'd fantasized about being the next teenage phenomenon, with a breakout bestseller before my twentieth birthday, twenty-five tops. I still remember one line from the essay that accompanied my application to the University of California. At seventeen, I wrote, "One day, I will write popular fiction for the masses." I agonized over that grandiose boast, convinced it walked the line between cheeky and earnest, naive and absurd. I could claim I didn't really mean it should the need arise, that I was only being ironic.

But I meant it.

I procrastinated so long finishing that college essay that by the time I applied, it was too late for the upcoming fall semester. I would have to begin mid-year. During those long, tedious months at home, before my new life as an independent college girl began, I had plenty of time to write a novel. I didn't. Not even a few ideas jotted down. No character sketches or outlines.

Mark had disappeared. I was nursing my wounds. Even if I hadn't been broken-hearted, it would have been impossible to be creative under my parents' roof. I needed to be *free* before I could write. Ideally, a Parisian garret, but a college dorm room would have to do.

In the meantime, daydreaming was way easier and more gratifying. In dreams, my books were already in shop windows and best seller displays, my face on the cover of *Rolling Stone*. Only it wasn't my face on the book jacket and in the magazines, at least not the way I looked in the mirror. Because *everything* would change when I was famous. My hair would be long and miraculously straight. All the kids who'd snubbed me in high school would want to hang out with me. Only it would be too late. I'd be in New York City or London, hobnobbing with rock stars and the international jet set.

All the while, what I was really doing was sitting around the house, eating and watching TV. Sometimes Ron called. Minutes later I'd hear his car idling out front.

What I didn't know back then was that the magic day when conditions were perfect for writing, or fulfilling any dream, would never arrive. It would only become harder, more complicated. Life doesn't stop happening so that you can pursue your dreams. It would take me decades to figure that one out, and sometimes I still forget.

When you're young, you can make yourself believe that when you fantasize and daydream, you are projecting the future. It's all out there, still possible. Now, with fewer years ahead of me than behind, I still daydream about finding my books in the bookstore, but in the jacket photo I look my age, a slimmer, more distinguished version of me, but still someone my grandson would recognize as his grandmother.

25

Over their spring break, we visit our daughters on the East coast. The plan is to fly to New York, take the train to Philadelphia, where none of us has ever been, spend several days sight-seeing, then back to Manhattan before returning to Sacramento.

New York is frigid and sleety, dirty snow mounded in the gutters. Philadelphia is colder still, with record-breaking snow storms within the five-day weather forecast. I'd reserved a suite at a downtown hotel, one bedroom with two queen-sized beds and a separate living room with a fold-out couch. The girls opt for the couch.

"I'll take this bed," Bob says, setting his bag down on one of the two beds. "That way I can stretch out."

I assume we would sleep together. We always have. I try not to overreact. Maybe it's because the bed is smaller than we're use to, but the length is the same, isn't it? Or he's uncomfortable with the girls being so close, on the other side of the door.

The next morning, I fill up at the all-you-can-eat breakfast buffet. What's the point in moderation when it's all "free?"

Flaky croissants, tons of fruit, oatmeal that's more granola and raisins than oats. Cream in my coffee instead of skim milk. Besides, I need something to buck me up. I didn't sleep well, wondering if the whole separate beds situation is an omen of things to come.

We spend two days bundled up in scarves, coats and mittens, trudging to historical sights and museums, entering steamy buildings and shedding layers of clothing, only to cover all but our eyes and noses as we step out of doors again. And we eat. When I'm not eating, I'm planning our next meal, snack, or coffee break. At least I packed wisely. A forgiving wardrobe of black, elastic-waistband slacks and shapeless tops.

The second day in Philadelphia the snow starts, coating tree limbs and dusting the centuries old brick buildings. It's lovely and picturesque when we are safe inside, gazing out a frosty window pane. Not much fun when we leave the hotel. Carolanne is bored. Glued to her phone. Her new roommate stayed in their dorm room over the break, and they are in constant contact.

We're glad she has a friend, a life she wants to get back to. One that doesn't revolve around us. Which is as it should be, as we'd hoped it would be. If only the revelation could have come before we ventured east and got caught in what will prove to be the biggest storm of the season. Even if we wants to fly home early, where it's a balmy 80 degrees, we can't. Most planes are grounded.

Sunday afternoon, my older daughter returns to New York for work. Carolanne withdraws even further.

"You want to go back to the city?" I ask.

"You and Dad wouldn't mind?" Hope blooms in her sea-green eyes.

"No point in all of us being stuck here."

We take a taxi to the station and put our youngest on a train bound for Penn Station. It's just Bob and me after that, with two more nights to spend in snow-bound Philadelphia. We seek out the few sights that remain open. There's a massive flower show at the drafty convention center. I ask a taxi driver what the local "must do's" are. Rather than more shrines to our nation's birth, she ticks off regional culinary specialties. Cheese steaks, of course, but also Tasty Cakes and something called Crab Chips. Devouring these regional delicacies becomes my mission, a cultural necessity.

We have the cheese steaks for supper, just a sandwich on a roll – not nearly so tasty as a good San Francisco sourdough – followed by three scoops of gelato. We track down the chips and Tasty Cakes in the snack aisle of a chain drugstore. They look just like Hostess Cakes, but the taxi driver said they were a must, so I pick out several of the gooier varieties, for later.

Sated, we call it a day and head back to the hotel, opting to walk rather than hail another cab. After days of awful weather, my hair is an unruly mess. Two blocks from our hotel, I spy a blow-out salon. I assume that with the girls gone, we'll be sharing a bed again. Good hair will boost my confidence.

"I'll be less than an hour. See you back at the hotel?" I say to Bob.

"No worries. I'll just watch a game on TV."

My hair comes out great, bouncy and shiny. I shove on a wool cap to keep it that way until I get back to the room.

Bob glances up from the TV as I enter the hotel room. He has that glazed, anxious-to-get-back-to-the-screen look. I pull the cap off and fluff out my hair.

"Happy with your hairdresser experience?" he asks.

"What do you think?" I give it a good toss.

He flashes me a thumbs-up, but his attention is already back on the boob tube. Not for the first time, I wonder if he even heard me, or if what came out of my mouth was like the senseless *wah-wah* squawk of the adults on *Peanuts*.

I'm deflated, but I know that complements aren't his thing. I sit beside him on the couch, pull off my boots and get comfortable. He drapes a leg over mine. I rest my head on his shoulder.

"I'm going to shower before bed," he says.

I click off the TV, undress and get into the bed that had been mine. Like a peacock displaying its plumage, I raise my hair up off my neck and fan it out over the pillow. Accompanied by a whoosh of steamy air, Bob comes out of the bathroom in his boxers. I scoot over to make room for him and pat the mattress.

He doesn't seem to notice the gesture and climbs into the other bed, "his" bed.

"Don't you want to sleep together tonight?" I ask.

"You want me to come over there?"

"Uh, sure."

We've been together over twenty years. Why is this so difficult?

He throws off the covers and crosses the divide between our beds. We kiss. Our hands roam. I sense that his mind is elsewhere or that he's half asleep. Yet we go through the motions, barely. It isn't awful. Nor is it satisfying, for either of us. I am at least grateful that my body doesn't betray me by making any disgusting noises, especially considering the way I've been eating. We drowse, my backside nestled in the curve of his front, his hand on my hip. The rare spooning feels more intimate than what preceded it.

Goaded by my mother's one piece of marital advice, I get up to pee. "Always urinate after intercourse," she once advised me, in that clinical tone of hers. "That way you won't get any nasty infections."

In the brief time I was gone, Bob left "my" bed and returned to his own.

I lean over him for a goodnight kiss. "Love you," he says.

"Love you, too."

I am sleepless in Philadelphia. I blame myself. He wasn't interested. Yet I pushed. And if there's one thing I've learned about Bob – perhaps it's true of most people – if he doesn't want to do something and I force the issue, I've gained nothing. Whether it's trolling for that first "I love you," for commitment, a marriage proposal, intimacy, or just a paltry complement.

I know this.

Yet I forgot, again. I am an idiot. And fat. And disgusting. And hungry. I slip from bed, shut the door behind me and huddle on the couch with the bag of Tasty Cakes. When they're gone, I eat a bagel I snagged from the breakfast buffet, smeared with peanut butter and jelly. I'm stuffed, but not satisfied.

Fuck him.

I am what I am, a 63-year-old wife, mother and grandmother. A grown-ass woman with extra chins, belly rolls, stretch marks, varicose veins, dark splotches on her wrinkled face and misshapen feet. Always somewhere in the process of digestion. Belching, farting or groaning, famished or comatose from stuffing myself sick. I'm a sugar addict. It tastes good. It takes my mind off what ails me, until it becomes what ails me.

I am lonely and scared, afraid that this is my life, all it will ever be.

Fuck everyone.

For making me feel that I'm not enough, that I'll never be enough, that I don't deserve to be loved and desired.

Fuck me.

Because whatever else I may be, self-absorbed, deluded, too sensitive, I'm not without the occasional insight. I do know it's only ever been about me, the ways I limit myself, judge and deny myself. I get that. Nobody else really cares. Not my husband, not my skinny sisters, not anyone, not really.

Fuck the whole, I-have-to-fix-myself-this-year plan.

What if I decide that I'm fine the way I am? That I don't have to change a thing. Just keep doing what I do, only enjoying it. What if I say it's all good?

I already know from experience that being some "ideal"

weight won't make me happy. I've been there and it didn't. I already know expecting people to treat me differently, to see me differently doesn't make it happen.

While my husband sleeps in the other room, I pledge to accept myself as I am. Period. That is the true journey, as well as the destination. Not reaching a certain weight. Not having my husband fall madly in love with me. Not being a massive success of any kind. But simply accepting. Being. Living. Appreciating. Lots of ing-ing.

Having talked myself out of feeling guilty for finishing off all the Tasty Cakes, I hide the wrappers, curl up on the couch and sleep, alone, digesting and at relative peace.

26

It's the official first day of spring.

Home from our frigid east coast vacation, I sit on the brown velveteen chair in the family room, beside Marmalade Jam's cage. Bob and I take turns keeping the guinea pig company. It's our way of communing with our daughter in absentia. Marmalade is the ideal cipher. He munches and grinds his hay. Those beady pink eyes never judge.

I ate like a major piglet while on our trip, and before, and since. The photos from yesterday, visiting Mom in the memory care facility with Juliet, brought it all home. I wore a tent of a tunic in a nice blue to bring out my eyes. But no shirt could disguise the fact that I'm twice as wide as my sister.

"You look amazing," she said, as I drove us back across the causeway, from Davis to Sacramento.

I made a sour face.

"You do," she said, jiggling her non-existent thighs, already with the short-shorts, though summer is still months away.

For a scintilla, I think, maybe she's right, that I suffer body dysmorphia and the fact that she is taller than me and I weigh fifty pounds more than she does, does not make me a heifer. Then I take another look at the photos. Four generations gathered around Mom's lumpy beige chair – my son and grandkids had also stopped by to visit. It would have been a nice one to post to Facebook, to share with far-flung family and friends. I can't do it.

That night in the Philadelphia hotel room haunts me. I know that I must get past it and back on track. The year is a quarter gone. First order of business, to fit into the size-fourteen jeans I almost managed to wriggle into two months ago.

Damage control. Regaining lost ground. Onward.

My big sister, Roxanne, says the three of us aren't late bloomers, but rather perennials. The opposite of those prom queens and football team captains who bloom early and seem to spend the rest of their lives reliving their glory days.

Our glory days remain always on the horizon.

I'm a daylily, a black-eyed Susan, a pink bleeding heart.

Hope springs eternal. Thank God for that.

⊖ ⊖ ⊖

Since retirement, my husband has spent hundreds of hours as a volunteer at the Sacramento Railroad Museum. He enjoys being a docent, leading tours through the world-class facility. He bought tickets for the museum's annual banquet honoring its hundreds of volunteers. It's an event I need to attend, to show my support for something he cares about. It's a sit-down dinner in a massive hotel banquet hall. I labor over what to wear and take extra care with my hair and makeup. Walking down the garishly carpeted hallway to the check-in table, I slow my steps and reach for Bob's hand.

"Are you embarrassed to be seen with me?" I ask, my expression sheepish. It's a dumb question, but it's how I'm feeling.

"I'm embarrassed to be seen with myself," he says squeezing my hand. "Besides, the average age in there will be 75. We'll be youngsters in this crowd."

As if that was the kind of reassurance I was looking for.

"I just feel like I look so shitty, so fat," I say, tugging at my skirt.

"Yeah, well, I'm the fat one," he says.

Right. After that mysterious bout with thyroiditis, his pants are still sagging.

"Besides," he says, "look around. You look better than half these people."

I look better than half the octogenarians. Not exactly a high bar.

He chooses a table where a few of his cronies from the machine shop, and their wives, are seated. I'm still licking my wounds, but manage to put on a cordial face and keep up my end of the chit-chat. I eat every scrap of my rubber chicken and polenta, all my dessert and most of Bob's. On our way out, I sweep up several of the party favors left on the tables and stuff them into my purse – little net bags of butter mints, a childhood favorite.

⊖ ⊖ ⊖

First Philadelphia. Now this. Strike two. I'm a slow learner, or stubborn, or both.

After the banquet, I'm itching for a fight. The only thing holding me back, keeping the venom bottled up inside me, is knowing that it won't do any good. Likely, I'll only feel worse. So instead of letting it out, I turn away from Bob in bed, barely managing a grunt in response when he says goodnight.

"Poor baby," he says. "All that chocolate cake give you a headache?"

He kisses my cheek and pats me. I feel like a farm animal.

The next morning, I settle into the chair beside Marmalade's cage. I sip coffee and browse the headlines. Bob stumbles into the kitchen, groggy eyed, wild eyebrows askew.

"Morning," he says, plugging in his phone. "How's the head bone?"

"Fine." Just as he'd had no clue how hurt I was that night in Philadelphia, he doesn't know I was upset at the banquet. I squint at him.

"Who me?" he says, turning around, as if I might be giving someone standing behind him the stink eye.

"Yeah, you," I say, returning to the paper.

"What?"

"You really want to know?"

"Do I?"

"Fix your coffee," I say.

He doctors his cup with a heaping spoonful of chocolate powder, then dilutes it with water. I join him at the kitchen counter, leaning forward onto my forearms so we're face to face.

"I was just wondering," I say, "Would you say you're satisfied with our marriage?"

"Of course. It's great." He slurps his makeshift mocha.

"Really? You think it's great?"

"Well, yeah, don't you?"

"Don't you think you might be happier with someone else?"

"Of course not."

"I mean, there's a lot of other women out there."

"I've already got you."

"Yeah, but you don't have to be with me. I mean it's your life. You could have anyone you want."

"Not really. Women aren't exactly beating down the door."

"In other words, you're with me because you don't think you could do any better."

I know he doesn't mean it that way, exactly. Still, it bugs me when he acts as if he doesn't know women find him attractive. I've seen plenty of evidence that they do.

He takes a thoughtful sip of coffee, caressing the warm mug with both hands.

"I'm sorry," he says with that hangdog expression, droopy mouth and eyes.

"About?"

"I guess I don't do a very good job of telling you what you mean to me."

"Aw." I give him a smiley frown, half up, half down.

"I admire you so much," he says.

"You admire me?"

"Yeah. I mean, I guess, I don't say it enough. It seems as if anywhere I go, people come up to me and tell me that they used to work with you and what a great boss you were, how much they learned from you, how much integrity you have. You never talk about your career. So, I forget. But then people remind me. It makes me so proud."

"Proud?"

Encouraged by my animation, his face lights up.

"I guess what I'm saying is, I know I should do a better job telling you how much respect I have for you. And it's not just the job stuff. Your kids have turned out so great. I know at the beginning I was critical of you for not disciplining them enough. But look at them now. I respect you so much for all you've done."

"You *respect* me?"

The newspaper is forgotten, coffee grown cold as he gestures with his hands.

"So much. And you're such a great cook. Indulging all our needs. Vegan for Carolanne. Meat for me. I guess I take it all for granted. I don't tell you enough. But you're amazing."

Admiration.

Pride.

Respect.

All great words. For a boss or work colleague. The kinds of

things you'd say at a retirement luncheon or in a eulogy. But I asked, and I'd gotten my answer. I have my husband's, my soulmate and life partner's respect and admiration. I guess it's more than some people can say.

I want to scream. I want to cry. I don't.

We are alone in the house. Well, not completely alone. Marmalade has taken cover beneath his purple plastic dome. Mocha slumps against my slippers. The cat sidles up to Bob and rubs against his pant leg. Absently, Bob reaches down to pat her. He grasps her upright tail and pulls his hand along its sinewy length. I am envious of that easy touch, that simple tactile response.

He can't, or won't, say any of the romantic things that I want to hear. I imagine that he doesn't say them because they aren't what's true for him and what he said was. He's tied to a woman he admires and respects rather than one he *loves*. I don't really believe it's his intention, but I feel like some charity case, albeit an accomplished one, one with a damned high degree of integrity, but a charity case nonetheless.

"But what about as a woman?" I ask. "I mean, are you happy with how it is between us. With how we are?"

"Of course," he says. "Aren't you?" He is solicitous, serious.

"Well, what about sex?"

"Yeah, I know. I guess there's always so much going on. I don't want to bother you. You do so much for all of us. There's the grandkids. Your writing. Your headaches. You have enough to deal with."

"It shouldn't be a burden, Bob."

His mouth droops, an exaggerated, hangdog frown that makes his chin pucker in a way that's hard to hate.

"I'm sorry I'm not meeting your needs," he says.

And there it is. We have punched all the buttons. Our

relationship in a nutshell. He's kind. He's good. I'm this amazing paragon he wouldn't dream of pestering with affection. And he's so sorry he's not meeting my needs, a well-worn phrase from some past marriage counseling session, not one of ours.

Strike three.

I have the sense of being managed. My emotions and words are landmines, and he's tiptoeing his way out of this volatile terrain with phrases and responses that have worked before, that have allowed him to extricate himself without bodily injury or blowing up another marriage.

I don't blame him for being wary.

I do believe he loves me. I'm just not sure what that means to him. And I can't help but wonder if we aren't both missing out. All his talk of respect and pride feeds into my fear that we're together because it made economic sense, because I'm steady and hard working, not prone to histrionics like his first wife and then there was the whole pregnancy thing. Good marriages have been made of far less, and, I imagine, far more.

Even our conflicts worry me. I can't call them fights. He won't engage. I poke and prod. I rant, then cry. He feels bad about it. He's apologetic. I don't think we've ever had make-up sex. Is that a real thing? Or is it just on TV and in the movies? No, it's a thing. I remember, from younger days.

He and his first wife fought. No holds barred. Shouting. Cursing. Awful stuff, sure, terrible for the kids to see. But she could push his buttons and get a response, in a way I've never been able to. Perhaps he didn't respect or admire her the way he does me. He's never bragged about her amazing integrity. But I'm betting they had make-up sex.

"Did you propose to her?" I once asked him.

"I guess I must have," he said, but claimed not to remember any of the details.

I was left to speculate. Did he plan it? Did he practice what he would say? Choose a special time and place? Get down on one knee?

All those things he never did with me. All those things I will never experience. I didn't remind him he never proposed to me. He would have argued that he had. Which I suppose is true, technically.

Years after we married, when we were going through our first round of marriage counseling, I recounted for the therapist my insecurities about whether Bob even wanted to be married to me. He gave Bob the homework assignment of addressing this by proposing to me. One evening, I came home from work to dinner on the table. During dessert, Bob knelt on the floor before my chair and said the words.

"Will you marry me?"

He slid my wedding ring off my finger, then back on.

It was too little too late, a homework assignment, not so different than being told what to do by my mother.

Or am I just being petty? Is there no satisfying me?

Perhaps, probably, I should shut up and be happy. I have a comfortable home, a decent pension, time to do the things I want, wonderful kids and now grandkids, and my husband's undying admiration and respect. He infringes little on my personal space, and for the most part we cohabit well. Is the one thing that's missing, that one huge thing, a deeper emotional and physical connection, worth jeopardizing all that?

I worry that one day he'll regret what he might have had with someone else, that we both will. I can't escape the grudging sense of having been cheated out of what's purported to be one of the reasons for living. If not *the* reason. True love. Body. Soul. Mind.

Ours must be some other kind of love. A smaller, practical kind, one based more on factors like income, credit rating and stability. Does love come in various intensities and flavors? Of course, it does.

Which brings me back around, again, to the fantasies, the fairy tales. Are they real or do we fabricate them, then choose to believe. Wasn't that the Tinker Bell notion from Peter Pan? That she only existed if you really, really believed in her. Perhaps love is like that. And I was doomed by cynicism, which tainted any chance I'd ever fall completely under the spell. Or, to circle around again – maybe I just haven't met the right man, or woman, or animal. I think I'm open at this point. And damn dizzy.

God, I have no fucking clue. I just want, once in my life, to really know someone and to believe in my bones, in my heart and head, that they know me, really know me, and love me anyway.

27

My total transformation isn't happening, yet growing out my gray—which I'd anticipated would be a huge hassle, with months of hiding my hair under a hat when I left the house is now the least of my worries. I leave it alone, and it grows. Go figure. And I'm not just growing out my gray roots, I'm rocking an actual style, the reverse ombré. When I tell people that, most don't get it, until I go through the whole explanation. Even then their faces don't exactly light up. That's okay. I'm a trendsetter.

Bob still hasn't said anything about it, but the general reaction is way better than the last time I went gray and was mistaken for my sisters' mother and my children's grandmother. I don't think it's because I look any better this time around, but rather that gray is now in style. It's a legit fashion choice, particularly with the young and edgy crowd. Not that I'm ever mistaken for young and edgy. But I do get props from twenty- and thirty-somethings with blue, purple, and gray hair. They smile and say, "Cool hair."

In this coffee shop where I've been a customer for years, the proprietress, a middle-aged woman who I imagine doesn't come by her dark hair naturally, comes over to my table. We've been saying hello, and *cómo estás,* for several years.

"I just had to tell you how *great* you look," she says. "I love it. Your hair, it's so ... " She pauses and does a little shimmy. "*Sexy.* Good for you."

Cool and sexy. Beats brave.

Even seeing my sisters doesn't get under my skin so much, not enough to send me running to the hair salon to undo my reverse ombré. Perhaps it's a sign of maturity. Or am I just being ornery? Only if I buy into the premise that not dying my hair is some political or feminist statement. I'm just an older woman, owning her years, end of story. People fear age. I'm no different. I'd love to look twenty years younger. But I don't think it's gray hair that makes you look old. It's the whole package. Health and vigor, how you move and feel. Being content with yourself.

Covering the gray isn't going to make me look, or feel, any younger. Taking better care of my body will. I know this. I do. Maybe I just can't multi-task as well as I used to. But my hair is cool, even, sometimes, sexy. That's not nothing.

$$\ominus \ominus \ominus$$

It's May, and I'm fat and happy. Well, not so much happy as complacent. My cell buzzes. It's what Bob calls "butt crack" early, before dawn. A familiar name appears on my screen.

"Hey, Bozo," I say.

"Did I interrupt you two lovebirds?"

I don't bother to respond. Roxanne doesn't expect me to.

"Hey, I've been thinking," she says.

"Always dangerous."

"I need to do something to shake things up."

"Just don't go back on those internet dating sites."

"No, not men. I've been feeling sluggish, flabby, I don't know, out of shape. I need a *reboot*."

She says the word like it's Sanskrit or something, a word she just learned and is trying on, to see how it sounds coming out of her mouth. It's a thing she does. Testing new words, new to her, with a lilt and a look. I can picture the look over the phone, as if to say, isn't that just the best word ever, can you believe I just used it, aren't I clever?

"A reboot, you say. Where'd you read that?"

"Oh, some website," she says. "Doesn't matter. I want you to come with me."

"Where?"

She's found a fitness "camp" in Southern Utah, the land of health resorts and lock-down rehab compounds for wayward teens.

"Come with me. It's not too expensive. I think you'll love it."

"It's a fat camp, isn't it?" I say.

She won't say it, but that's exactly what it is. I am offended – and relieved. I won't admit it to anyone but myself, but I do need a serious kick in the ass. More than she does. It occurs to me that she knows that. After all, she isn't flabby and out of shape. Sluggish? Maybe. But I am all those things, and then some. I suspect my sisters have been talking about me, again. Conspiring over what to do about their fat middle sister, again. Bob is likely in on it too, again. They've decided it's time for a group intervention.

All that crosses my mind. It might even be true. But I don't call her on it.

"When are you thinking about going for this *reboot*?" I ask.

"Soon," she says. "The only window I've got is the second week of June."

I look at the kitchen calendar.

"As in, two weeks from now?"

"We can do this," she says. "We need this."

I appreciate that "we."

"I'll ask Bob."

"He'll be fine with it. He'd do anything for you. He adores you – you know that, right?"

"Yeah, yeah, whatever."

"You crack me up," she says.

When I tell him, Bob is fine with the reboot. He thinks it's a fantastic idea. This doesn't surprise me.

28

New plan, always a new plan. And yeah, that's a good thing. I don't stay down for the count. I at least jerk my hand out of the cookie jar and take stock from time to time. As plenty of people before me have said – we try, we fail, we try again.

I tell my grandson that I'm going to fat camp for a week. He laughs in that way, eyes crinkled, like I've said something naughty or "adult," and that makes him feel special and maybe a little bit embarrassed for me too.

"By yourself, Grandma?" he asks.

"With Aunt Rocky," I say.

He mulls this over. His glittery eyes narrow. "Aunt Juliet, too?"

"Nope, just me and Rocky."

"Because Juliet's not fat?"

From the mouths of babes once again.

Elliott must have repeated the gist of our conversation to his mother that evening. She texts me, requesting I not refer to it as fat camp, that I not use judgmental words to describe people's bodies, even my own. She's right, of course. I should know better.

The next time my grandson and I are together, I call it "fitness camp."

"Not fat camp, Grandma?" I shake my head no. "Because it's a mean word?"

"That's right, sweetie. I shouldn't have said it."

At ages three and five, my grandkids don't need my self-deprecation.

I'll be spending a lot of money for a week of exercise and controlled eating. Will it be worth it? Like most things, that's up to me. I want to arrive primed, ready to jump into the program with both flat feet.

I read an article about sugar that says it's as addictive as cocaine. That rings true for me. One taste and my logical, thinking brain shuts down. Consequences – fear of migraine, colitis and all the rest – vanish. Poof. I must have more. Finding sugar, consuming sugar, becomes my whole world.

I decide to focus on just that one thing, eliminating demon sugar, which means most baked and packaged goods, and candy – empty calories I don't need anyway.

We leave for the desert in two weeks. Then it's four months until Hawaii and six months left in my year of fixing all that ails me. I get out the calendar and do the math. I always get out the calendar and do the math. Nineteen weeks left to fit into that bikini. At a pound a week, I'll be down twenty pounds by then. At two pounds a week, forty pounds down.

I don't know what I weigh, so I don't know what to subtract the twenty or forty from. Regardless, a pound lost is a pound lost. Twenty is good. Forty better. No use getting on the scale now. It will just bum me out and send me to the proverbial cookie jar for sure. I'll wait until I check in at fat camp, after my running start, after this sugar cleanse is underway.

No time to lose. Nineteen weeks will become no weeks in a snap.

I mean it this time. I always mean it. But this time I really, really mean it.

I try. I fail. I try again. You can do it, D.

29

By the June meeting of my book-in-a-year writing class, I'm back on the wagon, gearing up for my week at fitness camp. I resist the frosted scones. Plenty of white sugar in those babies.

According to my computer, I've amassed over 200,000 words on my work-in-progress, my magnum opus to twelve months of self improvement. The gruesome details of one degrading relationship and sexual encounter after another, fueled by a steady stream of cookies, toast and bowls of cereal.

I hope there are at least 50,000 usable words within the 200,000.

Two gems from our Saturday class stick with me. One is the suggestion that a good test for whether your writing is too abstract (code for boring) is to ask the question, "Can you pour chocolate sauce on it?" A writing analogy I can relate to. It reminds me of that college instructor who suggested I use fewer "emotion" words and more concrete imagery. I picture all the tangible, touchable, people and objects in my manuscript that I can pour chocolate sauce on, or marshmallow cream or caramel. The other bit of advice is that once I know everything that should go into the story, which I decide means that once I have exhausted my capacity for ripping off old scabs, I can start thinking about what order to put things in, what sense to make of all the material I've amassed. This gives me license to keep doing what I'm doing, getting it all out there. That's the entirely legitimate stage of the process I'm in. The generative stage.

There is a purpose to my self-flagellation. Thank God for that.

I am at the literal halfway mark in terms of my big year of fixing myself. I have stuck with the hair and writing parts. The rest is at least on my mind most every day. When it comes time to carve and edit, to make "art" of undisciplined memory, perhaps, ideally, yes, please, it will also be time to take care of my body.

I look around the room. It's a comfort to be among like-minded women, each of us plumbing our depths to produce a book. There is power in our shared intention, regardless the outcome for any of us.

After our Saturday session, the group of us go to lunch together, at a busy cafe five minutes by car from our teacher's home. The weather is idyllic. We sit outside, at a long table beside a creek, its banks overgrown with ferns, a canopy of trees overhead. I choose a healthful salad, something hippy-dippy befitting the Northern California setting, one of those towns where the sixties never ended. Locally sourced beets, pears, arugula, pumpkin seeds, fresh herb vinaigrette. Literal chocolate sauce, organic chocolate sauce.

In the glow of good food, wine, and the shiny faces of my new friends and comrades, Shelley takes my photograph on her phone and texts it to me. The green frames of my stylish new glasses pick up the background foliage. My hair is good, parted on one side, a sleek cascade of silver, gunmetal and brown. But, oh dear. My chin and neck are a series of pudding-like wattles. I earned those wattles. One for each 50,000 words.

Fat camp can't come too soon.

⊖ ⊖ ⊖

197

"I'm going to miss you," Bob says in bed the night before I depart for Utah.

He moves closer. Puts his arm around me. I freeze. Not because I don't want him to touch me, but because I'm bloated. Despite my best intentions of arriving at fat camp with a good head start, it hasn't worked out that way. I had a few good days and then, well, I binged, then I binged some more. It's what I do.

I feel sick. I really do. Yet I can't shrug him off, can't feign sleep, not tonight.

We move in the slow patterns of years. He is gentle, holding much of his weight in his knees and forearms, accustomed to thinking of himself as bigger, heavier, though we probably weigh about the same. I inhale, intent on holding my abdomen in, thinking that if I just hold on tight, there is less chance of my body embarrassing me. But a woman must breathe. And then there is the matter of relaxing enough that I can feel something, perhaps even experience pleasure.

There is that.

I exhale. My muscles soften. All of them. And then it comes, with a vengeance.

A short blast, a toot.

"Sorry about that." I re-clench all my sphincters.

"It happens," he says.

I giggle. Enough that I lose my tenuous grip on muscle control. Then it really comes. A long, sodden whoosh, punctuated by percussive toots in time with his thrusts. My body chooses that moment to expel a week's worth of accumulated gas. It goes on for days. The sound reverberates. I shake with sad, desperate laughter.

"Oh, my," he says.

"Sorry."

"It happens," he says, seemingly at a loss for any other words.

But I know it doesn't, not like that. I'm the only whoopee cushion in our bedroom. A human gag gift.

As Bridgett Jones so aptly put it, "And that was it. . . Right there, that was the moment I suddenly realized that unless something changed soon, I was going to live a life where my major relationship was with a bottle of wine and I'd finally die fat and alone ... "

Only, in my case, that's the moment I realize I'll never enjoy sex again and that my husband would be fully justified and vindicated in leaving me for a less gassy woman, for any woman at all. As I prepare to leave Bob to fend for himself for an entire week, I provide this auditory, olfactory, sensory memory to revisit each night as he lays his head on the pillow and contemplates my empty side of the bed.

Another brilliant outcome that could have been easily avoided if I'd only stuck with the plan, *any* of the plans. I failed. But I will try again. If I don't, I'll have to abandon my marriage, for both of our sakes.

30

Roxanne and I finally arrive at the Las Vegas airport, half a day late, after scrimping on an economy airline that charges extra for a carryon bag, for water during the flight, even for a seat assignment. As if a place to sit were an optional expense, one you could forgo to save fifteen bucks and still somehow arrive at your destination.

Vegas is surreal, even the little we glimpse on the walk through the airport and in the parking lot waiting for the shuttle van. A netherworld of slot machines, overweight tourists wearing too much glitter and spandex, mysterious limos with tinted windows and the occasional glimpse of a scantily clad woman inside, also wearing too much glitter and spandex.

The outside air feels like an oven set on a slow bake, for roasting nuts or drying out bread to make croutons, which I imagine is what happened to the natives, whose skin resembles fruit leather. Not a look I aspire to.

Our driver takes the highway that runs past a portion of the strip, high rise casinos planted in the desert, with their massive billboards and icons to world cultures. The pyramids and the Parthenon, the Statue of Liberty and Times Square. Then two hours over a rocky, monochromatic landscape, *Planet of the Apes* -style. The resort where we'll be staying was where *The Biggest*

Loser television show was filmed, where contestants vied to lose the most weight for a cash prize, where they were pushed to their limits, sometimes vomiting and passing out from exertion and heat. Nose pressed to the van window, I survey the desolate landscape and pray for an oasis beyond the next pile of rocks.

We arrive too late for the new guest orientation or dinner. The kitchen is closed, literally locked down for the night, nothing but hot water and herbal, non-caffeinated teas to tide us over. Our empty stomachs protest as we climb into bed and set the alarm for the next day's first activity, an assessment hike to determine our relative levels of fitness, so that we can be slotted with the appropriate hiking group. Our first weigh in, that moment of truth, won't happen until after the hike.

My sister and I wake early and watch the sun rise, the lightening sky striated with pink ribbons, craggy red mountains off in the distance. The hike will start at 6:30 AM and end before the sun gets too hot. Breakfast isn't until after the hike, so we're encouraged to grab a calorie-coded snack or two from the dining room. I chose a hard-boiled egg for 80 calories and an apple at 75. I resist the almonds. 100 calories for a measly 10 nuts. The same for a smear of peanut butter in a tiny tub.

The hike winds up and through the hills on the side of a canyon with a deep valley below and, across the valley, the dramatic red rock of the opposite side of the canyon. I keep pace in the middle of the pack, sucking down water and admiring the subtle earth-toned beauty of the desert floor at our feet, the hardy grace of ground-hugging brush and bristly cacti. Much of the desert is beautiful, even gorgeous, provided you don't succumb to heat stroke and become carrion.

I acquit myself reasonably well and am assigned to an intermediate hiking group. Roxanne's hips bother her, and she opts out of the hiking groups after this first foray, deciding to try the trail down the center of Snow Canyon, which is mostly flat terrain, and where you can go at your own pace without having to stick with a trail guide and group.

Back at the ranch, hot, sweaty and hungry, the two of us line up for the scales, along with the other newbies. I am guardedly optimistic. The last time I weighed myself, back at the beginning of March, I was still in the 170s, inching up, but still in there. I'd fallen off the wagon several times since, so I figure maybe I gained a few pounds, but I'd also had alternating bouts of more disciplined eating. Not exactly the "feast and fast" program – more like the "going off the rails, then exercising some restraint" program, – at least an improvement over flat-out abandon, what I call failing better. I hope the result of all this dietary indecision will be a wash, weight-wise.

I take my turn in one of two consultation rooms. The woman taking down my information is one of the leathery hiking guides. She is about my age, without an ounce of visible fat on her scrawny carcass. Per her instructions, I take off my shoes and socks and the exercise tracker on my wrist. I also empty my pockets and, of course, I already peed.

"Ready?" she asks.

I step up onto the fancy scale, position my feet on metal, foot-shaped sensors and grip the handles, sliding my thumbs into smooth thumb-shaped imprints. Music tinkles and the graphs on the screen in front of me slowly fill with percentages of fat and muscle for all quadrants of my body. At the bottom of the screen is one big number, presumably my weight. That can't be right. I look away. The music stops and the graphs and numbers freeze.

"All right," she says, "you can step down."

I pray that big number has changed, the way the numbers in the graphs kept hopping around as the gizmo completed its calibrations. It hasn't.

194.4.

I gained just shy of twenty pounds in a little over two months. I'd thought I had a long road ahead of me at 176. If I was at home, I would have sought solace in the fridge, in the cupboards. What the hell, I would have thought, what difference does it make now? Come on, D, let's make it an even 200. That's exactly where my mind would have gone.

But I'm not at home. I'm at fat camp. Where I belong. I haven't weighed this much since I was nine months pregnant. At least then I had an excuse. I really am as big as my husband, and he's half a foot taller than me – and a man.

What the hell?

It's funny, in an ironic sort of way. This year of all years. When I'm supposedly determined to get it together. I have, or had, a plan, for fuck's sake. To get healthy for my grandkids, to make my family proud, stop the migraines, my thighs chafing and my chins from bobbing on my chest. It's ironic, all right. And mule-headed. And just plain dumb.

My sister doesn't even want to know her numbers. For her it isn't about the numbers.

"I might want to look when the week is over," she says, "Or not."

We both know her numbers are already good. I don't share what I weigh, or any of my other stats, only that it isn't good, that I'm pretty freaked out.

"Oh, it can't be that bad," she says, "You look great. You always look great."

I squint at her. She squints back.

"Thank you," I say, and leave it at that.

"You're welcome."

"I do feel better."

"The sugar thing?"

"Yeah," I say. "No headaches, at least no bad ones." It's true.

While I've been eating way too much, I've at least avoided foods where sugar is one of the main ingredients.

"That's huge. Way more important than weight."

"I guess so." She punches me in the arm. "No, you're right," I say.

"You know I am."

"Let's go get some of that breakfast," I say.

"Now you're talking," she says. "We earned it."

$\ominus \ominus \ominus$

Early mornings at the "ranch" are my special time. Before sunrise. Before the hikes. Before breakfast. The air already balmy with the promise of another hot day, the air so thick and soft you can sift it with your fingers, stars and moon suspended above the mountaintops.

There are two areas for lounging at opposite ends of the swimming pool. Rattan couches and chairs beneath muslin canopies, kept lightly lit throughout the night. The one farthest from our room is mine, the same chair each morning, feet curled beneath me, notebook open on my lap, a cup of contraband instant coffee on the armrest beside me. This is Utah, and fitness camp besides, so no sugar, no caffeine. From my private perch, with only the occasional coyote howl or insect battering the light bulb, I have an hour or more to scribble in my notebook before the other guests begin to stir.

Away from home, it's easier to forgive myself, to see my missteps and backsliding as belonging to another time and place. Here in the desert, I expand to let in the light of potential, of possibility. I can see myself succeeding, a vision that so often eludes me at home.

I am the common denominator. I am the one who must change if I want change to happen. Brilliant deduction, D. For this I traveled across several states and handed over my credit card.

Why do you hate yourself? That was my mother's line. How could I not? I added that part.

I was always a moody, broody kid. It's there in the earliest childhood photographs. Sad eyes, quivering chin. That, "Please sir, may I have some more?" expression on my pitiable mug. As a girl, I concocted elaborate fantasies where I was locked away in a dungeon, arms shackled to the walls. Ragged, wasting away to nothing, I would die. Then everyone would be sorry. But it would be too late to make amends.

Good grief. I'm glad I wasn't my mother.

Where does this propensity for martyrdom come from? From being a middle child of resentful, unexpressive parents? Who the hell knows?

I claim to hate passivity. It's my main beef with my husband. But it's the way I was for so many years, perhaps the way I still am. When guys realized they could say anything, do anything to me, and I would just sit there, lie there, impassive, either a saint or an imbecile, were they goaded to see just how awful they could be?

I've been a drudge, what Mom would have called a doormat.

It never occurred to me to value kindness in a man. Boring. Or sincerity. Unexciting. I never trusted flattery, never believed it. Now I long for banalities about my eyes, hair and legs, all those things I used to dismiss as objectifying bullshit.

Women compliment me all the time, and I do the same in return. We are inclined to be kind and supportive with one another. Any random man's opinion becomes more important than a friend's, a sister's, or a stranger who approaches me on the street to say she loves my hair, my outfit.

What the hell, D?

There are lectures at fitness camp, a welcome break from

205

exercise. Nothing I don't already know after a lifetime of diets. *Losing weight is about calories in and calories out.* Who knew? *There's an emotional root or reason to most over-eating.* Headline news?

The sugar fixation predates adolescence and hormones run amuck. I remember being nuts for sugar going way back, fantasizing about it, sneaking it, stealing it, the rush, the high, not wanting to stop.

Mom was a nutrition Nazi. Nothing but whole grain breads, decades before brown bread was a thing, two to three fresh vegetables with every meal, back when the neighbors were eating canned corn and green beans, dessert a rarity. Candy was contraband, something to steal spare change for, to sneak and savor in secret. Mom was a hypocrite, too, preparing scrupulously balanced meals for us kids, while hiding her own stash of candy and treats in the glove compartment of her car.

When I was a kid, the only real consequence of sugar binging was an unusual number of cavities. Even in high school, I walked five to ten miles a day and didn't gain weight.

I can't remember a time when my mother wasn't dissatisfied with her appearance and trying to lose weight. Diets were what women did. By the age I am now, she'd had at least one facelift and round of liposuction. She didn't stop obsessing over her body until she was lost to Alzheimer's and forgot she'd ever cared. Now she says, "At least I've kept my figure."

I don't want to be like her, but I am, and my daughters have seen it all.

Hiking in the desert, sweating, eating good food and feeling good, it's easy to focus solely on me, my mind, my body. This safe-haven is a luxury. One most people can't afford.

I miss my husband, which surprises me. Our phone calls have a depth of feeling that face-to-face conversations don't.

Perhaps it's that I can imagine the emotions that I want to be there, that I believe should and must be there.

Every day I hike with a group of new friends, keeping pace with one of the women my sister and I have gotten friendly with over the past few days. She asks me details of my life, with an implied intimacy I only accept from relative strangers I'll likely never see again.

"So," she says, "You've been married close to twenty years. He must be a great guy. Tell me about him."

I blink at the red rock trail that winds up another jagged canyon.

"He's tall," I say, hesitating. "Great legs."

She laughs. The cascade of kinky curls poking out the back of her ball cap bounces.

"You're too funny. You sister warned me you were droll. I love it."

Am I droll, I wonder, making my sour, I'm-not-sure-how-I-feel-about-that, face.

"Your sister said you make great faces, too," she says, laughing.

I'm a type, a character, the cynical older woman, an amusing character to pass the time with at fat camp. My father used to repeat the old chestnut, "We say in jest what we dare not say in truth." I wonder at the truth behind the things I say about my husband. Not that there's anything wrong with being tall and having great legs. It's probably what I don't say that's more telling.

I resent his seeming lack of vices, weaknesses, nasty habits.

Perhaps I'm the one who settled. Is that really what I fear, rather than the reverse? And I hide all that by shoving it onto him, by finding affirmation in his every word and action that he doesn't really love me, want me, even know me.

I imagine I'm just a concept, a set of roles. The wife, the choice he made, the bed he must now lie in. Am I any different? Is anyone? We all make choices, every minute, every day. Sometimes the choice is not to choose, but rather to abide, to go along. Is being tall, having great legs, a good reason to choose a man, to stay with a man?

Is it any better or worse than him saying he admires me, respects me, is proud of me?

Would I be happier if he said *I* have great legs?

I would.

Why is it so important to have my body affirmed, appreciated, noticed, more than my mind, my heart? Perhaps it's cultural. Beautiful princesses lead beautiful lives. They are swept off their feet by beautiful men. They ride off together and live happily ever after. Is it possible to live happily ever after with a fat belly, a face covered with brown spots? Intellectually, I know it's foolish to even think it. Beauty doesn't guarantee happiness, or peace, or anything at all. Nor do fame or recognition.

I know all this. I do. And yet.

I want both. To be admired for those lofty traits Bob exclaims over and to be admired as a woman. What if I had to choose one over the other? My actions/reactions over the years seem to demonstrate that the cerebral stuff doesn't mean so much to me, that I don't value it. Perhaps because it isn't part of the fairytale iterations of love and romance, which are so often based on "love at first sight," on love of the perfect body, the perfect face. One doesn't spy integrity or generosity across a crowded room and be drawn to it, feel compelled to have it, to embrace it forevermore.

It's time to grow up. To stop waiting for some fairytale manifestations of what love and devotion should look like. I'm 63, which beats the alternative, as the old folks say. It's time to find joy and happiness in what is. Time to concede that the dreams I've held to for so long will never be realized and that they were likely the wrong dreams in the first place.

Is this what wisdom feels like? Or is this giving up?

I sip my tepid instant coffee and return to the open journal in my lap. I've reminisced through the end of Ron. Remembering has brought me up to where my youngest child is now, in her freshman year of college. I'd had experiences by her age that I'm grateful she hasn't, that I hope she never does. I don't think she will. She's stronger than I was, with a firmer grasp on who she is and what she wants for herself. Coming of age in the sixties, I believed inexperience was a curse, naiveté an embarrassment. There is wisdom in my daughter's innocence.

In my junior year of college I met Rick, who would eventually become my first husband. We were best friends. My first male friend. I felt safe with him, and we shared a dream. We both wanted to be writers. We became inseparable.

A few other early risers make their way to the dining room for hot water. Roxanne is likely awake in our shared room, getting ready for the day's hike.

Rick.

I write his name at the top of a new, blank page. I close the journal and my eyes, readying myself for another day in the desert, sweating out the poison.

31

After that humiliating creative writing class freshman year, when the professor suggested I stop writing and see a shrink, I didn't take another. For the remainder of my college career, I avoided the entire English department. When I discovered I could earn easy A's in Spanish classes, my major had found me.

Rick was a year ahead of me, a fellow Spanish Literature major and one of the few guys I ever encountered in language classes. He had wispy blonde hair he was forever flicking ineffectually off his forehead, and a slender, androgynous build. He always had some quirky anecdote or factoid to share with me. We began to save seats for one another and to meet up for lunch. I hadn't had a friend like this since high school.

He sometimes wore a jaunty scarf tied at the throat, its ends poking out like open scissors, clogs with woolen socks, a French beret, while I sashayed about in my latest thrift store finds, a forties pencil skirt, above-the-elbow gloves and a pill box hat. Though he was from West Sacramento, son of a fireman and his high school sweetheart, Rick spoke with an accent that was impossible to place. British tinged with something more exotic. After taking his order, waitresses would ask where he was from. A question he would evade, while I smiled enigmatically.

I was that odd girl, and he was that odd boy.

I felt more interesting when we were together, and safe, a

combination that was new to me. We were in our own, private movie. If I thought about his sexuality at all, I assumed he was gay, or perhaps ambivalent.

He took me places I hadn't been before. Exotic restaurants. Museums and concerts. There were books I should read. Movies I should see. Music besides rock that I should appreciate. Gaps in my education that needed filling. He seemed to adore me. Yet I required molding. A good friend of his, a former high school teacher and man he much admired, exclaimed, on meeting me, that I was a, "diamond in the rough." Evidently Rick thought so, too.

When I told him about my one disappointing creative writing class, he scoffed at the professor's insolence. Without having read anything I'd written, Rick said he knew I was a great writer. In return, I believed the same of him, though the few things of his I had read were so ornately worded, I couldn't figure out what they were about.

We were a mutual admiration society, an exclusive club. That's how it started. Funny how life is. You never know, you little imagine, when you first meet someone, the role they will come to play in your life.

Rick wined and dined me in a way I had never been before. No one else had needed to. In time, it became clear that his interest in me was more than intellectual, more than as a friend. I wasn't attracted to him that way, but it didn't occur to me to tell him. He was my best friend. He believed in me. Besides, I don't know that I'd ever thought of sex in terms of what I wanted. It was just what you did, what was expected.

I look back now and hate that I wasn't honest, for both of our sakes. I want to grab hold of my twenty-year-old self and slap some sense into her. Perhaps if Rick and I had stayed just friends, we might have actually helped one another.

Rick wasn't only eccentric. He was the most opinionated and

strident person I'd ever encountered. Once we were "out" as a couple, he became even more so, dictating what I should eat and wear, who was worthy of associating with, what we should and shouldn't do for entertainment.

I was raised in a household without raised voices, where overt conflict was avoided and disapproval was subtle and psychological. I refused to engage with Rick. I didn't know how. It was easier to abide by his "rules," and, nauseating though it is to concede, doing what I was told and resenting him for it, probably appealed to my martyr tendencies.

Before long, I was sewing all my own clothes with the natural fabrics he approved of. I stopped wearing makeup and painting my nails. I adhered to a strict natural diet and abandoned all frivolous reading material and friends. Meaning that I lost the few friends I'd had. I lost track of my celebrity crushes because I couldn't pick up magazines at the grocery store. I alienated my family and could only binge in the strictest privacy.

"You act like a Stepford wife," Mom said to me, "and you're not even married."

I now wonder how much of my relationship with Rick was just to spite her.

Rick loved that I wrote, but he felt that I needed guidance in that department, too. He suggested we keep a shared journal. An idea I thought was romantic, until I got my entries back with edits, corrections to grammar and spelling and suggestions in the margins for where I needed a metaphor, simile or stronger word. He tried to teach me calligraphy, too, so my writing would look better alongside his scrupulous penmanship.

After college we moved in together, working and saving our paychecks to fund a trip to Europe. We would live in Madrid, where, just before we met, he'd spent his junior year. We'd rent an apartment, write our break-out first novels, come home heroes, or perhaps not have to return at all.

Before leaving for Spain, I met Mom for lunch. She pressed some spending money into my hand.

"I hope you plan to see some things while you're in Europe, do some sightseeing," she said. "Enjoy this opportunity. You may not have another."

Her admonition would prove prophetic. I still have my first passport, issued in 1978. In the photo, I have the faraway gaze of a winsome poet, my hair a full Afro poof around my face, falling to the tops of narrow shoulders. That passport expired long before I would need another.

In our tiny studio apartment in Madrid, we adhered to rigorous writing schedules. There were rewards if we met our quota for words or pages. An evening stroll, dinner with cheap red wine in one of many small, neighborhood restaurants, or my favorite treat, *cafe con leche* and a warm *churro* in one of the bars that lined the *Avenida Princesa*, where our tiny apartment was. At major milestones, we might indulge in a visit to a museum.

When we needed clothing, his solution was to have his mother ship us my sewing machine. When I reached the point where I couldn't do a thing with my frizzy mat of hair, Rick cut it. That haircut broke something inside me. My hair had always been a major part of my identity. I hated it. I loved it. Shorn of my curls, I didn't know myself in the mirror. It was so short there was no way to curl it or pin it back, nothing to do but hide it under a massive scarf. In the only photograph I have from that year in Madrid, I'm in our tiny kitchen, hunched and forlorn. I'm wearing the same sweater as in my passport photo, but the light in my eyes, and that great poof of hair, are gone. I look like a badly coiffed poodle.

When we returned to the States, my sisters were full of questions. "How was Spain? Tell me everything. What did you see? What was your favorite part? Oh, it must have been so great, a whole year! I'm so jealous."

I wouldn't have told them the truth. We weren't the close friends we are today. I wouldn't have wanted them to know that I mostly saw the four walls of our one-room apartment at the top of six flights of stairs. One room, with a window onto the dank air well that ran down the middle of the building, crisscrossed with lines of dripping laundry. I'd stare up at the one tiny exterior window, no bigger than a cereal box, and imagine the city beyond our walls, teeming with people, with smells and sounds and life. We wrote and we edited and Rick typed it all up on a used Olivetti we bought at Madrid's huge open-air flea market. I did write a book, an awful, sanitized, coming-of-age tale about a teenage girl who was a lot like me. I'm still unable to reread it.

When we returned to the States, we were broke. Lacking any other options, we moved in with Rick's parents in West Sacramento, into his childhood bedroom.

His mother decided we needed to get married if we were going to live there. I knew it was a mistake. I knew it wouldn't last. Perhaps Rick did, too. Those didn't seem like compelling considerations. We were married in Reno, Nevada, at the county courthouse. It had to be Nevada. My one condition for going through with the marriage was that I not have to get a blood test, which was required in California but not Nevada. I was very squeamish about blood. Still am.

No blood test. That was my one condition.

I don't remember the date or if I ever had a ring. I remember piling into the car, Rick and his father in the front seat, me in the back with his mom, the smell of her cigarettes. I have no photographs from the day we married, only the ones in my mind.

It must have been spring, because of the dress I wore – pale yellow with a full skirt and split cap sleeves that fluttered in the warm breeze as we stood on the courthouse steps deciding where to go for lunch after the brief ceremony. Chinese or Mexican. My mother had picked the dress up at Macy's the day before. "You should at least have a new dress to wear," she'd said. She loaned me a string of beads, too, Victorian glass from her collection, a deep green, with flecks of black, like an exotic tropical beetle. After, she said I could keep them. Those beads are my only memento of that first wedding day.

⊖ ⊖ ⊖

I was 24. I'd just gotten married. I wasn't in love with my husband. I didn't even like him very much anymore, not after our miserable year in Spain. Perhaps he felt the same.

My initial route to motherhood was a result of the same brand of ambivalence. Rick had decided the cream for my diaphragm was toxic to more than sperm, and that olive oil ought to be an equally effective substitute. I was skeptical, but I didn't argue.

After one excursion with the olive oil, I was pregnant with my first child. Labor, natural childbirth at Rick's insistence, produced not only a baby boy but an epiphany. It was hard, physically and mentally, and I did it, on my own. While my muscles clenched and released, I had a rare clear thought: This child would be my responsibility. If it came to a choice between adhering to Rick's rules, keeping him from making a fuss, and doing what I believed was right for the baby, the baby would be my priority, plain and simple. That insight, that as a mother, choices would have to be made, important ones, was the first I'd come to on my own in many years.

There had been so many signs that Rick and I shouldn't be together—not as husband and wife. Yet it had seemed easier to allow one day to flow into the next, until I found myself five years into a life where I felt trapped. That state of complacency ended when I gave birth and recognized the responsibility I had to another. Having a child forced me to grow up, to find my backbone.

If it weren't for my son, now 37, I might still be going along. Of course, if it weren't for Rick, there would be no number one son, and that could never be.

Motherhood saved my life.

$$\ominus \ \ominus \ \ominus$$

The next morning, I occupy my usual spot beside the pool, balance my instant coffee on the armrest and open my journal. I reread the last few paragraphs from the prior day. It's been close to forty years since my son was born in Queen of the Valley Hospital in Napa. The sense of pride and determination I felt that day was new and unexpected, like yanking off shutters I hadn't realized were hammered shut.

Rick wasn't a bad person. But he wasn't good for me. Over time, by going along with his whims, I came to doubt my ability to function without him, to function at all. It was my fault, or perhaps no one's fault.

It would be another eighteen months before I walked out of the house to call my mother from the nearest pay phone. Rick was so afraid of what I was about to do, he wouldn't let me near our telephone. I walked several blocks to the public library and dialed her number. Twenty minutes later, I climbed into Mom's car with my son in my arms. I didn't go back, not even to get our clothes. I was done.

Perhaps because decisiveness was so rare for me, so underdeveloped, those two moments – the surety at birth that I would leave for the baby's sake, then finally doing it – though months apart, are fused in my mind.

I'd make plenty of mistakes after that. Yet almost four decades later, in a desert oasis a thousand miles from home, I relived the old pride I'd felt as a young mother. I'd proven something to myself: That I could be strong.

Off in the distance a coyote howls. Another picks up the song. Then another and another. Their yelps echo off the canyon walls.

I never regretted leaving his father and raising Fred on my own. We had some tough times. For years, I worked low-paying secretarial jobs. My lackluster college career hadn't prepared me for much else. There was no child support. Rick didn't work, so no blood to squeeze out of that turnip. The lawyer who helped me with the divorce said I was lucky Rick hadn't demanded alimony. We lived in crummy apartments. As a toddler, Fred, with a blonde Beatles haircut and winsome eyes, was shy but strong-willed, insisting on wearing his He-Man costume to daycare most every day. After close to two years cocooned with his dad while I was at work, rarely going outside or interacting with other kids, daycare was traumatic. Fred cried when I dropped him off on my way to work, and he was often crying when I picked him up ten hours later. It was a whole new world. For both of us.

At 37, he's an amazing dad and husband.

"You raised him right," his wife once told me. "He's such a good guy."

I don't know that I raised him right, but I am proud of him.

One of the hiking guides walks past and says hello. I set my notebook down. Enough, *nada más*. I will end the remembering there, with my 28-year-old self, a girl I can root for.

On the more pragmatic side of the ledger, if I keep going at this pace and continue to hash over the next thirty years of bad choices and missed opportunities, I'll rack up another 200,000 words and twenty pounds, easy.

Time to lace up those hiking sneakers and hit the dusty trail. But first, a trip to the dining room for a hard-boiled egg and half a banana with a teaspoon of peanut butter. Pure heaven.

32

Just as I always fall for a miracle diet at least once a year, whenever I come to a place like this – a spa or resort – I'm drawn to one of the instructor's pitches for the secret to emotional nirvana. There's buzz in the dining room about Glenda. I hear her name. My ears perk up. Her specialty is releasing negative energy. Exactly what I need. I've dredged it all up. Now it's time for an exorcism. I pull up a chair to listen.

"I actually felt negative thoughts floating away from my body," a chubby, rosy-cheeked blonde says, "like evil spirits."

"Wow," I say, inching closer.

"She finds where you hurt. She touches that spot and poof, bad energy gone! You should try it. That's what we're here for, right? What have you got to lose?"

Only ninety bucks. What the hell. I'm not having any beauty treatments. No facial or massage. It will be my one extra expense. I don't really believe all my bad juju will disappear so easily. But like losing weight without diet or exercise, how can I know unless I try?

I schedule an appointment with Glenda. We meet in one of the rooms where they do the weigh ins. She's Mormon. I know this, not from anything she's said, but because she has the requisite six children, she's very white and cheerful and fit, and I can see those special flesh-toned undergarments poking out from beneath her stretchy sports top. But because her long gray hair snakes around one side of her head in a stylish bohemian braid, she's a great yoga instructor, and her lovely eyes are grey and unflinching, I don't hold any of this against her.

"I'm glad you came to see me," she says, and I believe her. "Tell me about yourself and how you hope I can help you."

I do. I tell her so much. I tell her I've been dredging up old history and writing. I cry.

"I sense you are hard on yourself," she says.

I sniffle and nod. She hands me a tissue. She flips through one of her books, running a finger down the pages, searching for something.

"I don't know what this means," she says. "But this is the word I'm coming up with for you, for how you are right now. *Peevish.*"

"Peevish?"

"I know," she says. "It's not a word I even really know. But that's what it says. Does it mean anything to you?"

Oddly, it does.

"Do you want to feel this way?" she asks, crinkling her nose. "Peevish?"

We laugh. It's a ridiculous word, a ridiculous way to feel. My endemic ennui, self-hatred and angst are diminished by it, revealed for what they are, sheer, self-indulgent silliness. She makes two circles with her thumbs and forefingers, then joins them together like links in a chain. As we talk, she breaks the bond between the two circles, again and again. It's not a nervous habit. I know from what the woman in the cafeteria told me, that Glenda, whose grey eyes remain fixed on me, is breaking through my negative patterns. By her constricted brow, it looks like hard work. With each break in the chain, I will my stubborn synapses to yield, to release their hold on me. I want Glenda to succeed.

"Let's think of some words you like better than peevish," she says.

We brainstorm. Forgiving. Merciful. Peaceful. Amused. I like that last one a lot. It takes the peevishness and self-absorption out of being peevish.

"Let's try this," she says, writing in a fresh notebook.

At the top of the first page, she writes. "Emotional Exchange." Then the following:

1. I choose to feel _____.
2. I act like I feel_____.
3. I feel _____.
4. I am_____.

I plug my preferred word, amused, into the blanks. It's simplistic, but I get it. Plus, she's so earnest, and I really do love her hair. She writes her next suggestion in the book, something she calls the 10-10-10 to start each day. Ten minutes of reading and (sic) inspiring book (I imagine she was home-schooled, but don't judge her for it), ten minutes of meditation and prayer, ten minutes of writing.

"I bet you've already got that last part covered," she says. Her smile is kind, even respectful.

Glenda searches through her books some more. The grooves in her brow deepen. This is serious business. I'm glad. Because of the ninety bucks and because it would be so great to be healed so easily. Also, I like her and don't want her to be a quack. She gives me affirmations to repeat whenever I feel down on myself. She shows me how to do it, by tapping my chest with two fingers, over my heart, and repeating the words:

I love myself.
I honor myself.
I am grateful.

"You should repeat these a lot," she says, looking worried. I imagine she's thinking I'm a hard case, that it may not be enough.

"Try this, too," she says. She demonstrates how to repeat the affirmations tapping not only over my heart, but the top of my head, on my right temple, beneath my nose, then beneath my mouth.

It will take a lot of tapping and affirming to exorcise my peevish demons.

"I love your braid," I say. "Is it hard to do?"

Her face lights up. "Not at all. Would you like me to show you how?"

I say that I would.

She hands me the new notebook with the affirmations and the 10-10-10 written in it. It's mine to keep. She promises to find me in the cafeteria for a lesson in hair braiding.

⊖ ⊖ ⊖

That night, as the sun sinks behind the red cliffs, setting the sky ablaze, I join with others to walk a labyrinth. We have written our intentions for ourselves on slips of paper to leave beneath the stone at its center. Heads bowed, we wind round the switchbacks. I am in it. Knee deep in the woo-woo. Not the least bit smug or peevish. I inhale fresh, desert-sage scented air and mumble my affirmations.

At the center of the labyrinth, I pause in each of the four corners. I kneel before the stone. I close my eyes and mutter my intentions under my breath:

I am grateful.

I love and honor myself.

I am in love with my husband. I added this one to Glenda's script and the words feel sticky, like tugging at ragged Velcro.

I place my folded-up slip of paper in the small opening with the others.

I understand that dealing with the persistent sludge surrounding my marriage is important. I amplify my intention. To live fully in life's present incarnation. To release past hurts and grudges, and accept the good in it, or, if I can't do that, to...what? I don't know. Only that I am tired of playing victim, martyr, long-suffering peevish, shrivel-hearted crone. All that I don't want to be, all that I despise and disparage in others.

I retrace my steps, winding my way back out of the labyrinth. At each bend in the path, I tap my heart and murmur. *I am in love with my husband.* Thoughts intrude. But. But. He can't really love me. He doesn't even know me. And if he did, he'd love me even less. *I am in love with my husband.* But. But. I don't know his heart either. I can only know mine. Unless he shows me his. Unless I show him mine. *I am in love with my husband.*

I exit the labyrinth and find a stone bench. I search the starry sky. I make closed loops with my thumbs and forefingers. I break the circle. Again, and again. Releasing my reluctance into the soft night.

I am finding my way to the point of all this, *a* point of all this. It isn't about arriving at a place, or moment. It isn't about finding Prince Charming or he me. It isn't about reaching some magic number on the scale. It isn't about reaching any destination or milestone. It's about letting loose, cutting free, of whatever shackles have prevented me from diving into life, mind, body and spirit. Having my life matter, not because it's perfect, but because it's a gift, an opportunity.

Here I am. Midway into a year of change.

Happiness isn't hokey.

I've resisted happiness for being too simple, too trite and ordinary. A stubborn holdover from adolescence. I get it.

There's no more innate foolishness or simple-mindedness in contentment than there is in perpetual angst.

If I get out of my own way, I could have thirty or more years in which to continue sorting all this out, failing better, remaining open to the possibilities.

Wow. I wax profound. Why not? It's what I'm here for.

I'll repeat my affirmations and thump my heart, my temples and any place else that seems to need thumping. I will break through the sticking points, as easily as separating my thumbs and forefingers.

This is it. One more hike tomorrow. One more post-lunch digestive lecture, this one about how to bring the lessons home. I wish upon a rising star. I wish I could stay right here just a little bit longer. I wish to not forget how I feel right now. There is safety in being far from home, far from the familiar. I need to bring the safety home.

33

Fat camp, fitness camp, "fatness" camp, as my grandson has taken to calling it was good. Dry heat and an abundance of fiber. I pushed myself, and it didn't kill me. I got out of breath and overheated, and it didn't kill me, didn't even give me a headache. In seven days, I dropped five pounds and a couple of inches. Nothing like the amazing numbers contestants on reality TV shows manage, but it's a start. Seeing the number on the scale my first day, so close to 200, proved the kick in the pants I needed.

I'm home and determined to stick with the program. I watch my calories, eat fresh foods and avoid sugar. The days without headaches have become weeks.

I want to go back to the desert. They offer a special deal, up to four people in a room for one flat rate. Less than half what I spent for the first week. My daughters and a daughter-in-law agree to go. I sign us up. In the month before we are scheduled to fly to Las Vegas, I go into training. I hike the hills around our Calaveras County cabin, getting my heart rate up, going for the burn. I stick with the eating plan. I increase my daily steps from ten to twenty thousand and on my early morning walks, I tap myself silly and recite my affirmations.

By month's end, I've lost another eight pounds, on my own. I'm almost where I was back in January. Almost.

I'm stronger and more resilient than I've given myself credit for. I feel amazing and not in the least deprived. No refined sugar. No headaches, fatigue or despair. I can do this. I am doing this.

All the excuses I'd convinced myself were the reasons I wasn't losing weight were just that—excuses. I wasn't working hard enough, trying hard enough. I didn't want it badly enough. I got a perverse satisfaction from being fatter than I'd ever been before. I was goaded on by what I imagined to be the horrified looks from family and friends. How dare they? I'd show them fat.

Lessons learned. Lessons to not forget.

I do sweat.

My metabolism is not broken.

It really is just math.

34

I'm back in the desert with three of the young women I'm lucky to have in my life. The room is a standard, no frills motel room. My daughter-in-law and me in one queen-sized bed. My daughters in the other. Wet bathing suits and rinsed out sports bras over the shower rod. Piles of our belongings and four sets of power cords for phones and computers.

It could be awful. It isn't.

We do our separate things much of the time. Though I'm pushing myself more each day, the girls are in a more strenuous hiking group. Watching them goads me to push myself. One day follows another, and just by showing up and doing the program, I feel as if I've accomplished something.

One night, my youngest and I go with a group of other guests to a movie in town, our first off-campus excursion. It's a love story, touching, funny, sad. The lovers aren't big-time Hollywood movie star gorgeous, which makes them more relatable. The girl nearly dies of a rare illness, which makes the boy realize how much he stands to lose. On the drive back to the resort, my daughter is quiet. Instead of going straight to the room, we sit out by the pool, the air thick and warm.

We're still in the world of the film, left with the emotions it stirred up. She sighs.

"Have you ever felt like that, experienced that kind of love?" she asks.

The question catches me off-guard. I hesitate, wondering how deep, how honest to be with her, with myself.

"I don't think so," I say.

"That's what I thought," she says.

"I mean, perhaps I've felt it, but it hasn't been reciprocated, not the way I think of it. Does that make sense?"

"Yeah."

"It seems like most people settle for parts of it, pieces of the whole package. There are partnerships based on friendship, companionship, shared interests, chemistry or passion." This feels truthful and wise-motherly. "That movie, story book kind of love is rare, I think. Which I guess is why people write books and make movies about it. It makes a good story. It's what we all want, or think we want. In a way, it does us all a disservice, because it is so rare."

"Yeah, it seems rare," she says. "And it's what I want."

"We all do, sweetie."

Does Bob love me like that? What is *that*? Perhaps nothing more than two people believing in the same version of love, in the same story line. Perhaps I haven't experienced that kind of love because I don't let myself.

Is it a fairy tale?

I am beginning to think I could have it with my husband if I let go of the fear, the anger and resentment, if I accept him for what he is. It's a lot of if's.

I love and respect myself as I am.

I love and respect my husband as he is.

I pop the link between my thumbs and forefingers.

Can it really be so simple?

35

I am home from fitness camp and feeling damn good. I lost another five pounds and many inches. Over twenty pounds down in a little over two months, and no headaches. The size fourteen jeans that eluded me for so long are already loose. The size twelves are within sight. I pull out the calendar. Eight weeks until Hawaii. I could be down another ten to twenty by then, in shouting distance of goal well – maybe not *goal*, but good enough to leave the hotel in something other than a muumuu. By the dreaded holiday season, Halloween to New Year's, I'll be slinking into parties with my chin held high, tossing my reverse ombré.

I have high hopes. I have finally cracked the code. It really is just calories in versus calories out.

You got this, D.

I recite my affirmations, expressing gratitude, giving thanks.

$\ominus \ominus \ominus$

Being home is different, harder. In the desert, anything seemed possible. Now, it's Bob and me again. Most of the time we enjoy a platonic ease. I like him. I love him. But are we right, are we good, for one another? That was the intention that stuck in my throat at the center of the labyrinth. Coming home, nothing has changed.

As for Bob, he's thriving in retirement in a way that I have not. He's thrown himself into a new life. One that doesn't involve me. He has given me what I thought I wanted most – time.

Bob is not the problem.

He's just Bob.

Perhaps there is no problem.

Within days of unpacking my bags, it's time to hit the road again. I'm off to "Writers Camp," four days and nights in the Sonoma County hills with two dozen fellow writers and two authors to guide us through writing prompts and generative sessions. Four more nights where I won't have to lie down and wake up to the knowledge that my marriage isn't what it should be.

Repacking my bag, I toss in a pair of size twelve skinny jeans I haven't worn in years. They don't quite fit, but they're *so* close. If I stick with moderation and get in a few good hikes, in a few days they ought to slide right on, a reward for good behavior.

Shelley picks me up and we drive to camp together.

The setting is gorgeous. The hilly grounds of an extensive, well-established organic garden, planted with fruit trees, vines and vegetables. Benches and chairs for contemplation and creativity are tucked away midst the greenery. It really does feel like camp, the Girl Scout and family camps of my youth, trekking from the wood plank cabin I share with Shelley, down a dusty trail to the dining hall, farther downhill, winding through tended rows of vegetables, to picnic tables set under a grape arbor where we write and share, sunshine filtering through the canopy of leaves.

The first evening there's a presentation in the comfy, rustic meeting room. Before taking my seat on a lumpy couch along one wall, I rummage in the small pantry for a clean mug for some coffee. There's a row of mason jars on an open shelf, filled with a tempting array of snacks. Dried fruits and nuts, chocolate chips. I shake the jar of candies and put it back, settling on one plump dried apricot instead. It's been weeks without refined sugar, and I feel good. No point messing with success.

One of the speakers talks about the importance of reframing past events, particularly traumatic or painful ones. We don't want to get stuck in that place, he says, but as writers, we don't want to forget either. We acquire distance, we write about it and then we can reframe what's happened with the perspective of time.

"The past is the past," he says. "For a writer, it's a tremendous resource, a wellspring. But you don't want to become its victim."

I cradle my warm mug with both hands and nod in agreement.

No doubt I've heard or read similar thoughts before. But in this moment, it's as if he's speaking directly to me. My peers' faces blur. His words touch the exact place where I am. I set my coffee down on the arm rest. I lean in. I take notes. I circle words and draw stars and arrows around them.

In the desert, I'd concluded it was time to stop dredging up the past. Now, at camp, a gong goes off in my head. Reframing. This is the next task on my emotional to-do list. It's time to pull the stingers out of my memories, to emasculate them. It's time to find gratification in other ways, to stop wallowing and get over it already.

Just by writing it all down, then rereading and editing my emotional rants so the words make sense, half the task of desensitization has already been accomplished. Putting my editor's cap on has required that I take a giant step back, that I consider what my words say and mean, and that I separate what I've written from what I honestly remember and what I've conflated, exaggerated or filled in over the years, to pump up the emotion, to keep the anger and hurt a living, pulsing thing.

Reliving the past to wallow, to feel sorry for myself, and doing it to get it down right, as accurately as I'm able, are two very different exercises.

I'm a big girl now. A fact that is obvious in the mirror, but not always inside my head. Despite where my fantasies are inclined to keep taking me, I'm no longer the girl or the younger woman I was in those old movies. I've changed. How I view the past and the power I ascribe to it can change, too.

If I want it to, if I let it.

My writing feels good here at camp, natural and unforced. The prompts are ones that fit with where my thoughts are taking me. Or it could be that it's the other way around. Regardless, the words flow, and when the time comes for us to go around the circle and share what we've written, I'm comfortable reading my work out loud.

Our last afternoon, I have a "one on one" with one of two literary agents who have come for the day to meet with us aspiring authors. It is the first, and only occasion when I am anxious at camp. In the hours before we meet, I craft an elevator pitch for the book I'm working on. This book. About a woman of a certain age who is questioning her life's assumptions. A woman who came of age in the sixties, and is now *in* her sixties, and coming to terms with what her life has been. We meet outdoors after another amazing organic meal, the dishes drawing on ingredients from the gardens all around us. We sit opposite one another at a picnic table.

A vaguely exotic-looking brunette, I judge her to be a decade younger than I am. She'd told us all, earlier, that she's interested in women's stories and memoir. I'm hopeful. I begin my spiel. Her eyes never quite seem to focus. Her smile tightens, then freezes in one place. I've lost her attention. I never had it. I imagine I can hear her thoughts—*I'm being paid to be here, and I'm basically a nice person so I'll listen to this graying, desperate-to-be-published woman, whose story is not the least bit interesting.* I'm tempted to stop mid-sentence and slink back to my cabin to commiserate with Shelley.

When I finish, she blinks.

"Does that sound like something you might be interested in looking at, I mean, when I'm done?"

"Well, probably not *me*. But you should finish writing it, of course. I'm sure you'll find someone who's right for it."

I don't know what I wanted her to say. Liar. Of course, I know. *I love this so much. Send it to me the minute you're done. No, send it right now.*

Returning to the cabin, I swing by the meeting room with its tiny kitchen. I find a box of plastic baggies in one of the drawers and fill it with chocolate chips and roasted almonds. Shelley isn't in our room. I crawl under the covers, open a book and set the baggie beside me. I should never have met with the agent. She wasn't blown away by my story. She wasn't even listening.

Besides, I get it. Nothing about my story is extraordinary, sexy or shocking. It's a belated coming-of-age tale. A year to get it right before I lose the wherewithal to even know or care what that means. I need to shake this off. I will, but not before the chocolate chips are gone.

⊖ ⊖ ⊖

It's our last evening together. We have student readings in the lounge. Someone has brought a celebratory box of See's chocolates. I select one and savor it. I eye the box as it makes its way around the room. Someone sets it on a shelf. I will the woman sitting closest to the box of candy to send it around again. I need another. Just one more. She doesn't hear my telepathic plea.

232

As soon as the readings are over, I scramble over to the box of candy and pocket as many pieces as I dare.

The next morning, our last, I pull on the size twelve skinny jeans. They're still too tight. The waistband presses into my belly. The fabric clings to my thighs. I blame the chocolate. If I'd only stayed strong, they would likely have fit. Now that there's no use worrying about it, I sneak by the tiny kitchen to refill my baggie with chocolate chips. Knowing it's there, nestled in the pocket of my jacket, brings comfort.

Tomorrow is another day. Fresh start.

36

Home again. It's the first Saturday in nearly a month without someplace to be. Bob is at the Railroad Museum. He has back-to-back tour guide shifts for much of the day.

It's been two weeks since fitness camp. Writers camp triggered insecurities, which in turn triggered a few days of chocolate frenzy, which brought on my first migraine in a long time.

What part of "refined sugar is my poison'" do I not understand? I felt great for two months. This is not the time to pretend I haven't learned something important about my body and how it works. Like an alcoholic, or any addict, I had a relapse. A wake-up call. Time to regroup and reaffirm. I've come too far to blow it now.

On the plus side, I'm still twenty pounds down and holding.

Five weeks until Hawaii. At a pound a week, 167. Two pounds a week, 160. Either way, or someplace in between, I'll take it.

Gratitude.

Love.

Generosity.

Creativity.

Be good to guinea pigs, to all creatures great and small.

Reframing. That's what I need to do. Put the past in its place. Recast my role.

I drop into the brown chair beside Marmalade Jam and flip back through my notes from those high school years. Michael. Ron. Mark. Other guys who were too *wham, bam, thank you ma'am,* to warrant depiction. These scenes have their villains and their hapless heroine, little old me. Having now retold those stories, for what I hope will be the final time, I get that these people, these men, may have been the villains of my stories, but I was there, too. I wasn't some waif trapped in an abusive home or even a woman caught in a bad relationship with no way out, no where to turn, no resources. I had agency. I chose not to use it.

That's on me.

I get a text from my daughter-in-law. Their fridge has died. Can they bring over the contents of the freezer? Within the half hour, my son arrives with a loaded freezer bag. I help him find spots for ice cream and containers filled with some of the many baked goods his wife whips up for family gatherings. There are tubs of cookie dough and trays of buttery scones.

It's a test. It's always a test. Life is a test.

"How's the writing going, Ma?" my son asks, as he zips up the freezer bag.

"It's good."

"Cool. I'll get out of your hair."

I pick up my laptop and find my place. I've made choices in my life, ones I knew weren't good for me and that I knew I would regret. I've been unkind to myself. My mother's question comes back to me: *Why do you hate yourself?* Why did I? Hell, I don't know. It's a nasty habit, like smoking, drinking, stuffing myself until I want to puke.

I do know I'm tired of it.

I'm not the same girl who made a mistake, who got into a car on the side of the road, who kept getting into that car.

Ron didn't create the girl in the mirror, the one who was

supposed to ask why she hated herself. But he sure as hell didn't do her any favors. I imagine going back in time, standing at his car window and making a different choice. Short of that, I want other girls to see that they don't have to get into the car, they don't have to do things they don't want to, to pretend it doesn't hurt, to pretend it was what they wanted all along, to keep all that shame bottled up inside.

Ron was bad. There isn't any moment I can look back on with fondness, any part of him that touched any part of me in a way that wasn't hard, that didn't diminish, degrade and demean. He made me feel like an ugly girl who did ugly things. I wonder about all the other names in his little black book. How many girls he found who were like me. Lonely. Willing to do what he asked because it made them feel something.

I hope I wasn't the only one. And I hope I was.

A box of ice cream sandwiches my son brought over beckons. They aren't very big, just the right size for a child. But I know myself. One would become two, at which point I'd figure, why not eat the whole package and go buy a new one to replace it?

Instead, I wash my face and comb my hair. I should visit my mother. Increasingly, it's hard to make myself get in the car and go, much easier not to, to forget she's there. I hate myself for it. She is my mother, with no visitors but me and my sisters.

⊖ ⊖ ⊖

The smell closes around me the moment I enter through the sliding glass doors of the senior living facility. The air is stale, saturated with cooking, old sweat, urine and antiseptic cleaners. I breathe through my mouth as I walk down the hallway alongside the dining room. I press the buzzer to the memory care unit and wait to be admitted.

"Your mom is around the back," says the aide who opens

the door for me. "Keeping an eye on things." Her smile is both sympathetic and amused. Mom is a character. Which I suppose is better than being completely non-responsive, or incoherent, the way most of the residents here are.

I find Mom on a padded bench, her back rounded, her white hair held back with a girlish headband and she's staring fixedly at a closed door.

"How did you find me?" she says. "I'm surprised they let you in."

"It was easy."

"But how did you get through the roadblock? I understand all the roads are closed. And there's an electric fence around this place. We're so out of the loop here. Still, I hear things. I keep my eyes open. They don't like it. But it's important to stay informed."

I don't contradict her. Instead, I describe the world beyond the walls that contain her. Her eyes are wide with interest. She lets me hold her hand, something that would never have happened when she had her wits about her.

"You mean we're not at war?" she says.

"No."

"Well, that's a relief. I feel so out of touch sometimes. Thank you for coming."

"I'll try to come again tomorrow," I say, clasping her hand, the skin still soft and pliable.

"That would be nice. It's good to have someone to tell all the things that are rattling around in my head. You can't trust any of these people. You have to be cagey."

A woman leaning heavily on a walker pushes past us. She mumbles to herself, her gaze vacant and fixed.

"Watch out for that one," Mom whispers. "The walker is just an act. She's one of their spies."

I feel bad for not making it to see Mom every day. Even if she doesn't quite know who I am. Even if she doesn't remember that I've been. Even if every time I come it's as if it's the first time.

37

I'd been searching for Liz, my teenage friend after we moved to Mill Valley. We were good friends during confusing times, those early adolescent years when your best friend is your world. We hadn't spoken since I left for college at seventeen. She'd tried to contact me a few times back then, and I'd refused her calls. When I left Marin, I wanted to sever all ties to who and what I'd been.

I find her on Facebook. After a back and forth exchange of messages, we arrange to meet for lunch. At first sight of one another, we both burst into tears.

"I'm so sorry," I say, blubbering in the restaurant's foyer.

"Me, too," she says, shaking her head, though I don't remember her having done anything to be sorry for.

I might not have recognized her in a crowd, but it's Liz. Short, cute Liz with the wide open, blue-gray eyes. Slimmer than I managed to stay, her hair in a stylish pixie rather than the long, wavy dirty-blonde locks I remembered.

"But I should have talked to you," I say. "We should have stayed friends."

"I didn't blame you. I was an awful person back then," she says.

"You weren't."

"Well, I thought I was. Do you remember what your mother said to me that time?"

One evening, Liz had dinner at our house. It was raining, and Mom gave her a ride up the hill to her house, an act of kindness that she turned into an opportunity to get in a dig. Something Mom could never resist. As Liz was climbing out of the car, she turned to my mother to thank her for the ride.

"You have the low-slung ass of a peasant girl," Mom said, to my best, and only, friend, to a thirteen-year-old girl with no mother at home.

"She did have a way with words," Liz says.

"Such a bitch," I say.

"Yeah, but I guess I should thank her for it. When you're as short as I am, even a few extra pounds make a big difference. To this day, I can't look in a mirror without checking out my backside and remembering what your mom said. She thought I was low-class, didn't she?"

I shrug. Mom never liked any of my friends.

"I don't blame her. I was a mess. Dirty hair, shabby clothes, messed-up home life."

"It wasn't your fault."

I always wished my mother could have shown more compassion to my friends. It wasn't in her nature.

"I was so afraid of her," Liz says. "I never forgot what she said to you that time you found the hand mirror under your pillow. Oh, my God, so creepy."

Liz and I bust up laughing.

"Why, *why*, do you hate yourself?" We chant it together, imitating Mom's dramatic inflection.

Sitting in the restaurant, pecking at our salads, it's like coming home after a long time away, nearly fifty years. Mom *had* said some crazy shit. I hadn't made it all up. Liz remembered, too. It's an affirmation.

We reminisce about the time the two of us spent the night on Michael's houseboat. She was supposed to be at my house and me at hers, that ruse of so many teenage girls. We'd spread blankets on the flat roof, gotten high and stared up at the night sky. A friend of my boyfriend's mother joined us on the roof. He was an older white dude who reminded me of Popeye, with shaggy red hair and a grizzled beard.

"He molested me," Liz says, swirling sweetener into her tea. "It was awful. He was older than my dad."

I'd sensed her discomfort at the time, known something wasn't right, but I'd been busy with Michael. In the morning, we'd made our way home, keeping to the back roads in case our parents were out and about.

She'd tried to talk about what happened with the old dude. But my mind had been on other things. It was my fault she was there at all. I'd been too chicken to sneak out on my own.

The waitress refills our waters and removes empty dishes.

"You were special, one I didn't want to lose," Liz says.

"You, too," I say, though I had lost her.

We talk about those long afternoons walking up the highway from school, then hanging out at my house until she had to go home. When Michael and I hooked up, we became a threesome. Michael and me attached at the hip. Liz beside me, likely scurrying to keep up with Michael's long strides. The three of us dressed as much alike as possible, trudging along Shoreline Highway in our dusty cowboy boots and faded denim.

"You two were pretty cute," she says.

"Right?" I say.

My cheeks flush. Liz remembers. I wonder if Michael does. Perhaps not my name, but something about me, about us. You don't forget your first, do you?

⊖ ⊖ ⊖

A few days later, I post a photo of Mom at the Alzheimer's facility, smiling from her bench.

Liz, my new Facebook friend, "likes" it with a heart emoji. She replies with a comment, "That brings back memories."

So many memories. I hope that we can be friends – and not only on Facebook. But it won't be what it once was. We aren't girls anymore. I feel deep down sad for having pushed her away.

I drift into the kitchen and open the freezer. Like a sleepwalker, I rip open the box of ice cream sandwiches. I eat one, two, the whole box. I pull out a container of my daughter-in-law's dough. I arrange three scones on a plate and microwave them. Three scones become six become a dozen. My stomach aches.

I lie down.

When I wake, my head is pounding.

38

The end of September brings my second-to-last writing class, with one more to go in November. I am not where I'd hoped to be. I was moving in the right direction. Then I let it slip away, eyes wide open, as if I wanted to fail. The closer I get to the Hawaii trip, the more compelled I am to stuff my face. After the high of the summer, feeling great, no major headaches, success by any measure, I pissed it away, one indulgent day after another.

With one week until the long-awaited trip to Hawaii, I no longer expect that being in a literal paradise will bring Bob and me any closer. The trip now feels like an obligation, rather than a second honeymoon. For weeks, I've been eating like a drunken sailor. I need to be punished. I don't deserve to succeed. I lost over twenty pounds in three months. I've put ten of it back on in a few short weeks. I can't seem to stop.

I am ashamed.

Disgusted as I am with myself, looking back at where I was a year ago this time, deep in depression, eating entire sacks of Halloween candy, retching on the floor with migraine, I am doing a shade better. I am more conscious of the patterns. And I get to walk my grandson to kindergarten on weekday mornings. When I wake up, there is that to look forward to. With him, I am not my past. I am just Grandma. When I am with my grandchildren, my half empty cup is more than half full. That's the me I want them to see, to remember when it comes for remembering. That is not nothing.

I am in a philosophic frame of mind as Shelley and I carpool to our class in Sonoma County.

"You bring your own food this time?" she asks. Our prior class was just before my first stint at fitness camp. I'd been on my best behavior.

"Hell no."

We check into our rental, an idyllic cottage on a rural road, complete with a bottle of wine and a basket of fresh croissants on the kitchen counter. Shelley is watching her sugar, so the goodies are all mine.

I drive to our teacher's home that first afternoon for a one-on-one meeting. We discuss my progress and what remains to be done. I am candid about not having achieved what I set out to do with my year, about struggling to make peace with the past and to accept myself as I am, wrinkles, roots, emotional warts, all.

"These are feelings, experiences so many women go through," she says. "This is all so relatable."

"Yeah?"

"This story is really about finding and accepting who you are, right?"

I nod, a lump forming in my throat.

"It's the first time I've written about the rape," I tell her. "I mean I've tried writing about it as if it were a story, you know, as fiction. I even workshopped it. Not a good experience."

"I can imagine."

"The comments, especially from the couple of men in the group, were awful. I could tell they knew it was me."

"This is so important," she says. "Telling the truth of what happened to you. The rape, all of it. These are things so many of us have gone through and kept hidden, been ashamed of, been afraid to talk about, been told we shouldn't. Even if none of the other things you hoped to accomplish this year come to pass, the weight loss and whatever else, you will have told this story, you will have literally found your voice. That's huge."

I nod, close to tears.

The next morning, back in workshop, there's no point resisting the platter of pastries. They rest nicely atop the croissants I already enjoyed for breakfast. I eat enough to compensate for the times I haven't touched a crumb, enough to make up for the other women, most of whom don't seem to have any problem resisting. I notice every bite each woman takes. When someone goes in for a second or third slice of cake, it's my cue to do the same.

It's only cake. What's it there for, if not to enjoy?

I float on my teacher's words. It's like she said, I'm finding my voice. I will tell these stories, my stories, because it's time, past time. Others may see themselves in my experiences and take comfort in that. Or, I may decide not to share it. Either way, it feels good to get it out, and if self-expression requires massive quantities of carbohydrates, so be it.

Our leader gives us a few minutes to craft an elevator pitch, a sentence or two that doesn't so much summarize our stories as give enough information that a reader would want to see more. We go around the room, sharing what we've come up with. Here's mine:

After waiting a lifetime to be thin enough, pretty, sexy and successful enough to deserve love and happiness, a woman resolves to take one year—January to January—to learn how to stop waiting and be good enough right now. To get there she must revisit the roots of female shame.

"Oh, that really strikes a cord," one woman says. She's older than I am, seventies, with a professional, no-nonsense air.

"What you said about women's shame. We all have it." She's the last one of us I would have expected to hear that from. Her reaction reinforces for me how universal these feelings are, and how sad that is.

"And the preoccupation with the body and believing that to deserve love, we must be perfect," another woman says.

All around the glass-topped coffee table, I feel their support, their understanding.

That evening, several us go to a music festival on the grounds of a local college. The scene is reminiscent of hippie events of my teenage years, except that the revelers in tie-dye and fringe, passing joints, are white haired and past sixty. The others let loose and dance. I can't relax. I worry I'll look ridiculous, which I know is ridiculous, but I am what I am.

I wander the grounds. One of our group members finds me.

"You okay?" she asks.

"Yeah, just feeling a little out of it."

"Me, too."

It's funny how it happens sometimes. You meet someone and within minutes you're telling them the most intimate details of your life. I tell her about my marriage, about feeling too ugly to have sex. She tells me she has battled with bulimia, that she never believed she was thin or attractive enough, regardless what she saw on the scale or in the mirror.

"But you're gorgeous," I say.

"And you are one of the most beautiful women I've ever met," she says.

Women are like this. We say the things to one another that we long to hear from our partners and lovers.

39

Two years earlier, I enrolled in a writer's workshop in San Francisco, one convened by a seasoned and respected editor. I submitted a "story," a fictionalized recounting of that first encounter with Ron, to be read and critiqued by a group of others like me, a dozen aspiring writers with high hopes of impressing our leader.

We met on the third floor of a blocky decommissioned military building with a view of the Golden Gate Bridge. For four days, we dissected one another's stories. My day on the hot seat, I perched on a folding chair, ready to take it all in.

I'd stayed true to what happened that first time. I only fudged the ending. When Ron asks for the girl's phone number before letting her out of the car, I wrote the scene in such a way that the reader is left to speculate, and perhaps hope, that she had the sense to make one up.

As is typical for the creative writing workshops I've taken since retiring, I didn't participate in the group discussion of my own story. Instead, I followed the ping-ponging conversation with a detached smile, intended to project that I was open and receptive to whatever my classmates had to say. I was all those things. Still, I hoped my story would stand out from the others.

"I really dug this," said a handsome woman, mid-thirties, with a curtain of sleek blonde hair and expertly lacquered nails.

"It reminded me of that Joyce Carol Oates story, the famous one with the serial killer. I mean there's no murder, but it has that feel."

I tried not to glow too obviously at the comparison.

"You mean, *Where Are You Going, Where Have You Been?* I presume you all know it," said our leader. "It's been anthologized many times." His keen blue eyes swept the table, politely challenging. Some of us had heard through the aspiring writers' grapevine that he could be brutal in workshop. If it was true, he'd been on his best behavior with us.

My classmates nodded with varying degrees of conviction. I imagined some didn't know the story, while others disagreed with the comparison.

"So, this character, Ron," our leader said, "he reminds you of Arnold Friend."

"Yes," the woman with the orange nails said. "I believed in Ron. The guy is evil incarnate. I could picture him."

I loved her.

"I don't know." The speaker was an emaciated elderly man with a tight knot of a mouth. "The guy felt like a stereotype to me. There aren't really men like that."

"Oh, but there *are*," said a woman in flowing hippie garb, her eyes round with indignation.

Several other women nodded. They exchanged complicit glances. The three male writers shifted in their seats. My story had the group split along gender lines.

"Yeah, I don't know." The speaker, a young doctor in a peach polo shirt, shook his head. "I don't have a problem with Ron. Sure, there are predators out there. I get that. But the girl, the um, protagonist, she's too passive." He cast an unapologetic glance my way. I imagined he saw right through my ruse.

"The poor girl was frozen with fear," the hippie woman said, her tone strident. Our eyes met for a moment. I loved her, too.

"But wouldn't she have done something?" the doctor said. "I expected her to defend herself, or to at least scream."

"This is what happens," said the woman directly across the table from me. During introductions, she'd told us she was a therapist. She tapped the pages of my story, an authoritative gesture I found comforting. "Girls, women, freeze in these moments," she said. "I've heard it so many times."

"Then I guess I just had trouble relating to her," the doctor said, with a shrug. "She didn't seem to care what was happening to her, so I didn't care." He crossed muscled arms over his chest, a bemused expression on his conventionally handsome mug.

I peeled a strip of skin from my cuticle.

"I understand this is pretty common," our leader said. "That women, especially younger women, feel powerless in these situations. They internalize sexual assaults and often don't tell anyone."

One woman chewed her lower lip. Another closed her eyes and sighed. I imagined they had their own stories.

"That's right," said the therapist. "It's more common than we'd like to think. Even today." Her brown eyes drooped. "Girls are ashamed. They believe they brought it on themselves and that no one will see their side."

"Of course, just because that's the way things happen in life," the editor said, "doesn't mean it serves your fiction. It's hard to generate empathy for a protagonist who lacks agency, who's a passive observer, rather than an active participant. Action and reaction drive story and reveal character."

I stared at the page in front of me. The lines of my story fuzzed. I wrote "passive" three times, underlined it.

The hippie woman leaned forward. Her necklace – metal discs strung on a leather cord – clanked the tabletop. "On a different note," she said, "I wanted more of a blow-by-blow."

The editor raised his bushy brows. At the same time his mouth turned down. The doctor stifled a laugh.

"Oh, I see, very funny," the hippie woman said. "What I mean is, for me the meat of the story, so to speak, is all just sort of implied. We have the vivid details of walking along the road after school, the drive and the changing countryside. There's all that detail. Then we arrive at the climactic moment it's all been building to and the language, at least for me, becomes so much less descriptive. I couldn't picture what was happening in the car. I wanted it to be more fully orchestrated. You know, so I could *see* it." She waved her arms. Her full sleeves extended like the wings of some great bird preparing to lift off.

"I didn't need more," said the therapist. "I knew exactly what was happening."

"I certainly got the gist of it," said the dried up old man.

"I found it gratuitous." The speaker was a chubby post-graduate student who hadn't spoken more than a dozen words in two days of workshop. His cheeks flushed at the effort.

"Interesting," said our leader. "I'm reminded of the fable of the three bears. Not enough, too much and just right." He winked at me.

I had read somewhere that if reviewers have widely disparate views regarding what's working and not working in your writing, then you've probably got it about right. I tried not to beam too brightly. This guy was good.

"Well, I thought the poor girl was going to get herself killed," the hippie woman said. She sounded disappointed. I was tempted to blurt out that the girl thought so too, but that would have broken the workshop rules, and shown my hand.

"Me, too," the doctor said.

"Or at least more brutally assaulted," said the older gentleman.

"I was relieved," says the therapist. "What happened was bad enough."

I exhaled, gratified that the conversation had come back round to the view I preferred. It *had* been bad enough.

I gazed out the windows, their top halves canted to reveal patchy blue and white sky. The occasional seagull careened across my field of vision. A perfect San Francisco afternoon. As the discussion on my piece wound down, I gathered my papers and my thoughts. All in all, I was pleased. No one had suggested it wasn't rape. That had been my biggest worry. The doctor and then the editor had touched a sore spot with their comments about my protagonist's passivity. I scribbled a note to make appropriate changes in the next round of edits. I might have my girl resist more forcefully. Ron could hurt her. She might become a different kind of statistic.

I shoved my things into a canvas book bag and waited for the cluster of eager students pressing around the editor to dissipate.

"Thanks," I said, when I had him to myself. "That was a great discussion, super helpful."

"Good, I'm glad. You do setting well. It's a decent story."

"Good enough for your magazine?" I asked.

"Submit it. You absolutely should."

Which didn't answer my question. He'd made similar comments to most of us.

He held out his marked-up copy of my story. I reached for it. For a moment we were connected, each with a hand on my twenty-page manuscript.

"I have a question for you," he said, not letting go of his end. "Emily didn't give Ron her real phone number. She was smarter than that, right?"

I blinked. His discerning blue eyes were fixed on mine.

"I, I'm not sure."

"I see," he said, with a rueful smile.

And he did. He saw more than I'd intended to reveal.

Leaving the workshop, I climbed the steep concrete staircase to the road that leads down to Fisherman's Wharf. I paused midway and turned to look out over the choppy bay. A cool breeze ruffled my sweater. I rubbed my arms. I was grateful the editor hadn't pierced the flimsy veil of my charade in front of the others. But I imagined he wasn't the only one who'd guessed it was my story, or that I *had* been foolish enough to give Ron my phone number.

I read about a graduate writing program at a prestigious school back east somewhere. The students were given a prompt, to write about their most shameful moment. Something like nine of the ten students went on to have their shame-inspired stories published in respected literary journals. I imagined it didn't hurt that the professor was in a position where he could help them. Still, I took the point to be that shame makes for great stories. It shapes and illuminates character. We are fascinated by it, compelled to peer into dark places, to lift moss-covered stones and cringe at what slithers out. We are reminded of our own secrets.

I never told Liz, or anyone, what happened that afternoon.

Not then. Not ever. Not the truth.

Even in my fictional "story," I skewed what happened. I obscured what still shames me most. My complicity.

Shame adheres.

⊖ ⊖ ⊖

After the San Francisco workshop, I revised my story. I made it clear that Emily, my fictive protagonist, did give Ron her phone number and that, when he dropped her off, she is left wondering if he'll ever call, as if, even after what happened, part of her wants to believe it was a date, that she is split open and torn, wanting him to call, wanting to believe she now has a boyfriend, and afraid that she will have to see him again, be humiliated again, hurt again.

I submitted my revised short story to a different group of reviewers for comment. A few readers expressed appreciation for the portrayal of the teenage psyche, the poignant sadness of a girl so desperate for love and attention that she wonders if what just happened to her might be the prelude to a relationship. But despite the changes, the comments remained overall the same. Passive protagonist. Too predictable.

"The minute the stupid girl got in that car, we all knew she was going to be raped," one reviewer wrote. "I wanted you to mess with my expectations, to make things even worse for her, something besides just the assault."

Multiple reviewers said that the story should begin where I had ended it, that the real story was what happens to this girl after the assault. They were wrong. What happened that first time was a story unto itself, a life changing one. But they were right, too. What happened, and kept happening over the next two years, was what burned it into my psyche, what shaped my sexual identity.

I am still coming to terms with what kind of girl does what I did.

Part Three

40

September 30, we board the plane for Hawaii. Our hotel isn't the luxurious haven I had envisioned. Standard nondescript, furnished apartment decor, but there's a decent kitchen and a balcony with a view of palm trees and a triangle of shimmering ocean. We sit outside. The air is sweet and balmy. Birds find the balcony railing. They cock their sleek little heads at us, anticipating crumbs.

Bob's jaw is stiff. His hands clenched. He seems preoccupied.

"Anything you want to talk about?" I ask.

"Not really."

I imagine he's worried about his younger son, who's been struggling to finish law school.

"How's Bryan doing?" I ask.

"He seemed fine the last time we talked."

Bryan hadn't seemed fine to me.

"You know how when someone you love is unhappy or troubled, even if they don't say anything, you can sense it," I say. "Like when Carolanne was unhappy at school. She didn't want to worry us, but you could hear it in her voice, right?"

"I don't get those messages," Bob says. "I don't have intuition, or whatever it is. When someone tells me they're fine, I take it at face value. End of story."

Maybe it's true that Bob doesn't hear what isn't said, that he doesn't read body language, the nuances, the nonverbal cues inherent in virtually all communication. When one of the kids says, "I'm fine, Dad," that's it, end of conversation.

Maybe it's the same with me, with us. When I'm not actively bitching, he assumes I'm fine. When I get up in the night and don't come back, he assumes I have "simple" insomnia, or a headache. He believes the opposite of what I would, that it's nothing to do with him.

Out on the balcony, listening to the waves, I think I finally get it. All these years, I've felt dismissed, my feelings ignored, when more likely he hasn't heard me or even known that I was attempting to communicate with him.

Our patio chairs are inches apart, the setting is soft and languorous, yet I feel so alone, so cold inside. For years, I've tortured myself over the distance between us, felt guilty over it. I've lain in our bed and felt like an alien intruder. Has he really felt nothing, none of it? Does he think we're fine, that this is what marriage is? Is it, and I'm the one who doesn't get it?

That first night in paradise, we climb into bed.

"Thank you for bringing me to Hawaii," he says.

We kiss good night. It's sweet, but perfunctory. It's fine. We're tired. And I'm certainly not going to make a fool of myself the way I did in that Philadelphia hotel room. Besides, we have a whole week of days and nights to make it better.

His breaths lengthen. I lie there, wide awake, waiting for sleep.

⊖ ⊖ ⊖

In the morning, we have breakfast out on the patio. Coffee, cereal and fruit we bought at the supermarket the day before. Our second day on the island, we explore the rugged coast to the north of our resort in Hana. We hike down a steep trail to the beach below then back up again. I am red-faced and sweating.

It feels good, like my hikes in the Utah desert. We share a fruit smoothie on a windswept hilltop. That evening, we eat at a seafood restaurant with a view of lights twinkling on the bay. A gentle breeze sweeps through the wide-open windows. Bob scrolls through messages on his phone.

"Any news?" I ask.

"Not really."

He sets his phone down and reaches across the table. We hold hands and recount the highlights of the day. It feels like an effort. I feel the weight of us, all the ways we've disappointed one another, not been there for one another.

"Are you happy?" I ask.

"More importantly, are *you*?"

"Do you think I'm beautiful?" I swore I'd never do it again, never go there. I can't help myself.

His face puckers and seems to collapse in on itself. I don't know what this expression means, only that it isn't the reaction I was going for. His mouth is droopy with mock sadness.

"Poor baby," he says, squeezing my hands.

I don't think he's being sarcastic, or purposefully cruel. It feels more like empathy, as if he's commiserating with me. For what? That I had to ask? That he's unable to give me the answer he must know I want?

I always think I'm tossing him an easy one when I fish for compliments, for reassurance. There are so many things he could say that would make it all right, or at least better. It seems so simple. I can't let it go.

"It doesn't even have to be true," I say, smiling, keeping it light.

His expression remains playful, loving. Yet he has no words. It seems impossible that he doesn't get it, that he isn't just being stubborn or even cruel. For twenty-five years, I've been asking for what he can't or won't say. The man is a black box.

"I know it's silly," I say. "It's just that I've really been struggling with how I feel about my body this year."

I *hate* how I sound. But I can't stop.

"I know how hard it is to lose weight," he says. The hell he does. Bob is thinner than he's ever been. "I've complimented your weight loss. I've told you how much better you look, how proud I am of you."

"Better than what?" I say.

"You know what I mean."

"I really don't. Can't you say anything positive? Even if it's a white lie?"

"I can't think on my feet like you do. Words don't come so easily. I need to mull things over," he says.

What's to mull over? This isn't rocket science. Tell your wife she's beautiful, for God's sake.

In the last few books I've read, the men, the husbands, were fairytale perfect, devoted, thoughtful and loving. "You are magic," one husband said, reflecting on the children, the life, his wife had given him. "You are the most beautiful woman I've ever seen," said another, "My life began when I met you. You have given me the best years of my life." Night after starry night they fall asleep "tangled up" in one another's arms. Naked, of course. Have we ever said such things to one another? Anything close?

Rhetorical questions.

If I am his soul mate like my sisters are always telling me, if I am the most beautiful woman in his world, I will have to get there on my own, translating what he doesn't say and doesn't do, making my own meaning or finding it in the Hallmark cards he gives me.

Is romantic love a myth? Is everyone lying, exaggerating or only deluded?

○ ○ ○

In bed, the feelings from dinner cling to me. We are side by side, yet worlds apart. I feel like a prisoner inside my body, unable to move, unable to take his hand, to make the slightest gesture of reconciliation. I am ice. I am steel. I blame myself as much as him. It's gone on too long. I don't know how to start. It's unbearable. I slip out of bed and lie on the living room couch, an awful faux-leather, fold-out contraption that crinkles and rustles with my every move. After a few hours, I give up trying to sleep. When I crawl back into bed, Bob has migrated clear to the opposite edge. If he were to shift even half an inch further, he would tumble to the floor, taking the covers with him.

I am sad for both of us.

○ ○ ○

In the morning, he joins me on the balcony. We swap banalities about Kona coffee, birds and the weather, which is perfect.

"Well?" I ask.

His forehead rumples.

"Mulled anything over?"

"Not really."

I don't know whether this means he doesn't remember our conversation over dinner, or that the mulling didn't bear fruit, or that he simply can't be bothered. I know it's futile to press the issue, that now I'm only being masochistic.

I decide to come clean. I tell Bob what I've been working on all year, how I'm trying to figure out how to accept myself and my life, to reconcile with all of it, our marriage included.

"You're brave to do that, to take the time to analyze it all," he says. "Thanks for telling me. I thought you were still writing some kind of murder mystery."

Really? That was so five years ago. Did he even hear me say that some of it is about us, our marriage?

I know it's ludicrous, this harping on my appearance. Even if I do transform into a svelte, stylish senior cougar, it won't change anything between us, or who we are. I should just accept that he doesn't care what I look like. But I'm a dog with a bone. I can't let it go.

"So," I say. "I have to assume you don't say what I'm begging you to say because you don't want to, because it would be a lie, because attraction has nothing to do with why we are together."

He wears the same hang-dog expression.

I know he won't be mulling this over. There will be nothing coming from him to alter my perception of what we have, of what we are to one another. It's not that we're drifting apart. It's that we've never been together.

I am alone. As is he. I can't fathom an interior world devoid of emotional nuance. I don't want to believe it's true. There must be a secret, a lock to open, if I could only find the key. But what if he's right? What if he is and this is it?

I worry that he's hollow inside. Literally living from moment to moment, the emotional threads between us never taking root, never growing deeper. Other than about the children, we don't reflect or reminisce much about our past. Isn't that what lovers do? Old friends and siblings, too. Close relationships become as much, or more, about a shared history than what's happening right now.

I know so little about my husband. Childhood, past loves, anything at all. I keep scratching, hoping he'll finally reveal himself to me, assuming there must be a self to reveal, a rich interior monologue, a world of fantasy and dreams he's kept hidden. But perhaps not. As he scrolls through the news of the day out on the lanai, perhaps his mind is not elsewhere, not wondering what I'm thinking, not worried about our kids, not hoping that today, tonight, we reconnect. Perhaps there is none of that, each day a blank slate, wiped clean until someone interrupts his equanimity.

I get it.

If we stay together, I am the one who must adjust my expectations. There will be no meeting me halfway.

This is how you spend a week in paradise? And it truly is a paradise. Dramatic skies, darkened or bright with billowing clouds, the ocean a swirl of blues. We swim with the colored fish and sea turtles. And the trees, some with massive, symmetrical canopies, like a woman's skirt in full twirl, others wizened old men, gnarled and twisted, ropey tendrils reaching for the soil, for water, so ancient, both frail and solid.

⊖ ⊖ ⊖

The week in Hawaii has not been the respite we needed. So much beauty wasted on us.

On the plane ride home, I am resigned. I eat the sugared nuts and toffee we bought from a street vendor. I don't care that Bob is watching.

I consider him in the seat beside me. He turns and smiles. There is history here, whether articulated or not. I lean against his shoulder. He softens to accommodate me. I close my eyes. The engine thrums beneath my feet. It occurs to me that perhaps our brains don't even work similarly. My husband is a mystery, a hirsute presence in my life. Perhaps he finds me equally perplexing. Perhaps understanding one another isn't a prerequisite for love. He rests his hand on my thigh. I clasp his fingers as we hurtle through the sky, homeward bound.

41

We are home from Hawaii. The guinea pig squeals at the sound of plastic bags rustling in the kitchen. Luma preens on the kitchen counter. Mocha skitters on the wood floor, struggling for purchase on the slippery surface. I smooth his wispy gray-flecked hair and can feel ribs, the bony ridge of his spine through the fur. We've only been gone a week, yet I imagine he's aged.

Another round of holidays approaches. Halloween through New Years. I beg Bob, as I do every year, to hide the Halloween candy. Yet he returns from running errands and there they are, two chubby sacks of mini candy bars in his office. I don't really think he's taunting me. More likely, he just can't conceive the bounds of my sugar addiction, can't imagine that I will check on those sacks every day to verify that the plastic is still intact.

I am determined not to succumb to the candy this year, for though I've lost some ground and suffered headaches I could have prevented, I haven't, yet, been hit with anything so severe as last fall's devastating migraines. Candy headaches. Pure sugar headaches. I'd prayed to die, anything to stop the pain. I would be a fool to go there again.

This is progress. I am failing better. This is not nothing. Once a sugar addict, always a sugar addict; one taste and it's a slippery slope. Accepting this is progress.

This time last year, Carolanne and I were in darker places.

She worried she'd made the wrong choice and that she wouldn't fit in at Columbia. This year has been much better, with a new roommate and a cadre of friends.

Her name lights up my phone. I move into the family room, to sit beside her guinea pig's cage while we talk.

"What's up?" I ask, pressing the back of one hand to the cage. Marmalade snuffles my fingers.

"Just checking in."

"Everything okay?"

"Yeah, I guess so."

I want her to be blissfully happy, making friends that will last a lifetime, like all the movies about college promise.

"Hey, I wanted to run something by you," she says. "There's this program I want to enroll in. It's a year-long vegan cooking school."

"Concurrent with university?" I ask.

"Well, yeah, It's only two days a week."

"Would you keep your job, too?" She's been working more than half-time at a juice bar.

"Yeah, I love my job. It's the one thing keeping me sane."

"It's a lot," I say. "I don't want you to get overwhelmed. Just college is enough for most people."

"It's good to stay busy. And I can pay for it myself, with what I'm earning."

"If you think you can handle it."

"Thanks, Mom. You think Dad will be okay with it?"

"He just wants you to be happy."

"Yeah, that's what I thought. You know something?'

"Hmm?"

"I've been realizing how fleeting all this is. It's here, then gone. I just think I should do everything I can while I can, while I still want to. I'm not going to have another chance to be this age, with all this freedom. Right?"

We are three thousand miles apart, connected via the ether. Her voice in my ear. Her face in my mind. Marmalade the soft furry link between us. I have always urged my kids to go for it, to pursue their dreams. Those are the things you'll regret on your deathbed, or so I believe, the things you were afraid to try but never stopped wanting, like my dream of being a prolific author.

"I'm so proud of you," I say. "You're right. It is fleeting."

"Send me more photos of Marmie," she says.

I need a counseling session with my own daughter. With all the kids. My older daughter has taken a leave from teaching high school to become a veterinarian. She's brave. Bob, too. He's a rock star volunteer. Reinventing himself post retirement. Now that I have ample time to write and live my best life, I waste it. Maybe it's time for another reboot, another week at fatness camp to reset my priorities. But that's stupid. I squandered it last time. I need to lick this thing on my own.

I lift Marmalade from the cage and set him on the couch. I square up a shot on my phone, then another. It's a challenge to catch his fleeting expressions, those plump lips, the hint of an inscrutable smile.

What is it about the holidays, the approach of another new year? There is the inevitable annual reckoning and reconciliation. As the year winds down, the high hopes and plans hatched in January can't be put off any longer. They are either accomplished, well underway, or they've fallen to the wayside.

This Christmas could be my mother's last, or she could live to be 105. There's no knowing. Each day could be the last, for any of us.

Life *is* fleeting and precious. Why is it so hard to seize the day, harder still to hang onto it?

⊖ ⊖ ⊖

In the early morning, I wander into the kitchen and turn on the light. Before making my first cup of coffee, I cross the room to Marmie's cage to replenish his supply of hay and pellets and freshen his water bottle. He's on his side, beneath the hammock strung in one corner, pink eyes open wide, four little feet stretched out beside him as if he were trotting in his sleep. I stroke his white fur, the orange stripe down his nose. His plump belly is still warm. I'd been so sure we'd lose Mocha first. It wasn't supposed to be Marmalade.

"Oh, sweetie," I say, trying to ease his eyes closed.

Bob joins me beside the cage. He strokes the guinea pig's nose. His face crumples. I set my coffee down and put my arms around him. Bob sobs into my shoulder. Furry creatures bring out the heart in all of us. We pour our unselfconscious love and goodwill into them. He lifts Carolanne's precious pet from the cage and cradles him one last time.

"I'm gonna miss you, little guy," he says, "Such a good boy."

Our daughter has midterms. I will wait for the weekend before I tell her Marmalade is gone. In the meantime, I sew her a dress with lace from my mother's old curtains, channeling my thoughts and wishes for her into the seams.

When I do tell her, she cries, but it's not like the last time she lost one of her beloved pets. She was much younger then and I had worried for her. This time I don't. Carolanne will be fine.

42

I haven't colored my roots since last summer. Other than a little help from Paul, months ago, I've let it be. It's an accomplishment, one thing I haven't fucked up. I miss Paul, the time and attention he gave me. He said I had great hair, that I was amazing, and that he shared my vision for myself. Hyperbole or not, I miss it. I miss his smoky fingers. I miss having someone call me Goddess.

On Monday, I meet an old work friend for breakfast. I wait for her just outside a bakery café, admiring the gleaming case of pastries, cookies and cakes through the plate glass window. My hair is pulled back in a French braid that trails halfway down my spine, all the different colors woven together. I have on my favorite ensemble of the moment. A denim dress that covers all my lumpy bits, a tweedy pumpkin shaped sweater with batwing arms, black leggings and short boots. A woman – she's a little older and rounder than me, short, spiked hair, blonde streaks over red – exits the restaurant, so she sees me from behind first. She reaches the curb and turns to face me.

"Your highlights are absolutely perfect," she says, with a generous smile.

"It's mostly natural." I gloat. I can't help myself. "Just my gray coming in."

"Well. It's what we all want. You look fantastic."

"Thank you so much." I wish Paul could hear.

She steps off the curb then turns to face me again. "Love the outfit, too."

"Wow, you made my day." More than my day. I don't want to be too effusive, but damn. Maybe I really do have a future as a plus-size model for the mature gal.

Now I wonder, was that apple-shaped women coming on to me? I don't think so, not that I've ever had flirtation radar for either sex. I'm owning it, that's all. It's nice. Would it mean more coming from a dude? A nice comment should be a nice comment, regardless of whether the giver is someone I'd have sex with. It's not as if that's a possibility anymore. It's just a conditioned response. Pitiful. I'm 63 and twenty years into my third marriage. The body gets old and crusty, but the brain doesn't catch on. Mom is 95 and batting her lashes at the geezers in the dementia unit. She insists that all the woman are ignorant cows, while the men are intelligent, accomplished and "such good company."

Oh, Mom. Oh, D.

$\ominus$ $\ominus$ $\ominus$

I need a haircut, badly. The bottom six inches are stiff as a whisk broom. But I haven't wanted to risk it without Paul, who's moved to Los Angeles. I break down and make an appointment for a haircut with Juliet's hairdresser, a woman my sister swears has magic fingers, too.

The salon is in midtown Sacramento, on the main floor of a grey and white Victorian on J Street, up a wide wooden staircase, one of the city's many grand old homes.

Carmen is pretty, dark skin and gentle eyes, with long hair that curls down to her waist. She does a nice shampoo and conditioner, massaging my head as she works in the products, scratching my scalp with acrylic nails, getting deep into those spots behind my ears and at the base of my skull. I close my eyes and relax.

She snips away for half an hour, pulling out sections of hair to compare sides and make sure the layers match up. She frowns in concentration and only speaks if I say something first. Otherwise she's all business.

I bet it's not like this with Juliet. I picture them chatting away, giggling and enjoying one another's company, as the scissors snip and gnash and bits of hair waft to the linoleum. I suspect Carmen is comparing me to my sister and finding me a bit of a bore. I can't get my sister out of my head. She's in the room, watching, judging me.

"Does Juliet think I'm crazy for going gray?" I ask.

Carmen stops what's she doing and holds the open scissors away from my head.

"Oh, she wishes you'd color it," she says. "She says she doesn't get it."

Carmen doesn't say that *she* gets it, or that my hair looks good. She returns to the task. I imagine them talking about me, as Carmen slathers dark dye on my sister's roots. I imagine Juliet hoped I'd come to my senses and ask Carmen to make me a brunette again. I assume having now seen me, Carmen agrees with her.

Bitches.

She is a perfectly good hairdresser. But she's not Paul. She does what I ask, but I feel as if her heart isn't in it. He understood what I was after. He was so disappointed when his mother went back to black. "She chickened out," he said. "I guess she just couldn't see herself that way."

Sitting in Carmen's chair, I don't feel brave or beautiful. I don't feel like anyone's goddess. I wonder if I should chicken out, too.

When she's finished drying and styling my hair, Carmen hands me a mirror and turns the chair so I can examine her handiwork from the sides and the back.

"Is this what you wanted?" She sounds tentative, as if she hopes I'm happy with the results, but that she wouldn't be.

I pay with a credit card, overtipping because I'm guilty for harboring ungenerous thoughts about her. I stumble down the wood stairs to the sidewalk. Now it's confirmed, Juliet thinks I look like hell. In the moment, I want to confront her, to hear her to say it to my face. I know I won't. She means too much to me, and I do realize that she has no intention of hurting me, or making me feel bad.

I'm doing that to myself.

43

I make an appointment with the vet for Mocha, a quality of life assessment. I'm glad it's a vet who has seen Mocha before, in better days. He has an older dog, too. I ask him about the smell. He prescribes a medicated shampoo.

"It's old age," he says, scratching behind Mocha's ears. "He's not able to take care of himself anymore."

"How do I know when it's time?" I ask. The last time we were in this position, it was obvious. Miss Kitty was diagnosed with intestinal cancer. With Mocha, it's just the inexorable advance of old age.

"It's a very personal decision," the vet says.

He describes the extremes people go to. Carrying a massive dog outside to potty every few hours because he's no longer ambulatory. And that others don't. Opting to end a pet's life when it becomes the least bit inconvenient.

I already carry Mocha outside several times a day to do his business. But he's light as a baby in my arms, and I love the way he peers up into my eyes, so trusting and patient.

"I look for three things to gauge quality of life," the vet says. "Whether your pet is eating and drinking. Generally able to take care of elimination. I mean, a few accidents in the house is fine, but when incontinence is the norm, that is cause for concern.

Lastly, and perhaps most important of all, is he still happy to see you? Does he wag his tail, for example?"

Of course, this vet has already told me – when I shared with him how much trouble Mocha has with our wood floors – that he solved that problem by buying carpet runners that now snake through every room of the house, so his senior pet doesn't have to struggle so much. Still, the three-part test makes sense.

It's not so easy with humans. Mom often forgets to eat or drink, or she believes she hasn't had a meal and demands another, she's in Depends and, while she generally expresses gratitude for visitors, I have no illusions that she knows who I am.

Mocha still knows me. He follows me from room to room, sniffing for my scent. Perhaps it's that dog memories are more elemental, sensory based and distilled.

44

It's November and the last writers' meeting. Fifth of five. The next time I see these women, we should have all turned our manuscripts in for evaluation. This final session covers advice and suggestions for the revision process and next steps.

I'm not ready for revision. I'm still creating, still figuring out what the hell this year has been about. I want to go back to page one and start over. But this isn't fiction. I can't just roll back time and do it differently. The journey is what it is. I am where I am. There's no fudging that.

Small things. I'm back on the wagon and don't touch the tea cakes, tempting though they are. I'm practically salivating, imagining their moist nuttiness melting in my mouth. But no, I'm strong and virtuous as I rummage for a mid-morning snack in my book bag, a peeled hard-boiled egg and apple slices.

Yep, that's me. All or nothing. Feast or fast.

Whether I partake of the baked goods at each of these five classes has been emblematic of my year's journey. I see that. If this were fiction, I might find it amusing.

We go around the table, each of us providing a brief update on our progress, any challenges or setbacks.

One woman, the older woman who'd responded so viscerally to my theme of female shame, looks as if she's swallowed the proverbial Christmas goose.

"She's already finished her book," the teacher says, beaming at this senior paragon.

"Well, now comes the hard part, the revisions and all," the woman says, bashful, rouged cheeks flushed with pride.

Judging by the other expressions around the glass-topped coffee table, over-broad smiles and round slip-sliding eyes, I'm not the only one who's a tad envious. I imagine that our classmate followed the teacher's recommendations to the letter and completed her three forty-five minute sessions a day without fail, never permitting doubt or insecurity to interrupt her steady progress. I'm also betting she never binge watched half a season of *Weeds* at a sitting, several days running.

I take my turn meeting one-on-one with our teacher in her writing studio, a cozy cottage alongside the main house, connected by a wood plank walkway. She's lit the wood stove, and the small space is warm and inviting. I have a few prepared questions and clutch my latest journal, begun in October, my fourth notebook of 2017, a year of so many words.

"I think it's fine that everything won't be wrapped up with a tidy bow at the end," she says. "It's all right if you don't find your prince and live happily ever after. You're not Elizabeth Gilbert, and this isn't a fairy tale. It's life. I think it's even better this way."

"I hope so," I say. "I'm 63, for God's sake. It's time to figure this stuff out."

"Boy, that really resonates with me," she says. "If not now, when? Facing up to our age after a lifetime of dreams and ideals. Figuring out what worked and what didn't, where are we now."

That's what it is. Wanting to share what it was like coming up when we did, at a time when expectations for women expanded, while the reality remained that in the workplace and in the home, it was still pretty much a man's world. In many ways, the sixties and seventies were confusing, confounding times. The appearance of freedom and experimentation, the so-called sexual revolution and the rest, piercing the glass ceiling.

With the advent of the pill, birth control became, at least in my experience, something for the girl to take care of and worry about. This was before AIDS, before public health campaigns about the risks of sexually transmitted diseases. I never saw a condom – literally. Pregnancy was the only "issue." If you were sexually active, you were on the pill, you were "safe." I scarcely remember being asked. That's how my first pregnancy – and subsequent abortion – happened. I was a sophomore in college. I met a boy at a party. We went back to his apartment. He didn't ask about birth control. I knew I could get pregnant and chose not to say anything. I was that lonely for a connection. The moment felt more important than any consequences.

We had the fairytales of our mother's generation, their dreams for us, the sitcom lives on the television screen. Donna Reed and the rest. Ranch style homes, white shutters and green lawns, husbands who left for work in the morning with a peck on the cheek, then returned after five to supper on the table.

There were new expectations, too. That we would go to college, get jobs, have respectable careers, perhaps even earn more than our husbands, as I eventually did. Yet it still fell most often to the woman to raise the kids, shop, cook and clean. All that remained part of the pact, too. In my experience, it's the rare boomer marriage where it was a true partnership, a 50/50 proposition. The assumptions were there, a mixed bag of subservience and ambition. The roles, the expectations, didn't so much change as they multiplied.

I worked my way up from the secretarial ranks into a position in the state Capitol, where, with rare exceptions, the women held clerical jobs and the men did the fun stuff – writing and analyzing legislation. Female lobbyists were beautiful and sexy.

Their male counterparts were pushy guys with slick hair and expensive suits.

Talking with our leader in the writing class, a woman my exact age, I feel all those threads, the intense specificity of having lived through similar times, having shared a backdrop of history and experience that will never be repeated or experienced in precisely the same way. This is true of any time, any place, yet it feels important that I capture how it was for me, and others of my generation.

It's been a good meeting, yet I'm anxious, unsettled. Perhaps it's realizing that this year, this class, are nearly over. I make my excuses and leave early, grabbing treats from the coffee table on my way out. My stomach is uneasy. Driving away, the ache in my belly, in my ribs and sides, becomes a hole that must be filled. I consume the scones. The ache remains. At the junction with the freeway, I stop at a cafe for a slice of frosted lemon cake and a steamed milk. My stomach is iffy. Coffee wouldn't be good. I sip my creamy milk and consume the lemon cake. The waistband of my leggings digs into my belly, but the ache is still there, the hole isn't filled. I plan my next pit stop, Panera on Interstate 80.

I hope I can make it that far.

My world is reduced to anticipation of putting more into my mouth. All other thoughts recede. So much for the dream of getting rid of this belly. Of being able to get down on the floor to do puzzles with my grandkids.

When is a belly just a belly? When is it no longer an albatross, an impediment, a parasitic bowling ball affixed to my middle, spreading round the sides to my back.

What will I lament on my deathbed? Not the size of the belly. Not whether I ate the scones.

Fuck the scones. Fuck the lemon cake.

Should I? Shouldn't I? That's the game I play as I speed up

I-80. I picture the bakery case, the smell, the taste in my mouth. I exit the freeway. Of course I do. I'm an addict. The worm is in my head. I choose two sugar cookies, big as my outstretched hand, pumpkin-shaped with sugary orange frosting, as close to candy as a cookie can get, just sugar, butter and refined white flour. A baguette, too, and butter, several small tubs of it. I devour one cookie then the other, a continuous motion from the bag in my lap to my mouth, eyes on the traffic, blind fingers scrabbling on my shirt front, in my lap, for wayward crumbs. I'm nauseous after the second cookie, but the white bakery sack isn't empty. There's the loaf of soft French bread, still warm in the center. I'd meant to have it with dinner, to share it with Bob. I finish the loaf before I exit the freeway, minutes from the house. The wastebasket beside the gear shift is overflowing, candy wrappers from Halloween, evidence of other visits to Panera.

Bob is in the garage with the door up when I pull into the driveway. He reaches for the passenger side door.

"Let me help you bring your stuff in."

"That's okay. None of it's important. It can wait," I say, waving him off. "Leave it. I just need to lie down."

I drag myself into the house and collapse on the bed. I sleep for three hours, long enough to digest the ball of refined flour and sugar in my gut.

"I took your car to the carwash," Bob says, when I join him in the living room.

I can't look him in the eye. I imagine he emptied the garbage, saw the evidence of my debauchery.

"You want to see my project?" he says.

"Of course," I say, with a relieved exhale. "You finished?"

"Big presentation to the group Wednesday night."

"Show me," I say.

Bob enrolled in a program to become a certified naturalist. For six weeks, he's attended a three-hour class one evening

276

a week and field trips all day Saturday, to observe and record nature at locations throughout the Sacramento Valley. As his "capstone" project for the class, he put hours into a presentation on owl pellet formation. Owl pellets are these tiny potato-shaped agglomerations comprised of bits of the creatures that owls eat and can't digest – bones, feathers, fur – and that are held in a special organ until they are sufficiently compressed and can be hocked back up.

Bob returns with a glossy poster board. He holds it out for me with an excited gleam in his eye, as if he were presenting one of those giant ceremonial checks for winning a prize or scholarship.

"Wow. It's gorgeous," I say.

It is. Full-color illustrations of every phase of pellet creation, from the owl with a mouse's tail and hindquarters protruding from its beak to the finished pellet suspended midair, being spit back out.

"And here's the accompanying presentation." He hands me half a dozen laminated sheets. He's got a few actual pellets, too, wrapped in foil like tiny jacket potatoes. "These are to pass around. The kids can tear them apart and separate out the bones, the skull and whatnot. Sometimes you can reconstruct an entire skeleton."

"You did an amazing job," I say, meaning it. "I'll bet yours will be the best of the bunch."

"It's done anyway," he says, dismissive, yet by the set of his jaw, his smile, I can tell he's proud.

I've judged Bob sometimes – well, lots of times. For not being more contemplative, for appearing not to ponder what this business of life is all about. There's the presumption that those of us who agonize in our search for meaning are superior somehow, more complex, and that complex means better, deeper, more meaningful. Perhaps that's bullshit. I think of the hours he spent putting all this together. I can't know where his mind goes as he researches owl pellets, or anything else. I can't know where anyone's mind goes or doesn't go. Who am I to say my contemplative time is any more profound than his?

My mind was alive as I pinned the pattern to fabric and cut out a dress for my daughter, as the sewing machine whirred and a dozen pieces of cloth became something new. Perhaps Bob's thoughts are just as fluid when he makes something. The way he makes meaning and sense of life looks different, so different that I lose faith he cares, that he's looking at all, that he wants the same things I do. Peace of mind, love, appreciation, security.

I have waited all my life for a man to say the prescribed magic words to me, to perform the prescribed grand gestures. Lacking that, I have felt cheated out of my due of Lifetime movie moments. I have assumed I'm not good enough, that true, everlasting love hasn't happened for me because I don't deserve it, because I'm not beautiful enough, good enough, because I'm *me*.

He's with me, so I assume he must be what I deserve, that he must not be good enough either, that we must both have settled for less than we should have. I have no prince and he no princess, only each other.

Where does all this come from? What good has it ever done me? How do I stop?

It comes from stories, fairytales and romantic movies. It comes from having an emotionally distant father. It comes from wanting to be pretty and popular and to prove my mother wrong. It comes from wanting to impress people. It comes from a lifetime of never reaching that elusive place I aspired to, of never winning the boy's heart, never being pledged love ever-lasting, until death do us part. It comes from expectations that may have been wrong-headed, or at least misplaced and unrealistic. And is any of this good a reason, a logical reason, to hold my husband at arm's length until he utters the magic words?

By now I've ample evidence that he doesn't know the magic combination of words and deeds that will show me he's the one I've been waiting for. And they can't really be learned or coerced. Besides, it's been so long, it wouldn't feel sincere, just as the staged marriage proposal only made it worse. I have created a Gordian knot, a Catch-22. I am a woman who won't be satisfied, who can't be satisfied. That's the corner I've spent my life backing into, then defending.

He says he loves me.

We're still together after twenty years.

He cleaned up my candy and pastry wrappers and never said a word about it. I'm the one who rubbed it in my face.

I cling to the version of Bob as he was, as I perceived him to be, in the painful months before we married. I cling to the times he's hurt me, disappointed me, made me feel unattractive. Did he do these things, or did I just interpret his responses that way? Can I now choose to perceive them differently, have them affect me differently? Why let things that happened over forty, twenty, ten years ago matter so much, carry so much weight? Why is one harsh or hurtful word more resonant, more weighted, than "I love you" repeated one thousand times?

I've spent a lifetime lamenting what isn't.

I imagine lots of people feel this way, especially those of a certain age, past any number where we can pretend this business of being alive isn't more than half over. We've held onto these pictures, images of what we want, what we think we should be and have and achieve, and now it's time to go for it or shut up already. It's time to look at what I've been pining for all my life and ask if that's still it, do I need that anymore, or am I bigger girl now? Does my piano have more than one insistent sour note to plink?

θ θ θ

The next morning, I wake with a massive headache. I slip a migraine tablet under my tongue and wait for it to dissolve, hoping the pain will subside to where I can function. It doesn't. I can't do anything but take myself to a quiet, dark place until it passes. It's my fault. I invited this headache with each sugary bite and with full knowledge that this was the likely outcome. Did I do it on purpose? Did I make myself miserable so that there was no possibility I could be productive? Am I that foolish, that deep in denial, that addicted to sugar, that insane?

Have I changed at all, made any progress at all? I believe I have, though not in the clear, straightforward ways I'd hoped for.

I am getting there, by degrees. What's shifting most, perhaps, is where *there* is. I ask more questions. I don't let myself off so easily. I remind myself that eating won't help. I say it out loud. I write the words down. Sometimes it even works. I ask myself what *will* help. Like going for a walk or doing something for someone else.

It's fall, the season for binging, and I am binging. There is that. Yet I am conscious, more conscious than last year, perhaps than I've ever been before, of how I feel, physically and emotionally. I don't care so much about the tummy rolls and the waddle. I'd rather they weren't there, but if I feel good – meaning, mostly, if my head doesn't hurt – then I'm good.

It's a start, and it's November. Oh, my goodness.

45

I volunteer with a program that holds creative writing workshops for teens. We write to prompts, kids, adult mentors and teachers alike, then those who want to share their work by reading it out loud. The only feedback provided is positive: what we liked, what stuck with us. Today's session is good. The teacher provides a prompt to construct a found poem, one inspired by the words of others.

I remember things my kids and grandkids have said. Funny, memorable words and phrases. I jot them all down, then string them together to tell a story. From the mouths of babes. "Life is too big," my eldest said when he was three. "It's a beautiful world," my nephew's words at four or five, blinking at the view beyond the car window, sunlight slanting through the forest canopy, a pattern of splintered light and dappled shadow. "I did it by self," my three-year-old granddaughter's refrain, up tilted face filled with pride. My stepson's, "Does it hurt, Daddy?" as he stroked his father's wrinkled forehead.

The boy across from me in class is as big as a big man – broad, slumped shoulders, stubbly face. He's always huddled beneath a dark hoodie, never looks up. This morning, he raises his hand during sharing time, almost imperceptibly, just two fingers up then down, his arm held close to his body. But I see, and he sees me see. It's hard to decipher the name scrawled on his tented card. Twice, three times, the teacher leading the discussion calls for volunteers and doesn't see the boy's timid flag.

"Ruth," I say, "I think Raymond wants to share."

An expectant ripple courses round the tables set in a square.

"*Raymond?*" she says.

He blushes and blinks as if the light is too bright. He pulls the hood of his hoodie down to his nose then lets it go. He reads his poem about memories. How we want to hold on to some of them forever, how we'd relive them if we could, while there are others we wish would disappear, how it's all in our heads, all the time, that confusing swirl of memory.

I will never see that boy as big as a man the same again. He's now Raymond who ponders memories.

When I get home, I tell my husband about it.

"Very cool," he says. "He finally felt safe enough to share."

Bob gets it. I'm surprised. Perhaps I shouldn't be.

⊖ ⊖ ⊖

In the evening, the two of us attend an event at the Sacramento Poetry Center, readings from the eighth annual compilation of stories and poems from a long-standing writing group. It's my second year to be included in their chapbook. I'm anxious. A short nonfiction piece of mine is included, one I wrote this past summer after returning from fitness camp, about doing ten things I'd never done before. Now those accomplishments, the ways I pushed myself and was glad of it, feel far removed, almost fake. I fell from that high so fast, undid the progress, forgot the lessons learned, didn't value any of it enough to hold onto how good I felt. I almost don't go. I almost don't read.

But I do go. Another way I would likely not have pushed myself a year ago.

I stand at the microphone. In my reading glasses, the faces in the audience are fuzzed and indistinct, a sea of pastel smudges. This adds to my sense of disconnect. I find my place in the pamphlet and read about standing on a paddle board for the first time, sweating buckets and sighting a rare desert tortoise. What I wrote three months ago, so recent, yet so distant, these are joyous and triumphant words. Some of that spirit seeps back into me as I read. That was me challenging my body. Me connecting with my thoughts beneath the pre-dawn sky. Me finding physical strength I didn't know I had. Me headache-free and hopeful.

That was me. That can still be me.

46

I don't know how it happened. Well, I do know. What I mean is, there was no decision, no bright line I crossed. Bite by bite, choice by choice, day by day, since September I've regained all the weight I lost this summer, perhaps more. I can tell because nothing but the loosest of clothing fits. I won't get on a scale. That would just be masochistic.

I lost then regained close to twenty-five pounds in two months. This can't be good for a body. I could beat myself up over it. But what's the use? I regret it. I would prefer that it not have happened. But I could have stopped and I didn't. I could be forty pounds down by now if I'd stayed focused on that as something that mattered to me. It's all on me. Literally.

The Tuesday before Thanksgiving, Roxanne and I join Mom for a special meal at the Alzheimer's home. It's a buffet, out in the main dining room. Mother hasn't been outside the locked memory care unit in a long time. She's disoriented and uneasy.

"We're not supposed to be here," she says. "You're going to get me in trouble. I don't want to go back to jail."

"We're fine," Roxanne says. "Happy Thanksgiving, Mom."

Mom searches around her chair, at her feet, beneath her skirt. "Where's my purse? It has all my money. I won't be able to pay the rent."

"You left it in your room. It's fine."

"The hell you say. I want to go home, now."

"But it's Thanksgiving dinner, Mom," my sister says.

"Oh, you," Mom says. "You always were a bitch. I bet you stole my purse."

Our plates are cleared for pie. And with the first sweet bite, Mother's mood shifts. She rests her hands on the table. Her eyes are bright, as if she's just remembered something important.

"You know what's so wonderful?" she asks, with a pleased smile.

"What, Mom?" we say, in unison, though we both know what's coming. She asks us the same question at least once during every visit.

"That you all get along," she says. "You don't fight. You have no idea how rare that is."

"Yeah, we never fight," I say, kicking my sister under the table.

⊖ ⊖ ⊖

On turkey day, I put on a nice spread. We're a big group, sisters, children, grandchildren and a few added guests. When we go around the table saying what we're thankful for, my grandson says, "I'm thankful for Grandma and Grandpa."

I love this moment. So much.

The plan has been that between turkey and dessert, we'll all walk to the neighborhood park for a game of family baseball, my grandson's favorite sport. Though we've been talking it up for weeks, there are murmurs around the table. We are too stuffed to move. We hope he's forgotten.

"Is it time for baseball?" he asks, tugging at his father's shirt.

My son pats his stomach. He stretches his arms overhead and looks around the table, taking stock. "Um, maybe not, son. How about just a walk around the block?"

Elliott's face falls. His mouth goes pouty. His eyebrows form an angry v. "But you promised." He stomps his foot, a petulant child, something he rarely is. "We brought my bat and glove."

"There, there," my son says.

Elliott is on the verge of crying.

I whisper to my son, "We did promise. He's been looking forward to this. We don't have to play for long. Just a few innings."

So we troop the half mile to the park and choose teams. Elliott's face glows. We play several innings. My grandson gets a good high hit, a fly ball into center field. Bob catches it.

"You're out," Bob calls out, using his hands as a megaphone.

Elliott keeps running. He rounds third and slides into home, pumping his little fist.

"And I got a home run," he shouts back at Bob, bouncing like a pogo stick. "An in-the-park home run!"

Roxanne hams it up at the pitcher's mound, doing something approximating the running man, before each wind up. Juliet, in skinny jeans and a puffy vest, looks as young as her two sons. There we are, the three of us, mothers and grandmothers, still playing the parts Dad assigned us when we were kids. The funny one, the pretty one, the smart one.

In truth, my sisters are all those things and more. As for me, my belly is too big and my pants are too tight. I'm no good at bat. Or in the field. I guard third base with my granddaughter in my arms, meaning I won't be of much use if a ball does come my way. I hug her close and press my nose to her shiny black hair.

I'm lucky. I do know that.

⊖ ⊖ ⊖

On Monday morning, Elliott and I walk the six blocks to kindergarten. We sit in the cafeteria while he eats breakfast.

Cereal, graham crackers and fruit. The same choices every day. He watches every move the other kids make. I watch him watch, taking in the world, forming impressions.

"I want to make something for everyone for Christmas," I say.

"You mean sewing," he says.

I've been sewing up a storm lately. Using some of my mother's old fabrics to fashion new things for the girls.

"Yeah, something easy, like pajamas."

He jabs a pear chunk with his spork.

"Want to help me pick out fabrics?" He nods, the spork bobbing up and down in his mouth. "What about your family?" I ask him. "What kinds of designs for them?"

"Superheroes," he says.

"What about Carolanne and Grace?" I ask.

"Not superheroes," he says. "Animals?"

"That's good. Grace loves dogs, like wiener dogs—those are cute."

He grins, showing me his gums—three teeth missing along the top. "And guinea pigs for Carolanne," he says. I make a face, the corners of my mouth pulled down. "Too sad, right?" he says, matching my expression. "Because Marmalade is in heaven."

Our eyes meet. His are soft. He understands.

"He was so cute, right, Grandma?"

"He was," I say. "He really was."

On the weekend, Elliott accompanies me to the fabric store to make our choices.

"Can you keep it a secret?" I ask, pressing a finger to my lip. "Only you and I can know about this, okay?"

He lifts a bolt of fabric that's as tall as he is from the display. "I promise," he says, struggling to tip it into our shopping cart.

We decide on hedgehogs for Carolanne.

I receive an e-mail from my uncle, Mom's younger brother, her only sibling. He's in his eighties and lives in Washington. He's been promising to visit for several years now.

"I'm wondering if I should still make the trip," he writes. "If she won't recognize me, perhaps there's no point."

I understand what he means. I think that sometimes, too. Yet when I visit, there's almost always a moment when I feel a connection to the woman she used to be. It's as if she's trapped inside. If you aren't patient, if you don't give her enough time to relax into her thoughts, she stays trapped.

"She's still in there," my sisters and I say to one another when one of those moments happens, when we see a glimmer of the mother we remember.

That isn't the only reason we visit. I imagine that even when she doesn't seem to know who I am exactly, she senses the familiarity, the bond. She feels safe. She doesn't know me, but neither am I a stranger, not like the workers and the other patients. I'm some other thing. She can't put the words to it, but it's there, the connection that goes back, that touches something deeper. Daughter. Family. Home. Perhaps it's only that I want to believe this, what I need to believe when I take her hand.

I hope someone will be there to take my hand when the time for that comes, and that if they wonder if it matters anymore, they'll decide that it does.

47

Halloween and Thanksgiving. Done. Christmas and New Year's. On the docket. The annual trip to Bob's step-relatives in Southern California. Nine pairs of pajama pants to sew. Super-heroes done. On to the animals, beginning with hedgehogs for Carolanne, whales for Grace.

It's an in-service day at Elliott's school. Bob and I babysit so his parents can work. My grandson teaches me chess. Some of the moves he describes are so complicated, I guess that he's made them up. Once we get playing, the rules change mid-move, generally to his advantage.

I ask Elliott if he's kept our secret about the Christmas sewing project.

His dark eyes are merry. "I did, Grandma. I told my mom we're all getting 'fabric' for Christmas. She doesn't know it's really pajamas," he says, giggling with complicity so his shoulders wobble. "Only we know, right?"

I show him the pattern, sheets of flimsy tissue paper in the shape of legs. Long legs for the guys, medium ones for the women, shorter ones for him and his sister.

"For building the pajamas," he says. "Like Lego instructions."

He eyes my sewing machine, set up on the dining table, the folded fabrics and sheets of tissue paper.

"It's going to be that," he says, studying the photo on the front of the pattern, the perfect nuclear family in matching PJs.

I remember sitting at my grandmother's side as she sewed, knitted and crocheted. I believed there was magic in her fingers, wisdom in her puckered lips and wrinkled earlobes as she concentrated on the task at hand. When I was about Elliott's age, my family visited my grandparents in Oregon for Christmas. There was snow, a rarity for a San Francisco girl. Grandma Dorothy gave me the important task of rearranging her sewing basket. Rewinding strands of ribbon, bric-a-brac and elastic, tidying the pink satin pin cushion, the tiny glass jars of buttons and fasteners.

She made our red felt Christmas stockings. My sisters and I still use them every year. After over 60 years of use, the bells on the bottom haven't tarnished, the felt hasn't pilled or thinned and the tiny felt toys, trains and trees that decorate the stockings are still colorful, garnished with sequins and colored beads.

Now I'm Grandma Dorothy.

I compare the stockings I made for my children, and now the grandchildren, to my grandmother's. I wish she'd been around to remind me to buy high quality wool felt. The white felt I used for the grandkids' stockings is so thin you can see through it. I imagine that when my grandmother went shopping for materials, she didn't have to worry about durability, about the cheapness of some of the goods, synthetic fabrics that wouldn't last for more than a few years. I'm tempted to tear the ones I made apart and remake them in her memory, with the hope that, like the ones she made for us, they will still be taken out of storage each December, far out into the future, when my grandchildren have families of their own.

48

I've stopped weighing myself. I know it's bad news. I'm not prepared to do anything about it, so what's the use? Now that this year of transformation is winding down, here's my new thought: I took a year to reflect. I've done plenty of that. I need another year to act on it all. A cop out, perhaps. But better than beating myself up over what isn't. I'm sewing pajamas, spending time with family and friends, sorting through memories and checking them twice.

Christmas is hard enough as it is, without the added pressure of self-improvement.

It was a December, just before my fortieth birthday, when Bob and I started dating. It was Christmas two years later when he gave me that mother's ring, when I'd anticipated another kind ring. The Christmas after that I was pregnant, determined to have the baby with or without him. Two months later, prompted by my mother's intervention, we were married.

For the first several years of our marriage, we memorialized the holidays with a photo of our inexpertly blended family of seven. Several of these photos now rest in the dining room china cabinet. In the first one, I'm in the center with our baby in my arms, my daughter and son to my left. Bob stands on the far right, his two sons separating us. Even for the family photo, we'd lined up by sides – he and his boys, me and my kids.

Over the years, the borders blurred, but they never entirely disappeared. I remember thinking, when we were in the thick of it, with all the kids still at home, that step-parenting was the hardest thing I'd ever done, way tougher than being a single mom, struggling to pay the bills on my own. That sense has blurred now, too. It's not in front of me, so I don't often think about it. It wasn't perfect, yet our big slapped-together family survived, some of us more bruised by the experience than others.

Carolanne was always Switzerland. Neutral territory. Neither us or them, a child for us all.

⊖ ⊖ ⊖

Roxanne is living with us now, when she's not in Montana with one of her daughters. There's plenty of room to spare, the entire upstairs. My sister brings good humor into the house, an abiding optimism and energy that Bob and I tend to lack. She fills the quiet, lonely spaces that sometimes need filling. She also brings the flu, a nasty strain that hits all three of us, one after the other, in rapid succession, the week before we are due to drive to Southern California for the annual get together with Bob's stepmother and the extended family.

Weak from flu, we're tempted to cancel the trip. There are also devastating wildfires burning close to the party venue, parts of which have already been evacuated. Though he was the last to come down sick, Bob is determined to go.

The day of the trip, Bob hasn't eaten solid food in several days. He's gaunt and gray. I drive while he naps. We check into a hotel an hour and a half north of our ultimate destination. He has a few spoonfuls of soup for supper.

Next morning, I change into the dress I bought a few days before. It's voluminous, a sort of Mexican peasant dress, black with white embroidery around the neckline and sleeves. I think it looks all right and hope that the color scheme is dramatic enough that it passes for a party dress.

"You look handsome," I say, when he's got his suit on. "Too skinny, but nice."

Bob smiles.

"Am I too casual?" I ask, which I decide isn't really fishing for a complement, so it's okay.

He cocks his head and squints at me. "You look. . .festive," he says.

I wait, hoping for more. But no. He's packing his bag. I'm glad I didn't stick my neck out, didn't grovel. Letting it be shows progress, doesn't it?

The party is good. Everyone is kind and thoughtful. Several of the women compliment my hair. Women always compliment my hair.

"I love your dress," one of the spouses says. "Where'd you find it?"

"Old Navy," I say.

"*Oh*, I thought it was an ethnic costume, something 'cultural.' But it looks great."

I decide it's a compliment and don't parse it for hidden meanings. That too is progress.

⊖ ⊖ ⊖

Sunday morning, after the party, the advertised hot breakfast at the motel isn't happening. The power is out in the kitchen, and everywhere else. Another consequence of the fires that continue to spread, still only ten percent contained. Evacuees from area nursing homes fill the dim dining room, assisted by their care workers. Overnight, the grounds have been transformed into a gray winter wonderland. Fallen ash coats trees, asphalt, the roofs of cars. I start the car. It's hard to see out the windows for all the ash.

"Don't use the windshield wipers," Bob says. "They'll turn the ash to mush. Let the wind do the job."

He's right. As I accelerate out of the lot, clumps of ashes lift into the air like dirty snow.

Driving north from Santa Barbara, a thick brown blanket blots out the sun. It seems to go on forever, no edge in sight, as if all Southern California is burning. I recall the prior year's journey. As we'd motored up Interstate 5, mile after relentless mile, I'd fumed over what he'd said and not said. Not that he noticed.

This year it's there, but in the background, vague, amorphous, inconsequential. A sort of "it would have been nice, but oh, well," feeling. I don't say a word, about my "feelings," or much else. I wait for him to speak, to say anything other than banalities about when and where to stop. Mile after mile. Hour after hour. Tumbleweeds, roadside litter and trucks pulling into the passing lane, always on the uphill. I examine the silence, flip it over in my mind, checking both sides like a pancake on the griddle. Is it companionable or exclusionary, grudging or distracted? There's no knowing what it is for him. As for me, I can choose.

I decide it's just silence.

$\ominus \ominus \ominus$

Home again. Mocha is sound asleep. When I lean over his basket, he opens one eye. His tail flutters like a ragged feather duster.

The instant I hear his toenails on the wood floor, I whisk him outside before he has a chance to pee in the house. I cradle him and sniff his limp, musty paws. They have that stale cornflake smell. His rib cage and the ridge of his spine press into my hands. He seems to shrink more each day. My father was the same way in the months before he died. The body doesn't metabolize the way it once did. It begins to shut down. I imagine that has something to do with the way Mocha smells.

I sew. Finishing the hedgehogs and the whales. Tomorrow it's on to dogs for my stepsons.

In the afternoon, I visit Mom. She's on a bench with a clear view of the door to the outer hallway.

"How long have you been hiding in that room?" she says, after I come through the door and sit down beside her.

"It's not a room, Mom. Just the door to the lobby. They keep it locked so people can't wander in off the street."

"Well, that's a relief. Where are those other girls?"

"My sisters?"

She squints at me. I babble about Roxanne and Juliet, using their names, and their children's names, to reinforce any remnant of memory, to try to attach her question about "other girls" to her family.

The squint remains.

She rummages in her handbag and pulls out a ratty Kleenex. "One day," Mom says, "when I have lots of money, I'm going to buy a whole pile of these little sheets of paper for blowing your nose." She wipes her nose, refolds the soiled tissue, and stuffs it back into the stained handbag that never leaves her sight.

"I could fill your Christmas stocking with them," I say.

"*Really?*" she says. "I had no idea you could do that?"

⊖ ⊖ ⊖

I meet Shelley for our weekly session of gossip, moral support and cafe writing. I need all three. We only have a few weeks to finish and submit our draft manuscripts. Not that there's school credit or anything like that involved, and the money's spent. But during a year that's felt more like spelunking than mountain climbing, I kept writing no matter what else I wasn't doing. That is so not nothing.

We order from the tattooed barista who has complimented my favorite pair of oval earrings at least ten times this past year.

"I love circles," she says, like she has every other time. "It's such a powerful symbol of, you know, unity and ..." Her words trail off, as she waves vague circular patterns over the credit card gismo.

Shelley and I settle into our usual spots on the one cracked-vinyl sofa and matching chair.

"I have no idea how to end this thing," I say, sipping my almond milk latte. "I haven't accomplished anything I set out to this year. It's for sure not a success story."

"I disagree," she says. "You may not have met all of your goals, but you *are* different."

"You think?"

"You seem happier," she says. "More relaxed. You really do. There's a lightness about you that wasn't there before."

"Really?"

"Totally."

We sip our drinks.

"Yeah, I guess I am happy," I say. "Fat and happy, but still, happy."

"And, you wrote a book," she says, raising a finger to emphasize her point, like the good teacher she is.

"You, too."

We toast one another with our coffee drinks.

49

The week before Christmas is a flurry of cutting and sewing and inserting elastic. In addition to the superheroes, hedgehogs and whales, there are trains (for Bob), dogs, dog bones, dogs wearing glasses, and foxes. All five kids make it home for the holiday, plus two spouses and the grandkids. I use one pattern for all the adults, adjusting to account for differences in size and height.

On Christmas morning, as all the pajama pants are opened simultaneously, my biggest fear is that they will be too small for the guys. But they're massive, so long and voluminous it's comical. I offer to turn them all into M.C. Hammer pants by adding elastic to the ankles.

"Those are called joggers now," my son's wife informs me.

"I want joggers," my grandson says, though his pair fits just fine.

Everyone takes me up on the Hammer pants offer, everyone but Bob.

"They're perfect," he says, tucking the long cuffs into his new Christmas socks, so the legs poof like harem pants.

I take a group photo on the stairs, everyone with their new PJ bottoms over their clothes. I compare it to that first Christmas photograph from twenty years ago, when the lines between his, hers and ours felt so stark. Now, the lineup may look the same.

My husband, his sons and one daughter-in-law are grouped together in the top row. But it's not for the same reasons. The staging has more to do with height than family loyalties. They are the six footers. The grandkids occupy the bottom step, hamming it up. I imagine the borders of Switzerland now extend beyond Carolanne, to include the grandkids. And while I won't claim the relationships between step siblings are all close, we are a family, and in every family, no matter its configuration, there are stronger and weaker links. Not all siblings are so fortunate as my sisters and me.

Christmas Day coincides with my two daughters' fourth annual "non-vegan" day, the one day a year when they allow themselves dairy and eggs. Which means the day's menu revolves around packing in as many buttery, cheesy, creamy baked goods, candies, pasta and pizza as possible. Inspired by "The British Baking Show," my son brings homemade Brioche, and his wife makes a white chocolate-chip cheese cake, a buttery shortbread cookie and a to-die-for chocolate meringue cookie.

The next morning, I visit Mom with my daughters. We bring her gifts, a flannel nightgown and the knit Christmas stocking with her name on it. It's filled with those little slips of paper for blowing your nose, otherwise known as Kleenex, a tube of toothpaste, a new toothbrush and a few treats. She studies a package of cookies, turning it over in her hands, as if she has no idea what it might be.

"Just some cookies, Mom," I say.

"Well, *excuse* me. I guess I'm not up on all the latest things."

"Any wishes for the New Year?" I ask her.

"To enjoy another year, just like this one," she says.

I don't know what she sees before her. Not the locked memory care ward. Not the other residents, moving in senseless circles, mumbling into their chests. Not her own face in the mirror.

"I'm only in my sixties, after all," she says.

"And healthy. You could easily live to be one hundred," I say.

She laughs. But at 95, it isn't unlikely. The body is tenacious. It holds on.

⊖ ⊖ ⊖

Two days after Christmas, the family gets together again, this time augmented with my sisters and their children and grandchildren. We all trickle down the street to the park for another game of baseball. My grandson leads the way, anxious to lay claim to the field, concerned that some other group of holiday revelers might grab it first.

I'm covering second base, chasing a grounder, one eye on my sister Juliet, planning to tag her out, the other on the ball, when my feet get twisted and I'm falling. It seems to happen in slow motion. I'm aware of my body doing things it shouldn't. Twisting mid-air like a red vine, before I hit the ground with a heavy thud. There's pain, sharp and shooting between my ribs. Bob helps me up, and I limp to the sidelines.

"Where are you going, Grandma?" Elliott asks, shouting from across the field.

"Grandma's on the DL," Bob shouts back, using the baseball jargon.

The game continues.

The next day my ribs hurt like hell. Sitting still is okay, or lying on my right side, motionless. Anything else. Not so good. Which sort of puts a monkey wrench in my plans to start working off the extra holiday flab. Ah well, there's always next year.

⊖ ⊖ ⊖

My girls pack for New York, both headed back to school. Grace kneels beside Mocha's basket in the front room, one of three baskets placed throughout the house, so he's never far from a comfy landing spot.

"You don't smell so good, buddy," she says.

"Do you have any advice for me?" I ask.

"I don't think it's time, not yet," she says. "I mean, he doesn't seem to be in pain."

"Yeah, not yet. But soon."

She scratches behind his ears. "Goodbye, buddy. This might be it."

We've been saying the same thing about my mother for at least the last five years.

Both my sisters call, to check on how I'm doing after the baseball debacle.

"You were amazing," Juliet says. "You twisted in the air like three times. Elliott was so impressed. Me, too."

"Yeah, right," I say, laughing, then yelping and clutching my ribs.

"No, I mean it. It looked totally intentional. You had the moves."

"Don't make me laugh. It hurts too much."

"I wish I'd filmed it. Play of the day."

"Even if I didn't get the out?"

"Totally."

I hurt and I can't do much about it. Painkillers make me nauseous. Even so, what Juliet said makes me glow. I did have the moves. At least I tried. My body just wasn't up to it.

⊖ ⊖ ⊖

It's too early to get up, even for me. But I can't sleep. I'm not festering over something Bob said or didn't say, or because my fattest fat pants are suddenly too snug. It's just my damn baseball injury. I like saying that. Makes it seem more legit.

"I hurt myself playing baseball," I say, and eyebrows go up, like wow, way to go, grandma.

I've held off going to the doctor because I didn't want to face the scale. But it hurts like hell, even after a full week, so I go. When I tell the nurse that I don't want to get weighed, she shrugs and says, "Okay." Easy as that. My doctor says there's no point getting an x-ray. My sprained ribs just need to heal, which could take one to three months.

"On the bright side, you now have your doctor's recommendation *not* to exercise." His shoulders heave on that one, since he's been urging me to be more active for years.

50

I lie on my right side beside Bob, very still. Yet the sharp pain is there, beneath my breast and under my arm. I shift onto my back and doze, but only for a moment. My own snores wake me.

I ease out of bed, stifling a yelp as pain shoots up my side. If I can't sleep, might as well work on my conclusion. Whether I'm ready for it or not, the year is over. It's 2018. Time to wrap this up. I listen for Mocha's nails on the wood floor, but the old guy's been sleeping in later, just like Mom. I'll have to do this bit without his company.

If this were fiction, I could end it any way I liked.

I could leave Bob and move to the desert, or we could fall in love all over again and renew our vows on our twentieth anniversary, now only two months away. I could have a passionate affair or take a vow of celibacy. I could be as thin and fit as Juliet and get a job inspiring other seniors at a fitness resort. I could shave my head or find religion. I could devote the next five years to tracking down Ron and all the other girls he raped and telling their stories. I could sew a pair of flannel pajama bottoms a day and give them to cold people. I could open a guinea pig rescue or have a new career as a silver-haired, plus-sized model.

But this isn't fiction. None of that happened.

2017 was eventful, just not in the ways I projected back in January. I did learn things. Some of them things I already knew, but pretended I didn't:

- Sugar is bad for me.
- My hair grows fast.
- I am stronger, physically, than I knew, and I do sweat, some times a lot.
- My metabolism isn't broken; I just need to eat less and exercise more.
- Affirmations aren't magic, but they're nice nonetheless, affirming, so to speak.
- Writing isn't therapy, but it's therapeutic.
- My family loves me and brings me joy.
- I have been in some awful relationships.
- Bob is not one of them.
- He's just Bob, as I am relentlessly me.

My husband isn't going to transform into Prince Charming any more than I will become anyone other than who I am. If I understood my feelings for Bob, perhaps I'd know what, if anything at all, to do about us. But there are no clear signposts, no bright lights or shocking revelations, no clear right and wrong. He says there's nothing to know, no there, there. That's been a hard nut for me.

I'm beginning to wonder if it isn't that there's nothing to know, but rather that it can't be put into words. When I think, even when I only feel, actual words form in my mind. I speak inside my head, whole sentences and paragraphs. I craft monologues, harangues, speeches. Perhaps Bob doesn't do any of that. Maybe he doesn't think in words at all. There are all those books about how men and women are wired differently. Maybe that's it. Maybe he thinks in pictures or something even more amorphous, shapes or feelings that don't lend themselves to language.

Bottom line: I haven't learned his language, and he hasn't learned mine.

Years ago, a boy asked the question, "Is this all it is?"

I believe it is. Whether we consider it to be enough, a gift or a disappointment, is a choice, a matter of perspective, of personal investment.

I took a year to contemplate my inner navel. There is so much real suffering in the world, and here I stew in my tiny pot. I can say that, know it's true, yet it's still my reality. I can't help but be who I am, with all the opportunities I was born into, the chances I've had, the choices I've made. Perhaps others will see themselves in my story. Those who never feel pretty, lovable or accomplished enough. Those who have suffered shame and found it hard to wash off.

So, where am I? Metabolic age? Likely still 84, maybe more. Emotional maturity? I'd like to say I'm 63 going on 36. It has that synchronous, movie title ring to it. But 13 is more like it. Marriage? Enough said. That pile of jeans in the closet? Enough said.

I could blame the year. Trump. A tsunami of disasters of biblical proportions. Hurricanes, fires and famine. Mass shootings, genocide, the specter of nuclear war and the normalizing of white supremacy. Glaciers melting at an alarming rate. The apparent death of civility and decency, one tweet at a time. Trump.

And on the home front. Marmalade's quiet passing. Mom's continued decline. Mocha.

As if on cue, Mocha staggers into the hallway. He stumbles and thumps against the wall.

"Hey, buddy," I say, lifting him to my chest and sniffing his paws. I carry him outside. With a bit of assistance, he's able to hold up his hind quarters, enough to pee without sitting in it. Back inside, he settles into his basket and stares up at me, a slight tremor in his tail. I decide it's a wag.

My cell phone bleeps. It's Roxanne. She's spending a few days with her daughter.

"Hey, Bozo," I say.

"You're up early," Roxanne says.

"Butt crack," I say. "That's my time."

"Yep. We're two peas in a pod," she says. "Hey, did you get the e-mail about Mom?"

I hadn't. My sister tells me that there's an influenza outbreak at the home. No visitors until further notice. In a way, I'm relieved. After every visit, I feel so sad. She wouldn't have wanted this.

"I hope she doesn't get sick."

"I know," my sister says. "Not a good way to go."

"If I ever wind up like that. . .well, you know."

"Yep, we'll have a pact. We have to," Rocky says. "But it will be different for the three of us. We have each other."

"And we all get along," I say, mimicking Mom's refrain.

We may roll our eyes when she says it. But it's true. We speak the same language, one learned in childhood and steeped in a lifetime of shared experiences. We've even joked about what we'll do if we outlive any partners. The three of us will live together on a family compound, perhaps in three adjacent tiny homes. We can share meals and do crafts, or whatever it is old women do in their dotage. Juliet will be that crazy dog lady. Roxanne will redecorate every six weeks. I'll be Eeyore, bemoaning the loss of the love of my life and that I didn't appreciate him when I had the chance.

"That handsome man of yours still snoozing?" Roxanne asks.

"I just heard him go into the bathroom."

"Hey, here's an idea. How about you tear off those raggedy, flannel pajamas of yours, climb back into bed and surprise him?"

"I absolutely would," I say, "but my ribs are killing me."

"Uh-huh," she says.

So I have a confession, I made up that last part of the conversation, the bit about her saying I should climb back into bed with my husband. But, honestly, if it weren't for my baseball injury, I might. He's in the kitchen now, making a cup of coffee. Steam whooshes through the Keurig pod. The smell puts me in the mood for another. I think I'll wrap this up and join him.

One last thing. No resolutions this year. Well, just the obvious. Avoid sugar. Be kind to all the animals. Oh, and maybe I'll learn a new language.

ACKNOWLEDGEMENTS

Infinite gratitude to my husband and family for their patience, support and encouragement. This book would not have been possible without them.

Thanks to the friends and colleagues who generously reviewed the manuscript and offered valued suggestions, perspective and insight – Cynthia Romanowski, Joan Eddy, John Adler, Cass Bonfiglio, Linda Collins, Jan Haag, Shelley Blanton-Stroud, and Faye Satterly.

A special thanks and debt of gratitude to Ellen Sussman. This book was conceived, drafted and refined in her 2017 "Book in a Year" class and further nurtured at Sonoma County Writers Camp, ably facilitated by Ellen and Elizabeth Stark. Double thanks are owed to Shelley Blanton-Stroud who was my writing partner, latté drinking buddy and cheer leader throughout. And to our classmates on the book-birthing journey, a wonderful group of generous, talented writers whose spirit found its way onto these pages.

I am appreciative of the editors and journals that selected and published my essays, bits and pieces of which can be found in this memoir. The list includes: *Belle Ombre*; Editor Dinty W. Moore and Social Media Editor Allison Williams for pieces on the *Brevity Blog*; Marcelle Soviero, Editor-in-Chief, for essays in *Brain-Child* and *Brain-Teen Magazines; Memoir Mixtapes;*

Minerva Rising; Pure Slush Books; Split Lip Magazine; and, The Louisville Review.

I have learned and grown as a writer with the many authors I have had the opportunity to work with, including Robert Ray, Rebecca McClanahan, Debra Gwartney, Emily Rapp Black, Tod Goldberg, Joshua Malkin, Will Allison, Ayana Mathis, Kathy Fish, Lois Abraham, Jeff Knorr, Aaron Bradford, Janna Marlies Maron and Kate Asche. And from the conferences and workshops I have been fortunate to participate in, including the Squaw Valley Community of Writers, the Napa Valley Writers Conference, the *Kenyon Review* Writers Workshop, *Tin House* Nonfiction Workshop, *One Story* Summer Writers Conference and Hippocamp 2018.

Special thanks to the welcoming Sacramento literary community and the local and online writing groups I have been fortunate to participate in, including Gini Grossenbacher and Elk Grove Writers, Jannifer Kircher Carr and the Quills, River Town Writers and Team Haag, whose facilitator Jan Haag introduced me to the Amherst Writers and Artists method and whom I value as mentor, colleague, friend and meticulous copy editor. Thanks as well to the inspiring staff, workshop facilitators and youth writers with 916 Ink, a Sacramento based literacy nonprofit with which I have the good fortune to work and create new words.

Reviewing submissions with literary journals has proven invaluable to improving my own self-editing skills. A special thank you to *Narrative Magazine* Cofounder and Editor Tom Jenks, and Senior Editor Michael Croft, for the opportunity to serve as an Assistant Editor with *Narrative Magazine* for several years. More recently, thank you Donna Talarico, Founder & Publisher with *Hippocampus Magazine* for the chance to read nonfiction submissions.

A lazy river of gratitude for Administrative Director, Tod Goldberg and the faculty of the University of California Riverside, Palm Desert, Low-Residency MFA in Creative Writing and Writing for the Performing Arts, and to my friends and colleagues from that special time.

Abrazos to Guy Bennett of Otis Books, for allowing me to share *Gray Is the New Black,* and to Hannah Martin for making it beautiful.

Other Titles from Otis Books

Erik Anderson, *The Poetics of Trespass*
J. Reuben Appelman, *Make Loneliness*
Bruce Bégout, *Common Place. The American Motel*
Guy Bennett, *Self-Evident Poems*
Guy Bennett and Béatrice Mousli, Editors, *Seeing Los Angeles:*
    A Different Look at a Different City
Steve Castro, *Blue Whale Phenomena*
Geneva Chao, *one of us is wave one of us is shore*
Robert Crosson, *Signs / & Signals: The Daybooks of Robert Crosson*
———, *Daybook (1983–86)*
Neeli Cherkovski and Bill Mohr, Editors, *Cross-Strokes:*
    Poetry between Los Angeles and San Francisco
Mohammed Dib, *Tlemcen or Places of Writing*
Ray DiPalma, *The Ancient Use of Stone: Journals and Daybooks, 1998–2008*
———, *Obedient Laughter*
François Dominique, *Solène*
Tim Erickson, *Egopolis*
Jean-Michel Espitallier, *Espitallier's Theorem*
Forrest Gander, Editor, *Panic Cure: Poems from Spain for the 21st Century*
Leland Hickman, *Tiresias: The Collected Poems of Leland Hickman*
Michael Joyce, *Twentieth Century Man*
Lew S. Klatt, *The Wilderness After Which*
Norman M. Klein, *Freud in Coney Island and Other Tales*
Alan Loney, *Beginnings*
Luxorius, *Opera Omnia or, a Duet for Sitar and Trombone*
Sara Marchant, *Proof of Loss*
Ken McCullough, *Left Hand*
Gary McDowell, *Cæsura: Essays*
Béatrice Mousli, Editor, *Review of Two Worlds:*
    French and American Poetry in Translation
Laura Mullen, *Enduring Freedom*
Ryan Murphy, *Down with the Ship*
Mostafa Nissabouri, *For an Ineffable Metrics of the Desert*
Aldo Palazzeschi, *The Arsonist*
Dennis Phillips, *Navigation: Selected Poems, 1985–2010*
Antonio Porta, *Piercing the Page: Selected Poems 1958–1989*

Eric Priestley, *For Keeps*

Sophie Rachmuhl, *A Higher Form of Politics:*
    The Rise of a Poetry Scene, Los Angeles, 1950–1990

Norberto Luis Romero, *The Obscure Side of the Night*

Olivia Rosenthal, *We're Not Here to Disappear*

Noah Ross, *Swell*

Amelia Rosselli, *Hospital Series*

———, *War Variations*

Ari Samsky, *The Capricious Critic*

Giovanna Sandri, *only fragments found: selected poems, 1969–1998*

Hélène Sanguinetti, *Hence This Cradle*

Janet Sarbanes, *Army of One*

Severo Sarduy, *Beach Birds*

Adriano Spatola, *The Porthole*

———, *Toward Total Poetry*

Billie R. Tadros, *The Tree We Planted and Buried You In*

Carol Treadwell, *Spots and Trouble Spots*

Paul Vangelisti, *Wholly Falsetto with People Dancing*

Paul Vangelisti & Dennis Phillips, *Mapping Stone*

Allyssa Wolf, *Vaudeville*

————

All of our titles are available from Small Press Distribution.
Order them at www.spdbooks.org